FEDERAL CONFLICT OF INTEREST LAW

FEDERAL
CONFLICT
of INTEREST
LAW

BAYLESS MANNING

HARVARD UNIVERSITY PRESS
CAMBRIDGE, MASSACHUSETTS · 1964

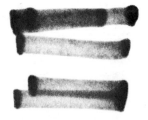

PREFACE BY ROSWELL B. PERKINS

The old adage that "a watched pot never boils" fails to survive the test of experience in the field with which this book deals. The more one examines the subject of conflicts of interest in government the more bubbling appears. Every indicator points in the direction of continued and more intensive concern with this field. The treatise which follows is timely, therefore, partly for the simple reason that the subject does not appear likely to become *untimely* in the foreseeable future.

The Report of the Special Committee on the Federal Conflict of Interest Laws of the Association of the Bar of the City of New York was issued in March of 1960 and published in book form a few months later under the title *Conflict of Interest and Federal Service*. The important events prior to 1960 are covered in the Committee's Foreword to that book. The key events since 1960 are traced briefly in the Introduction to the present volume, the most significant being the enactment in October 1962 of a revised conflict of interest law. The new law, which took effect January 21, 1963, incorporates many of the Committee's recommendations.

Instances of alleged conflict of interest in the executive branch continue to appear. A Secretary of the Navy under the Democratic Administration has disappeared from the scene under circumstances which, so far as appears from press reports, bear distinct resemblances to facts surrounding the resignation of a Secretary of the Air Force under a Republican administration. Even Presidents continue to be discussed. Whereas questions of propriety about acceptance of personal gifts were raised in the case of a Republican President, one now hears, in the case of a Democratic President, questions about family ownership of a federally regulated radio and television station. Needless to say, the resolution of such questions has become no less difficult.

Moreover, an area left unexplored by *Conflict of Interest and Federal Service* and by this volume—the conflicts of interest of Senators, Congressmen, and their staffs—looms larger and larger in the public eye. A highly publicized Senate investigation of the activities of a top Senatorial staff member has just closed. Therefore a recommendation made in the earlier book can be reaffirmed vigorously today, namely, that an independent and thorough study be undertaken of the conflict of interest problems of members of Congress.

Finally, the state legislatures are becoming a subject of increasingly sharp-focused attention. In New York, for example, the subject of ethics and conflict of interest with respect to members of the Senate and Assembly was one of the dominant subjects of the 1964 session of the Legislature.

Several factors contribute to the importance and special value of the present volume.

First, this book represents the most comprehensive treatment ever given to the case law and administrative regulation arising under the pre-1963 statutes. Although numerous unpublished and a few published efforts had been made to compile the law, these were modest ventures compared to the one here presented.

Second, although the spadework was completed before 1960, this study was actually written in 1963, after the legislative revision by Congress. Accordingly, the analysis of cases and rulings herein is made more valuable by insight into their pertinence today.

Third, the study includes extensive analysis of the law which took effect in 1963, including legislative history and comparisons with the pre-1963 provisions.

Fourth, interpretation of the law which took effect in 1963 will inevitably involve careful consideration of the case law and rulings under the former statutes, particularly since the new law was not, in many of its aspects, intended to change prior law. Anyone examining the new statutes can, with this volume, make ready reference to prior law.

Fifth, a study of the evolution and interpretation of the federal statutes is a key source of background material for those concerned with government service not only at the federal level but also at state and local levels. For example, this volume would be particularly useful in guiding those who are seeking to draft laws or ethical codes for public employees in state and city governments.

Bayless Manning, a professor at Yale Law School during the course of the work and now Dean-designate of the Stanford University School of Law, is unusually well qualified to write on this subject. After serving as Staff Director of our Special Committee, he has continued to be actively involved in both the legal and policy questions arising in the field of conflict of interest. He was a member of the President's Advisory Panel on Ethics and Conflicts of Interest in Government in 1961, participated in the development of the new federal legislation enacted in 1962, has worked with municipal governments and a Senate committee as a consultant in this area, and was a contributor to the recent symposium on conflicts of interest in the *Federal Bar Journal*. His book is a unique and valuable contribution to this field of law.

AUTHOR'S NOTE

Because an author's debts cannot be paid, it is the more important that they be acknowledged. Having an unusually large number of creditors in connection with this book, I should like to thank them all and name at least some.

Alexander C. Hoagland, Jr., not only was, as Roswell Perkins said in the Foreword to *Conflict of Interest and Federal Service*, the father of the study that gave rise to that book and this one, but also did much of the original basic law work that is reflected here. Assisting him at various times, and therefore me, were Mrs. Molly Epstein Cohen, William Kass, Robert Higgins, Edward Fowler, A. Edward Gottesman, and especially Donald Godiner. Anchoring all, Ruth Carter managed with flawless efficiency to maintain the files, the accounts, the typing, the paper flow, the office, and her own good nature.

The Association of the Bar of the City of New York and the Ford Foundation jointly made possible the research upon which *Conflict of Interest and Federal Service* and this volume are grounded. Bar associations and foundations are more conditioned to brickbats, but in this instance perhaps these two would be willing to accept a bouquet of gratitude. American society can be proud to have generated such institutions engaged daily in the effort to substitute light for darkness, order for confusion. Thanks should go too to those men who donate their time, skills,

and energies to such good works, men such as Roswell Perkins,
Chairman of the Association's Conflict of Interest Committee,
and the other lawyers of the Association who served as mem-
bers of the Committee in this enterprise: Howard F. Burns,
Charles A. Coolidge, Paul M. Herzog, Alexander C. Hoagland,
Jr., Everett L. Hollis, Charles A. Horsky, John V. Lindsay, John
E. Lockwood, and Samuel I. Rosenman.

Wives and children of authors are, of course, professionally
in the business of brunt-bearing. Even so, I owe an extra word
of thanks to my long-suffering family, for nearly all the basic
work on this book was done away from home and hearth, and
their forbearance has well exceeded duty's claim.

This book was written twice, once in 1961 after the publication of *Conflict of Interest and Federal Service*, and again in
1963 after the federal law regulating conflicts of interest was re-
vamped by Congress late in 1962. (I must confess to having
experienced an occasional unworthy twinge as I participated
in the work on the legislation, conscious that it would scrap
not only the old laws but also my new manuscript.) The new
law, Public Law 87–849, makes a significant contribution to the
field of public administration, and its enactment offers an example of our legislative process functioning at its best. Praiseworthy cooperative effort was invested in the legislation by men
in public life of both parties, of both houses of Congress, and
of the executive branch. There are many such, but among the
foremost stand Congressman Emmanuel Celler, Congressman
John V. Lindsay, Senator Henry M. Jackson, Senator Kenneth
B. Keating, Deputy Attorney General Nicholas Katzenbach—
and the young new President, who, from the very first days of
his truncated administration, played a central and personal role
at every stage of this legislative reform, and to whom this book
is dedicated.

New Haven, Connecticut   B.A.M.
April 1964

CONTENTS

xiii

FEDERAL CONFLICT OF INTEREST LAW

INTRODUCTION: PLAN OF THE BOOK

This is the successor and companion volume to *Conflict of Interest and Federal Service*.[1] Both deal with federal laws and practices regulating actual or potential conflicts between the public obligations and the private economic interests of government employees. The earlier volume is primarily an analysis of institutional facts and policy in this field, and concludes with a proposed program and proposed legislation. The present volume, by contrast, is not primarily critical in character. A book for working lawyers and public administrators, this volume is concerned solely with the federal law regulating conflicts of interest of federal employees. It offers a review, somewhat technical in character, of this field of law as modernized by legislation effective January 21, 1963.

This book, like its predecessor, is concerned primarily with the executive branch. Statutory provisions dealing only with members of Congress are not included here. Similarly, *ad hoc* statutory restrictions imposed upon particular executive offices and *ad hoc* exemptions granted to others are omitted as wanting in general interest.[2]

---

[1] Ass'n of the Bar of the City of New York, Conflict of Interest and Federal Service (1960) [hereinafter cited as Conflict of Interest and Federal Service].

[2] Examples of spot restrictions include 1 Stat. 67 (1789), as amended, Rev. Stat. § 243 (1875), 5 U.S.C. § 243 (1958) (Secretary of the Treas-

Chapters I and II of *Conflict of Interest and Federal Service* devote considerable attention to defining the scope of the term "conflict of interest." Since the same working definition is used here, a recapitulation of the definitional points developed in the earlier volume follows.

The term "conflict of interest," with related terms, has a limited meaning in this study. Any interest of an individual may conflict at times with any other of his interests. This book, however, is concerned with only two interests: one is the interest of the govern-

---

ury); 46 Stat. 797 (1930), 16 U.S.C. § 792 (1958) (FPC); 38 Stat. 717 (1914), as amended, 15 U.S.C. § 41 (1958) (FTC); 24 Stat. 383 (1887), as amended, 49 U.S.C. §11 (1958) (ICC); 52 Stat. 980 (1938), as amended, 49 U.S.C. § 1321 (1958) (CAB); 48 Stat. 1066 (1934), 66 Stat. 711 (1952), as amended, 70 Stat. 738, 47 U.S.C. §154 (b) (1958) (FCC). See, for other examples, 18 U.S.C. § 440 (1958), forbidding postal employees from contracting or acting as agents for contracting with the Post Office Department, and Rev. Stat. § 452 (1875), 43 U.S.C. § 11 (1958), prohibiting Bureau of Land Management officials from buying public land.

The often arbitrary and haphazard impact of the conflict of interest laws, and the consequent burden they have imposed upon the government's ability to recruit able personnel, have led Congress again and again to carve out special exemptions for particular offices or governmental programs having an apparent priority. This mass of spot exemptions has long been without form, philosophy, or favor. For a study and collection of exemptive statutes, see H.R. Rep. No. 2068, 86th Cong., 2d Sess. (1960). See also Conflict of Interest and Federal Service 66–69. Pub. L. No. 87–849, 87th Cong., 2d Sess., 76 Stat. 1119 (1962), effective January 21, 1963, makes a major change in federal conflict of interest law by repealing all the scattered exemptive provisions theretofore on the federal statute books insofar as they apply to "officers or employees of the executive branch of the United States Government, of any independent agency of the United States, or of the District of Columbia." Pub. L. No. 87–849, § 2. (For interpretation of the scope of this phrase, see ¶ 1B–3b; it should also be noted that any special exemptive provisions applicable on January 21, 1963, to officers or employees of the other branches remain in effect as to such officers and employees as exemptions to the corresponding sections of Pub. L. No. 87–849.) This broad repealer was thought possible as a result of the greater sophistication and more careful drafting of the general substantive restrictions contained in the new Pub. L. No. 87–849. Whether this optimism will prove justified, and whether Congress will no longer be called upon to provide new special exemptions, remains to be seen.

ment official (and of the public) in the proper administration of his office; the other is the official's interest in his private economic affairs. A conflict of interest exists whenever these two interests clash, or appear to clash.

A conflict of interest does not necessarily presuppose that action by the official favoring one of these interests will be prejudicial to the other, nor that the official will in fact resolve the conflict to his own personal advantage rather than the government's. If a man is in a position of conflicting interests, he is subject to temptation however he resolves the issue. Regulation of conflicts of interest seeks to prevent situations of temptation from arising. An Internal Revenue agent auditing his own tax return would offer a simple illustration of such a conflict of interest. Perhaps the agent's personal interest in the matter would not affect his discharge of his official duty; but the experience of centuries indicates that the contrary is more likely, and that affairs should be so arranged as to prevent a man from being put in such an equivocal position.[3]

This general statement concerning the character of conflicts of interest is, however, too broad. Many possible acts can put a government employee into a position where his personal economic interests conflict with his official duties. Yet in many of these situations we would not think of describing him as being in a position of conflict of interest:

The mint worker who takes home part of the daily product is an example. In a rather elemental way he is involved in a conflict of interest, but we call him a thief, not an offender against conflict of interest principles. His offense is an act of commission. Its criminal character depends entirely on what he does, not who he is. And his act—the taking of the money—is itself the evil consequence that the law seeks to prevent.

Similarly, the government contracting officer who accepts money from a contractor in exchange for granting him a contract puts himself in an extreme position of conflict between his official duty and personal economic interest. Again we have a specialized name for this offense, and again it is beyond the scope of this book. This

[3] CONFLICT OF INTEREST AND FEDERAL SERVICE 3–4.

offense is bribery. Unlike theft, it must involve an official. Its essential element is a payment to influence official action. It assumes a *quid* for a *quo;* the official is to do something in his official character in return for the payment.

But now assume that the same contracting officer simply receives a large gift from the contractor. There is no agreement or discussion about any contract, and the officer in fact does not give the contract to the donor. If this act is to be forbidden, it cannot be on a theory of theft or bribery. It must be on the theory that the conflict of interest set up by the gift is *likely* to lead to a warping of the official's judgment, or is likely to create the appearance of improper influence. If the official were not an official, the gift would be unexceptionable under federal law. The wrong arises entirely out of the undesirably inconsistent position of the official, first in his relationship to the outside party, and second in his relationship to his federal employer. The offense is an offense arising out of special status. The whole is greater than the sum of the parts: a subjectively innocent gift combined with a subjectively innocent official performing an innocent act can combine to constitute an offense against conflict of interest principles.

Regulation of conflicts of interest is regulation of evil before the event; it is regulation against potential harm. These regulations are in essence derived, or secondary—one remove away from the ultimate misconduct feared. The bribe is forbidden because it subverts the official's judgment; the gift is forbidden because it may have this effect, and because it looks to others as though it does have this effect. This potential or projective quality of conflict of interest rules is peculiar and important. We are not accustomed to dealing with law of this kind. It is as though we were to try to prevent people from acting in a manner that may lead them to rob a bank, or in a manner that looks to others like bank robbery.[4]

At one end of the spectrum, therefore, the problem of conflict of interest shades off into the statutory offense of bribery. At the opposite extreme, conflict of interest problems blend into differences over public policy—as where a senator declines to vote for the confirmation of the president of a private utility company as a Federal Power Commissioner. The problem of regulating conflicts of interest of federal employees will also be

[4] *Id.* at 18–20 (*footnote omitted*).

found to differ from the problems of controlling *ex parte* communication to official decision makers, the problem of influence peddling, and the problem of the appropriate role for WOCS and part-time consultants in staffing governmental functions.[5] Statutes dealing with these matters are therefore not treated here.

The last few years have been years of great ferment and activity in the field of regulation of the conflict of interest problems of federal personnel. In 1958 the staff of Subcommittee Number 5 of the House Committee on the Judiciary published its excellent *Report on Federal Conflict of Interest Legislation,* together with legislative proposals. In 1960 the Association of the Bar of the City of New York published the volume *Conflict of Interest and Federal Service,* to which this volume is the technical counterpart. The legislation proposed in the volume was introduced in both Houses of Congress. Other legislation was also introduced in 1960.[6] During the summer of 1960 the Subcommittee on National Policy Machinery of the Senate Government Operations Committee received testimony on the conflict of interest laws; it produced a report on the subject on February 28, 1961, entitled *Organizing for National Security— The Private Citizen and the National Service.* In 1961, one of the first acts of President Kennedy upon assuming office was to appoint a special three-man Advisory Panel on Ethics and Conflict of Interest in Government.[7] The Panel submitted its report in March of 1961.

Every one of these studies and reports concluded substantially the same thing. The federal laws governing conflicts of interest of government employees were judged to be archaic, inconsistent, overlapping, ineffective to achieve their purposes,

[5] These points are developed in some detail in *id.* at 20–24.

[6] For a history of legislative activities during this period, see H.R. REP. No. 748, 87th Cong., 1st Sess. 7 (1961).

[7] The members were Judge Calvert Magruder of the United States Court of Appeals for the 1st Circuit, Dean Jefferson B. Fordham of the University of Pennsylvania Law School, and the present author.

and obstructive to the government's efforts to recruit able personnel. Every one of them proposed new legislation.

On April 27, 1961, President Kennedy, acting on the basis of his Panel's report, sent a special message to Congress calling for a revision of the conflict of interest laws and submitting proposed legislation. Out of the recommendations of the Association of the Bar of the City of New York, the work of Subcommittee Number 5 of the House Committee on the Judiciary, the report of the President's Panel, the President's message, and other sources, the Congress fused, welded together, and, on October 23, 1962, enacted Law 87–849—a general overhauling of the federal law regulating bribery and conflicts of interest effective on January 21, 1963. The Senate Committee on the Judiciary explained the purposes of the new legislation in these words: "Insofar as the conflict-of-interest laws are concerned, the bill has two purposes. First, it would simplify and strengthen the conflict laws presently in effect. Second, in the interest of facilitating the Government's recruitment of persons with specialized knowledge and skills for service on a part-time basis, it would limit the impact of those laws on the persons so employed without depriving the Government of protection against unethical conduct on their part."[8]

Quoting from the President's special message, the Committee said "The fundamental defect of these statutes as presently written is that: On the one hand, they permit an astonishing range of private interests and activities by public officials which are wholly incompatible with the duties of public office; on the other hand, they create wholly unnecessary obstacles to recruiting qualified people for government service. This latter deficiency is particularly serious in the case of consultants and other temporary employees, and has been repeatedly recognized by Congress in its enactment of special exemption statutes."[9]

[8] S. Rep. No. 2213, 87th Cong., 2d Sess. 4 (1962).   [9] *Id.* at 5.

One major purpose of the new legislation is substantive: to take account of the government's staffing requirements and in particular to recognize that, under modern conditions, the government's reliance upon consultants and intermittent personnel demands separate treatment of such personnel in the conflict of interest laws.[10]

The other major purpose of the 1963 legislation is essentially technical in character. It is this technical aspect that in large measure dictates the structure and plan of the present book. Law 87–849 is a peculiar statute occupying a peculiar relationship to the laws that were already on the books at its effective date, January 21, 1963. Before that date, the body of federal conflict of interest laws was made up of seven provisions, though the term "conflict of interest" appears in none of them. These seven provisions deal with four problem areas—the four areas that are the subjects of the four chapters of this book. Three of the seven statutes, Sections 281, 283, and 216 of Title 18, deal in different ways with the problem of the federal employee who gives assistance to outsiders in their economic dealings with the government. One of the seven, Section 434 of Title 18, strikes at the problem of the official who acts on behalf of the government in a transaction in the outcome of which he has a personal economic interest. Two provisions, Section 284 of Title 18 and Section 99 of Title 5, impose restrictions upon the activities of certain federal employees after they leave government employment. One statute, Section 1914 of Title 18, is concerned with the federal employee who is paid by an outsider for doing his government job.

These seven statutory sections are totally disjointed—the product of a century of sporadic legislative response to the crisis, or apparent crisis, of the moment. They overlap, contain unjustifiable loopholes, and have no common core of drafting

[10] The special problems raised by the use of consultants are reviewed in CONFLICT OF INTEREST AND FEDERAL SERVICE, chs. 6, 8, 9.

technique or structure. Apart from the new special provisions in Law 87–849 concerning intermittent personnel, the major effect of the 1963 amendments is to bring to the older provisions a new element of integration, consistency, and tightness in drafting. The revisions do not point a new statutory finger at abuses other than the four categories covered by the seven earlier provisions; neither does the new legislation retreat from any of these four problem areas. The 1963 legislation is a basketful of separate unrelated substantive provisions, each of them a modernized redrafting of one or more of the original seven provisions. Even the organization of the 1963 legislation follows faithfully the group of predecessor provisions—each substantive section of the new having a matching counterpart in the old. (This statement does not quite hold in reverse, for the seven older substantive provisions are reduced in the 1963 version to five substantive sections, the two least important being absorbed by consolidation.)

Each of the sections of Law 87–849 is a relatively modest refinement of a predecessor. The changes made are minor in comparison with the substantive ideas left intact. As a result it is misleading and dangerous to think of the new statute as outmoding or discarding the predecessor provisions. Much of what was there, including judicial gloss, is picked up and carried forward by the 1963 legislation. The new statute and the older ones must therefore be viewed together as an integrated whole.

For another and independent reason, it is an error to think of the older statutes as being made obsolete by Law 87–849. Events that occurred before January 21, 1963, will continue to be regulated by the older provisions. In the normal course of events, those who serve in government employment after January 21, 1963, will be mainly concerned with the law as revised by the new legislation. But those whose service was, in whole or in part, prior to that date must continue to regard the older statutes as applicable to events before January 21, 1963. Judges, prosecutors, and counsel will for years to come need to have recourse to the law as it was before the 1963 modifications. The federal law regulating conflicts of interest is thus made up of a composite of the old and the new—and the new in turn continues much of the old. For these reasons, this book is devoted not to the 1963 legislation alone, but to the block of older statutes as well.

The book is divided into four chapters, each dealing with one of the four problem areas with which the statutes, old and new, are concerned. As a result, one chapter is very long, treating five related statutory provisions, one covers three statutory sections, and the other two deal with two sections each. To the extent possible, discussion of each statutory section has been organized according to a single recurring outline. Certain difficulties were found in doing this, and there are occasional unavoidable inconsistencies in sequence, but, on the whole, this system has proved successful in simplifying cross-references and in helping the reader to find a particular point of discussion in a hurry. For example, ¶ 3.2.1 in the analysis of each statute will be found to discuss the position of members of Congress under that statute.

A substantial effort has been made to avoid discussing any issue more than once. Frequently a single issue, such as the legal position of members of Congress, will be found to arise in the same form under several statutes. Cross-referencing is used in these instances. Most lawyers are by now relatively numb to the irritations of shuttlecock research in a world of loose-leaf law. But the reader who finds himself annoyed at being shunted about in this fashion is at least entitled to an advance apology for an unaesthetic solution adopted in the interests of space and economy.

Five appendices serve five special purposes. The first sets out the texts of the relevant statutes. The second is addressed to the special problem of military personnel under the statutes. The third is concerned with the problem of partners and associates of government employees. The fourth contains a note on administration and sanctions of the conflict of interest laws. And the fifth contains a detailed legislative history of each of the statutes discussed in the book.

Law 87–849 is a major legislative step taken after long deliberation, careful legislative study, and private research. As such, this body of legislation is apt to demonstrate considerable permanence and stability. Congress cannot be expected to refocus much attention on this area of the law until the new legislation and its administration have had time to settle down and experience has had time to accumulate. If such a prediction is valid, this is a good time to review and survey the field as a whole. Explanation of the new legislation is early enough to be useful and not likely for a while to be overtaken by events and new amendments.[11]

A final note should be added before we turn to a consideration of the statutory material. It is important to stress the limited role played by statutes in the field of conflict of interest regulation. The Senate, in its conduct of confirmation proceedings, has frequently imposed special conflict of interest standards not found in the statutes.[12] Congress may also bring strong pressures to bear through its investigatory process. Many relationships that might be legally acceptable, and not considered morally reprehensible conflicts of interest, may be politically very sensitive and politically unacceptable. And, finally, many agencies of the government have developed their own operating

[11] For an excellent review of the new legislation, see Perkins, *The New Federal Conflict-of-Interest Law*, 76 HARV. L. REV. 1113 (1963). On the same topic, see also Memorandum of the Attorney General, 28 Fed. Reg. 985 (January, 1963). For the legislative history of Law 87–849 see Appendix E. For general bibliography in the field, see 13 THE RECORD OF THE ASSOCIATION OF THE BAR OF THE CITY OF NEW YORK 323–30 (May 1958).

[12] The Senate's role in this regard is discussed at length in CONFLICT OF INTEREST AND FEDERAL SERVICE, ch. 5.

rules and their own internal regulations for dealing with the problem of ethics as it affects their own operations.[13] No one called upon to consider a question of conflict of interest in the federal service will have done his job unless he has weighed and investigated, in addition to the statutes in the field, the applicable administrative regulations, likely Congressional response, and the general political environment.

[13] See Appendix D.

CHAPTER 1. ASSISTING OUTSIDERS IN GOVERNMENTAL DEALINGS

A major concern of the federal statutes on conflict of interest has been to inhibit government employees from assisting outsiders in certain of their dealings with the government. Together they reflect the philosophy that the loyalty of the government man is to the government, that he should not serve two masters whose economic interests are adverse.

Prior to January 21, 1963, three separate sections of the Criminal Code were addressed to this object, Sections 281, 283, and 216.[1] By force of Law 87–849, these have been incorporated into two statutory sections, Sections 203 and 205.[2] Section 203 is closely modeled on the predecessor Section 281, and Section 205 on Section 283. These sections are discussed here in pairs in parts A and B of this chapter. Section 216 has no successor, as such, and is discussed in part C.

[1] 18 U.S.C. §§ 281, 283, 216 (1958).
[2] 76 Stat. 1121 (1962). As amendments to the Criminal Code, these sections automatically become 18 U.S.C. §§ 203, 205 (Supp. IV, 1963).

PART A

SECTION 281 AND SECTION 203 (1963)

1A–1. GENERAL

Section 281 has often been referred to as the keystone of the conflict of interest laws. Its closely similar successor, Section 203, will likely enjoy a similar position.

1A–1a. SECTION 281

Section 281 reads (omitting a special provision regarding retired military officers):

> Whoever, being a Member of or Delegate to Congress, or a Resident Commissioner, either before or after he has qualified, or the head of a department, or other officer or employee of the United States or any department or agency thereof, directly or indirectly receives or agrees to receive, any compensation for any services rendered or to be rendered, either by himself or another, in relation to any proceeding, contract, claim, controversy, charge, accusation, arrest, or other matter in which the United States is a party or directly or indirectly interested, before any department, agency, court martial, officer, or any civil, military, or naval commission, shall be fined not more than $10,000 or imprisoned not more than two years, or both; and shall be incapable of holding any office of honor, trust, or profit under the United States.

Essentially Section 281 forbids the government employee to accept pay for serving outsiders in matters before the executive branch where the government has an interest. Its coverage extends to members of Congress as well as to employees of the executive branch, and it is very broad in its application to any "matter in which the United States is a party or directly or indirectly interested." On the other hand, it is limited to compensated services only and, being restricted to matters before

the forum of the executive branch, does not apply to court proceedings.

Though Section 281 differs in significant respects from Section 283, discussed in part B of this chapter, the two sections overlap substantially.

1A–1b. SECTION 203 (1963)

The text of Law 87–849, including Section 203 effective January 21, 1963, is set forth in Appendix A.

Section 203 contains three subsections. The first subsection is closely similar to Section 281, which it supersedes. The second subsection is directed toward the outsider who makes or offers to make a forbidden payment to the government employee. The third subsection sets forth a special rule for certain intermittent employees of the government.

Interpretation of Section 203 requires reference to Section 202, where certain definitions are contained, and to Sections 205 and 207, which in some respects modify Section 203.

Law 87–849 specifies that Section 281 is to be "supplanted" by Section 203,[3] but this statement requires interpretation. See ¶ 1A–5.

1A–2. BACKGROUND

1A–2a. SECTION 281

Like others of the conflict of interest statutes, Section 281 arose out of the administrative abuses of the Civil War. The necessity for the enactment of the statute in 1864 is not very clear from the record. In 1853, Congress had passed the predecessor to Section 283 in direct response to scandals involving fraudulent claims against the government.[4] The 1864 statute largely overlapped the 1853 act, though it did somewhat ex-

---

[3] Pub. L. No. 87–849, Section 2; 76 Stat. 1126 (1962).
[4] See ¶ 1B–2a for the background of Section 283.

tend restrictions of the earlier provision to a wider group of matters and proceedings. Little mention of the 1853 statute was made during the debate on the 1864 statute.[5] The likely cause for the enactment of the 1864 act was that abuses had continued and grown worse with the war, scandal was in the air, public opinion was aroused, and Congressional action of some sort was politically demanded.

Until 1963, the 1864 predecessor of Section 281[6] was not substantially modified.

A detailed abstract of the development of Section 281 appears in Appendix E.

1A–2b. SECTION 203 (1963)

A direct outgrowth of Section 281, Section 203 shares its history. The particular legislative background of Law 87–849 is discussed in the Introduction. Appendix E contains an abstract of its legislative history.

1A–3. COVERAGE

Who is subject to the conflict of interest restrictions of Sections 281 and 203? The question involves two separate components. Is the employer a federal governmental body subject to the statute, and does the person in question have the kind of office or employment relation that brings him under the statute? Unfortunately the answers to these questions are often not clear.

The coverage of Section 203 is virtually identical with that of the older Section 281, but minor improvements in drafting have been made.

---

[5] At least one Senator noted the overlap, however. CONG. GLOBE, 38th Cong., 1st Sess. 561 (1864).

[6] Act of June 11, 1864, ch. 119, 13 Stat. 123.

1A–3.1. Federal employer

1A–3.1a. Section 281

Section 281 applies by its terms to "the head of a department, or other officer or employee of the United States or any department or agency thereof." It is not important for purposes of the statute to distinguish among these categories listed; it is sufficient if the person in question falls into any one of them—and the categories overlap. The problem then is to determine the joint outer limits of the entire phrase.

Both "agency" and "department" are defined terms in the Criminal Code. The definition of "agency" is very broad, encompassing virtually every imaginable governmental organ, including "departments." 18 U.S.C. § 6 (1958) provides:

The term "agency" includes any department, independent establishment, commission, administration, authority, board, or bureau of the United States or any corporation in which the United States has a proprietary interest, unless the context shows that such term was intended to be used in a more limited sense.[7]

Nothing in the history or gloss of Section 281 suggests any intention to use the term in a more limited sense.[8]

Despite the breadth of this definition of "agency," however, it does not extend to the full reach of Section 281. One is subject

[7] Title 18 of the United States Code is itself positive law, enacted as a block in 1948, with the definitions included as part of an integrated statute. The statutory definition of "department" is less broad, since it refers to the ten Cabinet departments only: State, Defense, Treasury, Justice, Post Office, Interior, Agriculture, Commerce, Labor, and Health, Education and Welfare. 18 U.S.C. § 6 (1958).

The Federal Bureau of Investigation has been held to be an "agency" under 18 U.S.C. § 6 (1958). United States v. Stark, 131 F. Supp. 190, 194 (D. Md. 1955). See United States v. Bramblett, 348 U.S. 503 (1955) regarding the status of the Disbursing Office of the House of Representatives.

[8] The words "or any department or agency thereof" did not appear in Section 281 until 1948. Act of June 25, 1948, ch. 645 § 281, 62 Stat. 697.

to the statute if he is an officer or employee of "the United States," whether or not he is an officer or employee of a "department" or "agency" as defined. The officer or employee of the agency is surely an officer or employee of the United States; but the latter category is the more inclusive and therefore the critical one in determining who is covered by Section 281.

In some situations it may be clear that the employer is some kind of federal government entity and yet remain uncertain whether the employee is covered by Section 281.

Judiciary. The best illustration is offered by the judiciary and employees of the judicial branch other than the judges themselves. There is no case law on the application of Section 281 to such personnel, and no discussion of the matter appears in any of the legislative history of the section. Some special considerations of policy might argue for special legislation applicable to the judicial branch, but in view of the stark simplicity of the language in Section 281, it is difficult to escape the conclusion that judges would be held to be "officers of the United States" for purposes of the section, and federal court employees to be "employees."

Legislative employees. Employees of the legislative branch are not specifically referred to in Section 281, as they are in Section 283. But the breadth of the general language of Section 281 and the fact that members of Congress are themselves covered make it fairly clear that the section is applicable to legislative employees.

Uniformed services. The position of uniformed military personnel under the conflict of interest laws, including Section 281, is discussed in Appendix B.

District of Columbia. Personnel of the District of Columbia government raise another area of doubt. Their employer is evidently governmental and federal, but it may be questioned whether the basic policy underlying Section 281 requires that all employees of an essentially municipal government should

be subject to the strict disabilities of the section in their relations with agencies of the national government. There is no
judicial authority on the issue.[9] The Attorney General has
opined that the commissioner of deeds of the District of
Columbia is subject to a predecessor of Section 281.[10] As the
main support for this conclusion, the Attorney General relied
upon earlier determinations that a notary public for the District
of Columbia is an "officer of the United States" and, but for
a special statutory exception enacted in 1906, is subject to the
predecessor of Section 283.[11] For this and other reasons, one
is led to the surprising conclusion that notaries public of the
District of Columbia are "officers of the United States" subject
to Section 281.[12]

[9] In one case the Supreme Court has held that a justice of the peace of
the District of Columbia is an officer of the United States, though the
decision is not best known for this holding. Marbury v. Madison, 5 U.S.
(1 Cranch) 137 (1803).

[10] 28 OPS. ATT'Y GEN. 131 (1910). An earlier opinion, 18 OPS. ATT'Y
GEN. 161 (1885) held an assistant attorney of the District of Columbia
not to be covered by a predecessor of Section 281, but the ground was
that he was not an "officer," not that he escaped coverage because his
employer was the District of Columbia. The opinion is today doubtful
authority, in any case, because of its reliance upon the now weakened
case of United States v. Germaine, 99 U.S. 508 (1878), discussed in note
21 *infra*.

[11] 28 OPS. ATT'Y GEN. 131, 133–35 (1910).

[12] The details of this point are a bit intricate. The special exemption
appears in Act of June 29, 1906, ch. 3616, 34 Stat. 622. It was adopted
as an amendment to § 558 of the Code of Law of the District of Columbia,
Act of March 3, 1901, ch. 854, § 558, 31 Stat. 1189, now § 1–501 of that
Code. The 1906 exemption statute did not refer by section number to
any conflict of interest section. Its operative language said merely that
"the appointment of any person as such notary public . . . shall not
disqualify or prevent such person from representing clients before any
of the departments of the United States Government in the District of
Columbia or elsewhere . . ." But the accompanying Senate Report of
the Senate Committee on the District of Columbia said that the amendment
was intended to exempt such notaries from REV. STAT. § 5498 (1875),
predecessor of present-day 18 U.S.C. § 283 (1958); the Report did not
mention the predecessor of Section 281 or any other conflict of interest
statute. S. REP. No. 4012, 59th Cong., 1st Sess. (1906). The Report
used the same language as the amendment in speaking of permitting

Altogether, existing authority and the bare language of Section 281 indicate that the officer or employee of the District of Columbia is covered by the section.

Government corporations. Employees of governmentally owned corporations are subject to Section 281 by force of the definition of "agency" in 18 U.S.C. § 6.[13]

Non-appropriated fund agencies (PXs). The protean forms of modern government plague alike the statutory draftsman and the counselor. Post exchanges on United States military posts are operated under the auspices and supervision of the federal government, but are self-supporting and do not share in federal fund appropriations. Their legal status has caused trouble. In 1942 the Supreme Court held that a post exchange could not

---

practice before "the departments," but in floor debate Representative Bartlett, the proponent of the bill, said three times that the amendment would permit such notaries to practice before the Court of Claims *or* the departments. 40 CONG. REC. 6839 (1906). Unfortunately for Mr. Bartlett's position, (1) REV. STAT. § 5498 (1875) prohibited prosecution of claims in courts as well as before "departments," but nothing in the history of the 1906 amendment refers to judicial proceedings; (2) the amendment does not mention the Court of Claims; (3) while REV. STAT. § 5498 (1875) and its modern successor 18 U.S.C. § 283 (1958) apply only to "claims" and these are opened to notaries by the language of the 1906 amendment, the range of forbidden activities under Section 281 and its predecessors is much broader than the exemption language of the 1906 amendment. With some pride, Representative Bartlett announced on the floor: "I drew the bill myself . . ." 40 CONG. REC. 6839 (1906). The best way out of the first of these difficulties is probably to interpret "departments" in the 1906 amendment to mean all three coordinate branches of government, an avenue suggested by the definition of "department" in 18 U.S.C. § 6 (1958). There seems to be no best, or even good, way out of the other difficulties.

The uninstructive case of Hall's Safe Co. v. Herring-Hall-Marvin Safe Co., 31 App. D.C. 498 (D.C. Cir. 1908) is the only opinion relying on D.C. Code § 1–501.

[13] The House of Representatives Report accompanying the 1948 criminal code points out that the definition is intended to cover government corporations in which stock is not actually issued as well as those in which it is, but it is not intended to include corporations in which the interest of the government is custodial or incidental. H.R. REP. No. 304, 80th Cong., 1st Sess. A6 (1947).

be properly subjected to a California motor fuel tax;[14] the decisions are in dispute on the issue whether PX employees are employees of the United States for purposes of the Federal Tort Claims Act;[15] the Judge Advocates General of the Air Force and the Army also disagree.[16]

Are employees of non-appropriated-fund agencies such as PXs subject to the restrictions of Section 281? The only lead available is a statute passed in 1952 that refers to such agencies as "federal instrumentalities" but provides that their employees are *not* to be considered federal employees for certain limited purposes.[17] The conflict of interest laws are not among those mentioned in the 1952 statute. A modest inference is thus available suggesting that some agencies may be considered as federal employers, even though operating without appropriations.

Perhaps there is a difference here between Section 281 and Section 216.[18] The latter adds to the phrase "officer or employee" the word "agent." If a court were to conclude that PX employees are not "employees" of the United States for purposes of Section 281, it might nonetheless conclude that they are "agents" of the United States acting for it in an important aspect of the administration of military posts.

1A–3.1b. SECTION 203 (1963)

Section 203(a)(2) restricts the activities of any person "at a time when he is an officer or employee of the United States in the executive, legislative, or judicial branch of the Govern-

[14] Standard Oil Co. v. Johnson, 316 U.S. 481 (1942).
[15] *Compare* Faleni v. United States, 125 F. Supp. 630 (E.D.N.Y. 1949) *with* Daniels v. Chanute Air Force Base Exchange, 127 F. Supp. 920 (E.D. Ill. 1955).
[16] *Compare* 6 DIGEST OF OPINIONS OF THE JUDGE ADVOCATES GENERAL OF THE ARMED FORCES 436 (JAGAF 1955/35 1955), *with* 4 DIGEST OF OPINIONS OF THE JUDGE ADVOCATES GENERAL OF THE ARMED FORCES 551 (JAGAF 1954/8232 1954).
[17] 66 Stat. 138 (1952), 5 U.S.C. § 150k (1958).
[18] See ¶ 1C–3.

ment, or in any agency of the United States, including the District of Columbia." The word "department" does not appear in Section 203 as it does in Section 281. It is unnecessary because included in the definition of "agency" appearing in 18 U.S.C. § 6 (1958). See ¶ 1A–3.1a.

Evidently the language of Section 203 clears up a good many of the questions discussed at ¶ 1A–3.1a respecting the application of the statute to employees of agencies that are connected with the federal government but are peripheral to it. Judges and employees of the judicial branch are subject to Section 203. The same is true of employees of the legislative branch. Employees of government corporations continue to be covered because such corporations are included within the statutory definition of "agency." Employees of the District of Columbia are explicitly covered by Section 203.

The position of employees of non-appropriated agencies remains as uncertain under Section 203 as it is under Section 281.

The balance of the discussion at ¶ 1A–3.1a remains applicable to Section 203.

1A–3.2. Officer or employee

In some situations it may be quite clear that a government department or agency is involved, but may be quite unclear whether the person in question should be viewed as a federal "officer or employee." In this respect there are substantial differences between Sections 281 and 203. The changes are mainly additional, however, and most of the learning accumulated regarding the coverage of Section 281 continues to be relevant to Section 203.

1A–3.2a. SECTION 281

Until the adoption of the Criminal Code in 1948, the predecessors of Section 281 did not use the term "officer or employee of the United States." The corresponding language in the earlier versions was "head of a department, or other officer or clerk in the employ of the United States."[19] This phraseology raised a problem of interpretation, for it opened the possibility that an employee might not be of sufficient status to be considered an "officer" yet might be considered to be more than a "clerk." If the words "officer" and "clerk" were not considered to blanket all possible categories of federal employment, a hole would be left in the coverage of the section,[20] and in that case it would be necessary to establish special criteria for determining who was an "officer" and who was a "clerk." Such a reading would make relevant the substantial body of case law that has accumulated in various contexts defining the scope of the term "officer of the United States."[21] Cases arising under the predecessors of Section 281 prior to 1948 must be read with this earlier statutory language in mind, though the courts were not always careful to indicate which category they considered the defendant at bar to occupy.

In 1948 the language of the section was extended without

[19] Act of June 11, 1864, ch. 119, 13 Stat. 123; Act of March 4, 1909, ch. 321, § 113, 35 Stat. 1109.

[20] This argument was advanced before the Attorney General but rejected by him in 40 Ops. Att'y Gen. 294, 299 (1943).

[21] Three different, though often overlapping, views interpreting "officer of the United States" can be distinguished in the cases. A leading case is United States v. Germaine, 99 U.S. 508 (1878), holding that the phrase "officer of the United States," in a criminal law against extortion, means the term in its constitutional sense; that is, a person holding formal appointment pursuant to U.S. Const. art. II, § 2. But in Steele v. United States, 267 U.S. 505, 507 (1925), the Supreme Court suggested a retreat from this proposition in favor of the view that legislative intent is the determinant and in some statutes a broader use of the word "officer" is indicated. The third view is illustrated by McGregor v. United States, 134 Fed. 187 (4th Cir. 1904), where the court relied upon United States v. Hartwell, 73 U.S.(6 Wall.) 385 (1867) to support its view that the nature of the office itself is the determinative element. The McGregor court held a third-class postal clerk to be an "officer" for purposes of indictment under the predecessors of Sections 281 and 216, since the position required an oath of office and "established the idea of tenure, duration, emolument, and duties." Id. at 196. The Germaine rule is clearly in disfavor in the modern cases and the term "officer of the United States" is interpreted in the context of the particular statute in which it occurs. See 40 Ops. Att'y Gen. 294 (1943) and Appendix thereto.

comment to cover any "officer or employee of the United States." This phrase closes the gap that may have arguably existed in the earlier versions. In so doing the broader phrase undercut the relevance of cases concerned with distinguishing officers from employees or clerks. What is the scope of this joint term setting the coverage of Section 281?

The modern cases agree that the phrase "officer or employee of the United States" has no fixed content and that its interpretation will vary depending upon the statute involved and the situation at hand. Care must be used, therefore, in using as analogies interpretations of the term as it appears in other statutes —even other conflict of interest statutes. Abstract generalizations are of limited value. The decided instances are collected in the margin.[22]

1A–3.2b. Section 203 (1963)

Section 203 continues to apply to one who is an "officer or employee," as does Section 281. The new statute does nothing to crystallize further the content of this phrase. See ¶1A–3.2a.

[22] There have been no cases arising under Section 281 interpreting the 1948 term "officer or employee." In the following instances the person in question was held to be an "officer" or "clerk" under a predecessor of the section: United States v. Reisley, 32 F. Supp. 432 (D.N.J. 1940), 35 F. Supp. 102 (D.N.J. 1940) (contact representative in the Veterans Administration); United States v. Long, 184 Fed. 184 (D. Ore. 1911) (land office clerk); United States v. Booth, 148 Fed. 112 (D. Ore. 1906) (land office receiver); McGregor v. United States, 134 Fed. 187 (4th Cir. 1904) (postal clerk); 28 Ops. Att'y Gen. 131 (1910) (commissioner of deeds of District of Columbia). In the following instances, dicta have indicated that the person in question was subject to a predecessor of the section: 29 Ops. Att'y Gen. 199 (1911) (city postmaster); 28 Ops. Att'y Gen. 131 (1910) (notary public); 24 Ops. Att'y Gen. 557 (1903) (post office superintendent); 14 Ops. Att'y Gen. 482 (1874) (pension agent).

In the following instances the person in question was considered not to be subject to a predecessor of the Section: 37 Ops. Att'y Gen. 204 (1933) (attorney for receiver of national bank); 18 Ops. Att'y Gen. 161 (1885) (attorney for the District of Columbia). The last cited opinion is particularly doubtful because of its heavy reliance upon the Supreme Court's narrow interpretation of "officer" in United States v. Germaine, *supra* note 21.

1A–3.2.1. Congressman

1A–3.2.1a. SECTION 281

Members of and delegates to Congress are specifically covered by Section 281. Indeed, in its origins, the Civil War predecessor of the section was aimed solely at members of Congress.[23] Resident commissioners were added in the 1909 revision.[24] The disabilities of the statute attach immediately upon election or appointment and are not postponed to the date of oath or entry on the payroll.[25]

1A–3.2.1b. SECTION 203 (1963)

Under Section 203, members of Congress and members-elect continue to be subject to the restrictions of the section, as in the case of Section 281. The earlier term "delegate" has been dropped in Section 203 as being obsolete.

1A–3.2.2. Intermittent employee; Special Employee

1A–3.2.2a. SECTION 281

One need not be on a regular government payroll in order to be an "officer or employee of the United States." One who

[23] CONG. GLOBE, 38th Cong., 1st Sess. 93 (1863) (regarding S. 28). *Cf.* the original act as finally passed, Act of June 11, 1864, ch. 119, 13 Stat. 123, May v. United States, 175 F.2d 994 (D.C. Cir. 1949); United States v. Quinn, 111 F. Supp. 870 (E.D.N.Y. 1953), 116 F. Supp. 802 (E.D.N.Y. 1953), 141 F. Supp. 622 (S.D.N.Y. 1956); United States v. Johnson, 215 F. Supp. 300 (D.Md. 1963).

[24] Act of March 4, 1909, Ch. 321, § 114, 35 Stat. 1109. A resident commissioner has been defined as "an official agent sent to the national capital by an unincorporated territory such as Puerto Rico . . . [who] may speak but not vote in the House of Representatives." SMITH AND ZURCHER, DICTIONARY OF AMERICAN POLITICS 268 (1944).

[25] The phrase "either before or after he has qualified" was added in the 1909 revision of the criminal laws to settle the question, earlier court opinions having been inconsistent on the point. 42 CONG. REC. 1755, 1762–65, 2123–25 (1908); Act of March 4, 1909, ch. 321, §§ 112–115, 35 Stat. 1108. See United States v. Dietrich, 26 Fed. 676 (C.C.D. Neb. 1904). The Attorney General had early opined that a Congressman-elect not yet sworn into office was subject to the 1864 predecessor of Section 281. 14 OPS. ATT'Y GEN. 133 (1872).

serves in a government position without compensation (a WOC), or who is paid only for the time when actually employed (a WAE) is nonetheless an "officer or employee." The regular but part-time worker for the government is also an employee. Modern government has constant recourse to technical consultants called in from time to time for expert advice. These advisers do not always realize that, by accepting appointment as paid or unpaid consultants to perform occasional or intermittent services, they become "employees" for purposes of Section 281, and subject to all its disqualifications.[26]

A separate, though related, question is whether the intermittent employee, having once been characterized as an "employee" under Section 281, is restricted by its provisions only during the time he is working for the government, or whether the section pursues him as well during periods when he is doing no government work. See ¶ 1A–4.6.

1A–3.2.2b. SECTION 203 (1963)

The new legislation effective January 21, 1963, makes a radical and important change in the application of the conflict of interest laws to many government employees whose services are intermittent. A major purpose of the 1963 legislation was to remedy the failure of the existing conflict of interest statutes to deal with the special problems of the consultant and of other intermittent employees of the government.[27]

[26] 42 OPS. ATT'Y GEN. No. 6 (Jan. 31, 1962); 40 OPS. ATT'Y GEN. 294 (1943); 40 OPS. ATT'Y GEN. 289 (1943); U.S. Civil Service Comm., EMPLOYMENT AND COMPENSATION OF EXPERTS AND CONSULTANTS, A GUIDE FOR FEDERAL EXECUTIVES 18–20 (1954). See discussions *infra* of the application of the other conflict of interest statutes to WOCs, WAEs, and intermittent employees, particularly ¶ 2–3.2.2.

The impact of the conflict of interest statutes on the private economic life of those accepting government consultancies and other intermittent governmental employment can be drastic. The deterrent effect of the statutes upon government recruitment of intermittent personnel has been a major factor in the reform efforts that resulted in the new Pub. L. No. 87–849, effective January 21, 1963.

[27] H.R. REP. No. 748, 87th Cong., 1st Sess. 4, 13–15 (1961); S. REP. No. 2213, 87th Cong., 2d Sess. 6–7 (1962).

The new legislation approaches this problem by defining a separate class of employees as "Special Government Employees." These "Special Employees" are in substance intermittent and temporary employees. They are closely defined by Section 202. That section provides that "special Government Employee"

shall mean an officer or employee of the executive or legislative branch of the United States Government, of any independent agency of the United States or of the District of Columbia, who is retained, designated, appointed, or employed to perform, with or without compensation, for not to exceed one hundred and thirty days during any period of three hundred and sixty-five consecutive days, temporary duties either on a full-time or intermittent basis . . .[28]

Several important features of this definition should be noted. Under the new legislation, it is apparent that some identifiable and formal act is contemplated as the process by which one becomes an "employee." This had been assumed in the case of Section 281 but was not stated. The formal act by which one is "retained, designated, appointed, or employed" is of crucial importance under Section 202, for the employee's status as a regular employee or a Special Employee is determined by the terms of his appointment or retention. That is to say, Section 202 turns the definition of Special Employee on the question whether the employee was appointed to serve no more than one hundred thirty out of any consecutive three hundred sixty-five days—not on a *post hoc* determination at any particular time that the employee in fact worked less than one hundred thirty days in the preceding three hundred sixty-five days. A consultant would, for example, be a Special Employee if his appointment provided that, however long it might run into the future, the consultant would not be called upon to perform governmental services for more than one hundred thirty days out of any consecutive three hundred sixty-five days. The section also makes it perfectly clear that the employee may remain a Special Employee even though

[28] 76 Stat. 1121 (1962), Section 202(a).

his labors on behalf of the government require his full time and even though his one hundred thirty days are consecutive. For purposes of the classification as a Special Employee, it is immaterial whether he is paid or not paid for his governmental work.

It seems quite clear that under Section 202 the employee's working time is not to be computed on a minute-by-minute or hour-by-hour basis. In principle, the employee will be considered to have worked a day for the government if he has worked part of the day. At the same time there is doubtless a *de minimis* limitation on this method of computing; a one-minute telephone call in which the consultant agrees to show up on the following Thursday is hardly enough in itself to count as a "day" of his one hundred thirty allotted days. Some difficulties in computing days of work may be expected to arise despite the fact that the statute seeks to make the character of the appointment rather than past performance the key to classification as a Special Employee. For example, an employee who has worked full time for two hundred and fifty consecutive days will surely not be viewed as a Special Employee even though his original appointment may have specified that he would work only one hundred thirty days out of any three hundred sixty-five consecutive days. The facts as well as the form of appointment will doubtless play an important part.

In addition to its general provisions regarding Special Employees, Section 202 contains some more particularized provisions. A part-time United States Commissioner is to be viewed as a Special Employee regardless of the form of his appointment or the amount of time he actually works. Similarly any person serving as a part-time local representative of a member of Congress in the member's home district or state will be considered a Special Employee—again regardless of the form of the appointment or the amount of time actually worked.

By exclusion, Section 202 appears to provide that no employee of the judicial branch may be a Special Employee. It is not at all clear why the statute should make it difficult for the judicial branch to hire consultants just as it is becoming evident that the judicial system and its administration are in need of new technology and modernization—matters on which outside consultants have typically been most helpful in private industry and in other branches of government. Nonetheless Section 202 appears to limit the definition of Special Employee to employees of the executive or legislative branch, employees of independent agencies, and employees of the District of Columbia. The exclusion of the judicial branch from this enumeration can only be interpreted as deliberate.

Members and employees of the uniformed forces are treated specially by Section 202. See Appendix B.

Classification of an employee as a Special Employee is a matter of considerable significance under the new legislation. The conflict of interest restrictions applicable to Special Employees are appreciably different from those applicable to regular employees. The differences will be noted in subsequent discussions of the substantive restrictions contained in the new legislation.

In any case, it is clear beyond argument that the intermittent or temporary employee is to be considered an "officer or employee" for purposes of the new conflict of interest legislation, including Section 203. Whether a particular person occupies the special status of a Special Employee is a subsidiary question.

1A–3.2.3. Non-employee; independent contractor

1A–3.2.3a. SECTION 281

A consultant may be deemed an "employee" in spite of the fact that he is unpaid and that he may have been called for a brief consultation only once. But there must be some actual employment relationship to invoke Section 281. One does not become an "employee of the United States" merely by voicing an opinion on government matters to a federal official at a cocktail party. The distinction may be shadowy in a particular case, and each situation must be judged on its own facts. Formalities can play an important part. In the ordinary situation, a person will not be considered to be a consultant-employee if he does not bear a formal appointment, is not enrolled on the personnel roster of the relevant agency, has no government personnel file in his name, and has not been sworn in or signed the customary oath of a government employee. Other factors that might be relevant can be conjectured. Is the person's advice solicited frequently? Is it sought by one official, who may be a personal friend, or impersonally by a number of persons in a government agency that needs expert counsel? Do meetings take place during office hours? Are they conducted in the government office, and does, perhaps, the adviser maintain a desk or working materials in government facilities?

Of recent years, careful counsel have become increasingly conscious that the edges of the government employment relationship are blurred and that relatively little contact with government operations may be needed to open the risk of classification as an "employee of the United States" subject to the disabilities of the conflict of interest laws.

Conflict of Interest and Federal Service develops in some detail the point that the simple categories of "employee" and "non-employee" are no longer adequate to describe the multiplicity of ways in which modern government gets its work done. The hybrid intermittent employee—partially in and partially out of government service—is an illustration. Remaining to be considered is the position of the more-or-less independent contractor.

Services may be performed by employees. But services may also be performed by persons who are not "employees"—those who are considered by the law to be "independent contractors." The family doctor and the building contractor are familiar examples from daily life. It is clearly understood that Section 281, while applicable to those who render services to the government as "employees," is not applicable to those who render services (even the same services) to the government as "independent contractors." But there are difficulties in applying this clear understanding.

The federal government has always turned to outside contractors for most of the material goods and equipment it consumes. The arsenal concept has been the exception. In recent years, as government has grown in size and complexity and its functions have become more technical, the federal establishment has increasingly turned to outside contractors not only for goods, but for services as well. Especially in the area of defense, the government has contracted out research and development tasks, turned over vast operations to private enterprise under management contracts, engaged outsiders to make elaborate analyses of and recommendations on alternative governmental policies, and enlisted private citizens to help in the dispensation of public research funds.[29] The contracts spelling out these intricate arrangements display an infinite variety of terms defining for each situation the work objectives, the compensation, the methods of operating, the degree and kind of checking and supervision, the way in which the work is to be staffed, and so on. Each contract is individually negotiated and, most frequently, is unique.

These modern techniques of governmental staffing have been considered more efficient in many areas than the alternative route of using in-house government personnel, and have made it possible to turn to government use and public advantage the talents of many men who would not have been willing to become regular government employees.[30]

[29] See CONFLICT OF INTEREST AND FEDERAL SERVICE, chs. 6 and 8.

[30] The proper scope of governmental contracting out is a growing topic of controversy. Two interesting papers on the subject were delivered at the 1960 Annual Meeting of the American Political Science Association: Heyman, The Problems and Benefits for the Government in Administra-

But if a project is done by personnel hired as direct govern-ment employees, they are subject to the restrictions of the conflict of interest laws, including Section 281. Can this result be avoided by the device of writing an employment arrange-ment in the legal vocabulary of "independent contractor"? The answer to this question, so stated, must be no. But the problem then becomes one of distinguishing the "true" independent con-tractor who should not be considered an "employee of the United States" for purposes of Section 281 from the "true" employee who masquerades behind a paper reading "independ-ent contractor."

Here, as in the fields of tort law and labor law where the same problem is familiar to every lawyer, it has proved exceedingly difficult to lay down functional criteria for distinguishing be-tween "employee" and "independent contractor." And, it may be unnecessary to say, case authority is apt to have little trans-fer value from one context to another: an "employee" for some purposes of classification may (and should) be considered an "independent contractor" for others. The most helpful point for inquiry is the degree of operational control exercised by the party to whom the services are being rendered. The key term is not "contractor" but "independent." If the contract narrowly specifies the work in detail, it looks less like that of an independ-ent contractor. And if the work of the asserted "independent contractor" is in fact closely supervised by regular government employees, he runs a risk of being considered an "employee," however his working arrangement may have been drafted. Other factors may, of course, be weighed as well. How is the person rendering service paid? What are his working condi-

tion by Contract (prepared as part of a project for the Brookings Institu-tion); Dupré and Gustafson, The "New Public Administration": Problems and Benefits for the Contractor in Government by Contract. See House Comm. on Government Operations, *Avoiding Conflict of Interest in De-fense Contracting and Employment,* H.R. Rep. No. 917, 88th Cong., 1st Sess. (1963).

tions? What was the history of bargaining that led to the arrangement? How is the government accustomed to have similar jobs done? What were the formalities of contracting, swearing in, bonding, etc.?

Canons of statutory construction are of their usual usefulness here, "through form to substance in protective legislation" canceling out "narrow construction of criminal statute."[31] Better to ask whether in the particular situation the person rendering services occupied the kind of inside position that could be taken advantage of in the manner forbidden to an "employee" by the section.

At present there is little material under Section 281 that helps to delimit the inside boundary of the independent contractor— the same boundary that marks the outside edge of the regulatory reach of the statute.[32] In an earlier day it was not so necessary to explore these edges. It was clear that the employee of a company providing goods and supplies to the government was not a government employee, and neither was the company. Service contractors, working close to the heart and nerve of inside government operations, did not exist. They do now. It may be predicted that some will seek to use the "independent contractor" form as a device to avoid conflict of interest and other restrictions applicable to government employees—and that in due time these efforts will be challenged in the courts. Little more can be done now than to point to the problem, note

[31] See 40 Ops. Att'y Gen. 289 (1943); 40 Ops. Att'y Gen. 294 (1943).
[32] The Attorney General has opined that an attorney for a national bank receiver is an independent contractor and not an employee of the United States for purposes of the predecessor of Section 281. 37 Ops. Att'y Gen. 204 (1933). See also 18 Ops. Att'y Gen. 161 (1885), discussed at note 22 *supra*. Of collateral relevance at best are the holdings and discussions of the term "independent contractor" in the following federal opinions concerning statutes other than the conflict of interest laws: Metcalf v. Mitchell, 269 U.S. 514 (1925); 37 Ops. Att'y Gen. 193 (1933); 19 Decs. Comp. Gen. 284 (1939); 13 Decs. Comp. Gen. 101 (1933); 12 Decs. Comp. Gen. 322 (1932).

its increasing relevance, and recommend to the counseling lawyer that he draw upon his professional judgment grounded in other fields of law where he has encountered the problem.

1A–3.2.3b. SECTION 203 (1963)

Section 203 adds nothing to the earlier discussion of the position of the independent contractor as such. As noted in ¶ 1A–3.2.2b, the language of the new statute does, however, put more stress upon a formal employment relationship as a prerequisite to the application of the statute.

1A–3.3. Other persons
1A–3.3a. SECTION 281

Section 281 forbids designated persons to receive compensation for certain acts. It does not forbid the payment of such compensation to such designated persons. Legal action against the payor must be grounded, if at all, on the theory that he is an aider and abettor. See Appendix D.

The application of Section 281 to partners and associates of government employees is discussed in Appendix C.

1A–3.3b. SECTION 203 (1963)

Unlike Section 281, Section 203 contains a separate subsection (c) dealing with outsiders who make payments to government employees that the employees are forbidden by law to receive, thus making it no longer necessary to rely on an aider and abettor theory to catch up with the seducer. The substantive rule applicable to such outside persons is discussed in ¶ 1A–4.7.

See Appendix C for discussion of the application of Law 87–849 to partners and associates of government employees.

1A-4. Substantive offense

Any person covered by Section 281 commits a crime if he

directly or indirectly receives or agrees to receive, any compensation for any services rendered or to be rendered, either by himself or another, in relation to any proceeding, contract, claim, controversy, charge, accusation, arrest, or other matter in which the United States is a party or directly or indirectly interested, before any department, agency, court martial, officer, or any civil, military or naval commission . . .

Corresponding language is in subsection (a) of Section 203. Very similar in its drafting, that subsection makes it a crime if a person subject to the section

otherwise than as provided by law for the proper discharge of official duties, directly or indirectly receives or agrees to receive, or asks, demands, solicits, or seeks, any compensation for any services rendered or to be rendered either by himself or another . . . in relation to any proceeding, application, request for a ruling or other determination, contract, claim, controversy, charge, accusation, arrest, or other particular matter in which the United States is a party or has a direct and substantial interest, before any department, agency, court-martial, officer, or any civil, military, or naval commission . . .

Viewed as a whole, the substantive offense under Section 203 differs from that under Section 281 mainly in that the new statute makes exception for certain special services listed in Section 205, and contains special provisions applicable to intermittent employees, and other outsiders who are not government employees. The offense under Section 203 in some cases overlaps the offense under Section 205. See ¶ 1B-4.

1A-4.1. Compensation

1A-4.1a. Section 281

To be guilty under Section 281 the person covered must be one who "directly or indirectly receives or agrees to receive, any compensation . . ." The courts have been clear that such receipt of compensation is not only an element of the crime, but the very gist of the matter. Unlike Section 283, in which compensation is not a factor, Section 281 is built on the assumption that the government employee who is paid for services in matters in which the United States is interested poses a greater threat than the employee who performs the same services gratuitously. As was said in *United States v. Booth*:

Whether the service in itself was of a proper or improper nature is not now very material: . . . inasmuch as *the essence of the statutory offense is,* not receiving, or agreeing to receive, compensation for proper or improper acts, but *the receiving, or the agreeing to receive, compensation for service of any kind,* rendered or to be rendered by himself in relation to any proceeding or other matter or thing, *without regard to its character,* in which the United States is directly or indirectly interested, before any department or officer. [Emphasis added.][33]

The same point was emphasized by the court in *May v. United States:*

If the money was received by May as compensation for acts done by him for the Garssons, it is immaterial that those acts were patriotic, legitimate and within the scope of his official duties as a Congressman . . . So, if a Congressman receives compensation for services rendered by him to a person in relation to any matter in which the United States is interested, before any Government department, he is guilty of violating the statute, even though the service rendered was a proper act on his part. A Congressman cannot legally receive compensation from a private person for doing his duty in respect to something in which that person and the United States have interests. *The gist of the offense is the receipt of compensation, not the nature of the act done by the recipient in consequence thereof.* [Emphasis added.][34]

[33] 148 Fed. 112, 117 (D. Ore. 1906).
[34] 175 F.2d 994, 1006 (D.C. Cir. 1949). A payment made to an employee for services he is obligated to perform as part of his official duties would also be a violation of 18 U.S.C. § 1914 (1958) if the employee is within the class of those subject to that statute. See Chapter 3.

Interpretation of the term "compensation" has never been litigated as such, but a contingent commission,[35] a share of partnership profits,[36] and an interest in a company[37] have appeared in the cases, and any pecuniary benefit would presumably serve. The cases offer no guidance on nonpecuniary benefits such as, for example, support in the government employee's efforts to be admitted to an exclusive club, but the policy of the statute would clearly be subverted if such benefits in exchange for services were not considered to be "compensation."

Nor has there been any substantial judicial construction of the meaning of "receipt" of compensation under the section. The statute itself makes any "indirect" receipt as culpable as a "direct" one, but it is not at all clear how far the concept of "indirect" receipt may reach. In *United States v. Quinn*,[38] a member of Congress whose partners rendered compensated services before the Bureau of Internal Revenue on behalf of certain taxpayers was indicted under Section 281. Defendant's motion for acquittal was granted on the ground that the evidence failed to establish that, in receiving a share of partnership profits, Quinn had received compensation with knowledge that it was for services which, as a member of Congress, he could not have legally performed under the section. Implicit in this analysis is the assumption that the receipt of the compensation by the partnership would not in itself constitute "indirect receipt" by the partner in government service in the sense in which the term is used in Section 281, at least where the government partner did not know of the source of the payment to the partnership. The court injects an element

[35] Beavers v. Haubert, 198 U.S. 77 (1905); Muschany v. United States, 324 U.S. 49 (1945).
[36] United States v. Quinn, 111 F. Supp. 870 (E.D.N.Y. 1953), 116 F. Supp. 802 (E.D.N.Y. 1953), 141 F. Supp. 622 (S.D.N.Y. 1956); 40 Ops. Att'y Gen. 183, 184 (1942).
[37] United States v. Cowart, 118 F. Supp. 903 (D.D.C. 1954).
[38] *Supra,* note 36.

of "knowledge," unmentioned in the statute, but it is not clear just what the defendant must have knowledge of to make out the offense. In the actual circumstances of the *Quinn* case, the defendant had personally received a distribution from the partnership based upon calculations that included the tainted compensation, so the precise question of receipt *vel non* was not before the court.

It is interesting that though the *Quinn* court had no difficulty in "imputing" the acts of the partners to the defendant, (1) it would not "impute" to the defendant the partners' receipt of the compensation with knowledge of its source, and (2) it would not impute to the defendant the partners' knowledge of the source of the compensation and thereby supply the missing element to the defendant's personal receipt of compensation. Somewhat similarly, the Attorney General has indicated that an employee may, without violating Section 281, retain his interest in a partnership rendering services forbidden to him under the section, if he is careful to see that he personally receives none of the compensation for those services.[39] Both the *Quinn* court and the Attorney General seem in agreement that the compensation must actually come into the hands of the defendant. In appropriate circumstances, however, it is a safe guess that a principle of "constructive receipt" would begin to operate, and the "indirect receipt" language of Section 281 would be used to prevent a government employee from evading the section by storing up compensation in a partnership or other vehicle against the day when he leaves government service.

Section 281 forbids not only receipt of compensation for the prohibited services, but also "agreeing to receive" such compensation. While most cases arising under the section have involved actual payments of compensation,[40] some have been

---

[39] 40 Ops. Att'y Gen. 289 (1943).

[40] A receipt of compensation was alleged or proved in the following cases: Burton v. United States, 131 Fed. 552 (E.D. Mo. 1904), *rev'd,*

predicated solely upon the defendant's agreement to receive compensation.[41] In several cases, the indictment has alleged both an agreement to receive the compensation and the receipt.[42] The Supreme Court has held that such an indictment is not duplicitous, and that a defendant can be convicted of both offenses arising out of the same transaction.[43]

Literally read, Section 281 would prevent the government itself from paying its own employees, since it forbids all compensation for services, not simply compensation from extra-governmental sources. To avoid this absurd result the courts have assumed that there is no offense if the compensation in question is, in substance, paid by the government. In the usual case under the section the source of the compensation is quite ap-

---

196 U.S. 283 (1905), *aff'd*, 202 U.S. 344 (1906); Beavers v. Haubert, 198 U.S. 77 (1905); Muschany v. United States, 324 U.S. 49 (1945); Opper v. United States, 322 F.2d 719 (6th Cir. 1954), *aff'd*, 348 U.S. 84 (1954); United States v. Driggs, 125 Fed. 520 (C.C.E.D.N.Y. 1903); McGregor v. United States, 134 Fed. 187 (4th Cir. 1904); United States v. Booth, 148 Fed. 112 (D. Ore. 1906); United States v. Mitchell, 163 Fed. 1014 (D. Ore. 1908), *aff'd*, United States v. Dunne, 173 Fed. 254 (9th Cir. 1909); Egan v. United States, 287 Fed. 958 (D.C. Cir. 1923), *appeal following remand*, 5 F.2d 267 (D.C. Cir. 1938); United States v. Baneth, 155 F.2d 978 (2d Cir. 1946); May v. United States, 175 F.2d 994 (D.C. Cir. 1949); Finnegan v. United States, 204 F.2d 105 (8th Cir. 1953); United States v. Olster, 15 F. Supp. 625 (M.D. Pa. 1936); United States v. Reisley, 32 F. Supp. 432 (D.N.J. 1940); United States v. Quinn, *supra* note 36.

[41] United States v. Long, 184 Fed. 184 (D. Ore. 1911); Dahly v. United States, 50 F.2d 37 (8th Cir. 1931); United States v. Adams, 115 F. Supp. 731 (D.N.D. 1953), *appeal dismissed on stipulation*, 209 F.2d 954 (8th Cir. 1954).

[42] *E.g.*, Burton v. United States, 202 U.S. 344 (1906); Egan v. United States, 287 Fed. 958 (D.C. Cir. 1923), *appeal following remand*, 5 F.2d 267 (D.C. Cir. 1925).

[43] Burton v. United States, 202 U.S. 344 (1906). The *Burton* holding has been followed in *Egan v. United States*, *supra* note 42, and has provided authority for similar holdings in connection with other criminal statutes as well. *Cf.* Read v. United States, 299 Fed. 918 (D.C. Cir. 1924) (forgery and uttering forged instrument); Ekberg v. United States, 167 F.2d 380 (1st Cir. 1948) (demanding and obtaining a valuable thing by false pretenses).

parent, but in some situations it is not so clear. *Muschany v. United States* was such a case.[44]

In the *Muschany* case, the War Department desired to obtain land for an ordnance project. To expedite the acquisition, the Quartermaster General contracted with one McDowell to secure purchase options. McDowell's compensation was to be 5 per cent of the sale price (to be taken out of the sale price and paid by the vendor). The option form provided that if the government condemned the land, it would pay compensation equal to the negotiated option price. By this method, 270 options were obtained and almost half the contracts were closed. Criticism of the prices and manner of purchase then developed, and the War Department repudiated the contracts and turned to condemnation. The landowners claimed the option price as refused, on the theory, *inter alia*, that the contracts were void as against public policy—that the payment of McDowell's commission by the vendors constituted a violation of the predecessor to Section 281. The Supreme Court upheld the validity of the contracts and held for the landowners. In its view, McDowell was the agent of the government and not of the vendors. While in form his commission was paid by the vendors, they were not paying him a fee contingent on his securing a government contract for them. In substance, his compensation was being paid by the United States. The court recognized the temptation for McDowell to inflate the sale price to the detriment of the government, but felt that while Congress could have prohibited this type of contract, it had not done so. The War Department had made a policy decision to conduct the acquisition in this manner and it was bound by it. The court said:

The evidence indicates that in reality McDowell was the Government's agent and that his commission, although nominally paid by the vendor, amounted to a payment by the Government to him as

[44] 324 U.S. 49 (1945).

its agent . . . It is the Government here who pays the contingent fee and pays it not for securing a contract from the Government, but a contract for the Government. . . .

Here the pay was for services rendered to the Government. In form the vendors agreed to pay the compensation but actually the United States was the payor. As stated above it was merely a convenient way in which the Government's promise to pay its agent could be met.[45]

The court's language must not be construed, however, to imply that it is a defense under Section 281 to show that the defendant's acts were a "service" to the government. The key finding in the *Muschany* case is that there was no outside compensation paid to McDowell, not that his services benefited the government.

The *Muschany* case was not a criminal prosecution, and the equities of the situation were hardly with the War Department. But the decision is worth noting because it illustrates that the source of compensation may sometimes be in legal doubt—and that, in another case, the court's conclusion as to whose "agent" the employee was might come out the other way.

1A–4.1b. SECTION 203 (1963)

As in the case of Section 281, services performed will not violate Section 203 unless the services are compensated. The new section is somewhat broader than the old in that it also forbids the government employee to ask, demand, solicit, or seek compensation for services forbidden by the statute. Otherwise the discussion at ¶ 1A–4.1a is applicable to Section 203.

1A–4.2. Services

1A–4.2a. SECTION 281

In order to charge a crime under Section 281, the indictment must allege that any compensation received has been or will be

[45] *Id.* at 64–65, 67.

for "services rendered or to be rendered by the recipient or another," and this nexus must be proven at trial if a conviction is to be sustained.[46] It is not sufficient for the government to allege and prove that money or other thing of value has passed or an agreement to pay has been made; in addition, the government must show that there have been or will be services, *and* that the payment was for the services rather than a gift.[47]

Under Section 281, it would appear that any act undertaken on behalf of a person other than the actor may be a service. The following have been, directly or indirectly, held to be services: using official influence to procure government contracts on behalf of private individuals;[48] giving special information or assistance to private individuals in connection with public lands;[49] representing private individuals before government officers, agencies, departments, etc.;[50] arranging interviews with government officials on behalf of a private company seeking to present its views on pending legislation;[51] intervening with government officials on behalf of private parties having contracts and other dealings with the government;[52] advising a

[46] *E.g.,* United States v. Quinn, *supra* note 36.

[47] *See, e.g.,* United States v. Cowart, 118 F. Supp. 903 (D.D.C. 1954).

[48] Beavers v. Haubert, 198 U.S. 77 (1905); Opper v. United States, 211 F.2d 719 (6th Cir. 1954), *aff'd,* 348 U.S. 84 (1954); McGregor v. United States, 134 Fed. 187 (4th Cir. 1904); United States v. Baneth, 155 F.2d 978 (2d Cir. 1946); United States v. Driggs, 125 Fed. 520 (C.C.E.D.N.Y. 1903).

[49] United States v. Booth, 148 Fed. 112 (D. Ore. 1906); United States v. Mitchell, 163 Fed. 1014 (C.C.D. Ore. 1906), *aff'd,* United States v. Dunne, 173 Fed. 254 (9th Cir. 1909); United States v. Long, 184 Fed. 184 (D. Ore. 1911).

[50] Burton v. United States, 131 Fed. 552 (E.D. Mo. 1904), *rev'd,* 196 U.S. 283 (1905), *aff'd,* 202 U.S. 344 (1906); Dahly v. United States, 50 F.2d 37 (8th Cir. 1931); United States v. Waldin, 122 F. Supp. 903 (E.D. Pa. 1954); United States v. Quinn, 111 F. Supp. 870 (E.D.N.Y. 1953), 116 F. Supp. 802 (1953), 141 F. Supp. 622 (S.D.N.Y. 1956); 14 OPS. ATT'Y GEN. 133 (1872); 40 OPS. ATT'Y GEN. 183 (1942); 41 OPS. ATT'Y GEN. No. 4 (1949).

[51] McMullen v. United States, 96 F.2d 574 (D.C. Cir. 1938).

[52] May v. United States, 175 F.2d 994 (D.C. Cir. 1949).

private company of the status of its tax returns, informing the
company that it was entitled to a refund for overpayment, and
preparing amended returns and claims for credit;[53] and appraising
lands of claimants in an eminent domain proceeding and
offering expert testimony on their behalf with respect to the
value of such lands.[54]

It is clearly established that if there are services rendered or
to be rendered, the proper or improper nature of these services
is irrelevant under the section.[55] All that must be shown in this
regard is that the defendant performed services and that he was
compensated therefor. Under this statute any service may be
performed, unless it is performed for pay. On the other hand,
any service, even if proper or praiseworthy in itself, becomes
tainted or criminal if the defendant is paid for rendering it.[56]

In order for there to have been a "service," however, the defendant
must have either performed certain acts on behalf of
private parties, or intended to perform these acts in the future.
If the defendant receives or agrees to receive compensation, but
does nothing and intends to do nothing for the payor, even
though the compensation passed for services which the recipient
promised the payor to perform, Section 281 has not been
violated.

The important case on the point is *United States v. Reisley*.[57]
Defendant, a contact representative in the Veterans' Administration,
in the course of his work received the record of one Barile,
who was clearly entitled to disability benefits. Instead of forwarding
it to the adjudication department immediately and in

[53] United States v. Olster, 15 F. Supp. 625 (M.D. Pa. 1936).
[54] United States v. Adams, 115 F. Supp. 731 (D.N.D. 1953) (indictment
dismissed on other grounds), *appeal dismissed on stipulation,* 209
F.2d 954 (8th Cir. 1954).
[55] United States v. Booth, 148 Fed. 112 (D. Ore. 1906); United States
v. Olster, 15 F. Supp. 625 (M.D. Pa. 1936); May v. United States, 175
F.2d 994 (D.C. Cir. 1949).
[56] See text accompanying notes 33 and 34 *supra.*
[57] 35 F. Supp. 102 (D.N.J. 1940).

the usual course of business, Reisley retained it for about two weeks. In the meantime he told Barile that he was a physician and, for $300, would procure an additional disability award for him. After Barile agreed to pay, defendant permitted the file to go to the adjudication department. The department awarded Barile the amount he was properly entitled to. Barile paid defendant $100 on account. The court felt that while defendant was guilty of obtaining money by false pretenses, he had not violated the predecessor of Section 281 because there was no evidence that any actual services were rendered or agreed upon. The court said:

The gravamen of [the] crime is that the defendant received compensation for services rendered to Barile before the Veterans' Administration. There was no evidence that the defendant rendered services to Barile, in the sense of advancing his claim, before the Veterans' Administration. On the contrary it is clear that the right of Barile to receive additional benefits had already been approved and that Barile therefore required no help from the defendant. In fact the success of the defendant's scheme was entirely dependent upon his ability to retard the progress of the Barile record toward formal adjudication. The government urges that his releasing of the Barile record after his agreement for compensation with Barile constituted the rendering of a service to the latter. This action, which merely neutralized his previous disservice, was not the service he had agreed to render, however, and I do not think that it was rendered before the Veterans' Administration within the meaning of the statute. . . . In [this statute] . . . Congress dealt with that threat to the integrity of governmental action which arises when a Senator, Representative, departmental head or other federal officer or clerk sells his influence to a claimant against the government. It is the trading for pay of the prestige or power which comes with the defendant's position in the government that is dealt with by this section. If no other government official knows of the defendant's interest in the matter at hand, if the latter argues no claim, appears before no department or governmental body on behalf of the one who pays him, makes no appearance by himself or agent in the matter in which the United States has an interest, and does not himself take favorable action in his own department upon the matter, it is obvious that he has not utilized his position with the government or his influence with his co-workers to serve the claimant who has paid him. Whatever his offense if he receives pay for imaginary services falsely represented to have been rendered in a matter already decided by others in the claimant's favor, it is not that contemplated by the statute upon which the defendant before me was indicted. Because of the absence of evidence as to actual services rendered to Barile by the defendant his conviction cannot stand.[58]

The *Reisley* case has been criticized.[59]

Just as Section 281 prohibits both the receipt of compensation and the agreement to receive compensation, so it makes criminal both the past and present rendition of services and the agreement to render services in the future. Most of the cases decided have alleged or established services rendered. A few have dealt with agreements to render services.[60] The only case in which it affirmatively appears that a defendant was indicted for and convicted of both rendering services and agreeing to render services is *Burton v. United States*.[61] There is no specific discussion of whether the two acts constitute separate and distinct offenses, both outlawed by Congress. It is probable that the *Burton* holding covers present and future services as well as receipts and agreements to receive compensation, and that the former, as well as the latter, is a distinct offense.

Generally, cases arising under Section 281 involve instances in which a government employee is accused of having violated

[58] *Id.* at 104.
[59] For example, *Federal Conflict of Interest Legislation*, A Staff Report to Subcommittee No. 5 of the Committee on the Judiciary of the House of Representatives, 24–25, 50–51 (March 1, 1958).
[60] Dahly v. United States, 50 F.2d 37 (8th Cir. 1931); United States v. Waldin, 122 F. Supp. 903 (E.D. Pa. 1954); United States v. Adams, 115 F. Supp. 731 (D.N.D. 1953), *appeal dismissed on stipulation,* 209 F.2d 954 (8th Cir. 1954).
[61] 131 Fed. 552 (E.D. Mo. 1904), *rev'd,* 196 U.S. 283 (1905), *aff'd,* 202 U.S. 344 (1906). See note 43 *supra,* and accompanying text.

the statute in that he received or agreed to receive compensation for services which he himself rendered or agreed to render in the future. Ever since its enactment in 1864, however, the section has provided that a government employee is subject to criminal sanctions, even if the services are rendered by someone other than himself, so long as he is compensated for them. This situation is most apt to arise when a person covered by Section 281 is a member of a partnership and his partners render or agree to render services which the government employee is forbidden to perform under the statute. See Appendix C.

One final point relating to "services" should be mentioned. The conflict of interest statutes have not been construed to prevent government employees from prosecuting their own personal claims against the government so long as the exercise of their official influence or position is not involved. See ¶ 1B–4.1a. Section 281 does not often raise a problem on this score, since the language of the section does not read easily upon the situation of one appearing *pro se;* one does not usually render "services" to himself, nor does he often compensate himself for such services. But questions of this kind can arise under the section when the facts are changed only slightly. May the government employee assist a business enterprise of which he is the sole owner?—sole owner, with his wife?—sole owner, with his wife and son?—one-half owner, with the other one-half owner inactive in the management of the concern? Or, to use a different example, what of the government employee who is the administrator or executor of an estate, or a guardian or trustee under a will? A sufficiently rigid reading of Section 281 would bar him from assisting the estate or trust in its tax matters, while as a fiduciary he might not be able to avoid close attention to such matters. In some situations it appears that the only safe route for the employee is to accept no compensation for his work, or resign as fiduciary. In other situations the employee's personal estate might be so intimately connected with his fiduciary estate that he could bring himself within the *pro se* exemptions. There are no cases or other interpretive materials on these questions.

1A–4.2b. SECTION 203 (1963)

The discussion at ¶ 1A–4.2a is applicable to the element of "services" under Section 203, with the exception that Section 205 lists certain exemptions that have the effect of permitting some services under Section 203 that are forbidden by Section 281. These exemptions are discussed at ¶ 1B–4.7.

1A–4.3. Transactions

1A–4.3a. SECTION 281

A government employee may lawfully be compensated for many kinds of services. Section 281 forbids such compensation only if the services are "in relation to any proceeding, contract, claim, controversy, charge, accusation, arrest, or other matter in which the United States is a party or directly or indirectly interested . . ." The scope of this language is manifestly broad; just how broad is hard to say.

The terms in the quoted list overlap. Some are redundant altogether. All surely fall within the inclusive term "or other matter." The key term, then, is "matter in which the United States is a party or directly or indirectly interested."

The courts have squarely rejected the argument that Section 281 is limited to "matters" in which the United States has a proprietary interest, as opposed to a governmental, nonpecuniary, interest. One issue in *Burton v. United States* was whether, for purposes of the section, the United States had an "interest" in an investigation by the Post Office Department to determine whether a company had used the mails to defraud. All the judicial opinions in the *Burton* case agreed that the United States did have an "interest" in a mail fraud order inquiry even though it had no pecuniary or proprietary stake in the matter. The lower court said:

Counsel [for the defendant] have called attention to several cases . . . in which the words "interest" and "interested" are found in statutes relating to disqualification of parties, witnesses, and judges in legal proceedings—that is, suits pending in the courts—and to cases involving the right of appeal in suits in which the state is interested as a party or otherwise. In these cases it has been held generally that the "interest" referred to must be a pecuniary or property interest, and counsel for the accused contend that the interest of the United States contemplated by section [281] is only that kind of an interest, . . . and that the matter or thing pending before the department within the purview of that section must be one in the determination of which the United States may gain or lose something of value. These cases involve statutes relating generally to suits or actions at law wherein property or property rights are involved. The witnesses and judges whose "interest" in the matter was made a disqualification were such as had no other duty to discharge in the cases except, so far as the witnesses were concerned, to testify, and, so far as the judges were concerned, to render judgments and pass upon rights of property or other valuable rights, which afforded the subject of the particular litigation in hand. The Legislatures which enacted the statutes construed in those cases obviously had primarily in view the narrow sphere of the subject of litigation, which, of course, was property . . . The legislative vision need not and did not extend beyond the effect of the pecuniary interest of the witnesses or judges in the individual cases. Is this the measure of duty or obligation of the United States in the matter of inquiries or investigations pending before its executive departments or bureaus? I think not . . . In my opinion, the government of the United States is interested in the matters of inquiry and investigation pending before its executive departments, looking towards the enforcement of its laws, . . . It follows that, in my opinion, the United States can be and is interested . . . in the matter alleged to have been pending before the Post-Office Department. [Footnote omitted.][62]

In its final opinion in the *Burton* case, the Supreme Court stated:

[62] 131 Fed. 552, 557–58 (E.D. Mo. 1904).

It is said that, within the meaning of the statute, the United States is not interested in any proceeding or matter pending before an executive Department, unless it has a direct moneyed, or pecuniary interest in the result. Under this view, Senators, Representatives and Delegates in Congress, who are members of the bar, may regularly practice their profession *for compensation* before the executive Departments in proceedings, which if not directly involving the pecuniary interests of the United States, yet involve substantial pecuniary interests for their clients as well as the enforcement of the laws of the United States enacted for the protection of the rights of the public. Such a view rests upon an interpretation of the statute which is wholly inadmissible.[63]

Several other cases have expressly applied the principle that the government does not have to have a pecuniary interest in a matter to be "interested" within the meaning of Section 281 and its predecessors. In *United States v. Booth*[64] and *United States v. Long*,[65] it was held that the United States had a direct interest in its public lands and in their disposition pursuant to law. The court in the *Long* case found a dual interest of the government:

An application for the purchase of land from the government under the timber and stone act is, in effect, the inauguration of a proceeding through which to acquire land from the government, and in which the government is an interested party. It is an interested party in two aspects: First, in its governmental aspect, to see that the laws are enforced and obeyed; and, second, in its proprietary right, as the owner of the land the title to which is sought to be acquired from it.[66]

And the Attorney General has concluded that the United States is interested in the filing and prosecution of patent applications before the United States Patent Office. He opined:

The purpose in filing and prosecuting a patent application is to secure a statutory monopoly for the prescribed period through the

[63] United States v. Burton, 202 U.S. 344, 372 (1906).
[64] 148 Fed. 112 (D. Ore. 1906).
[65] 184 Fed. 184 (D. Ore. 1911).
[66] *Id.* at 186.

granting of a patent by the Commissioner of Patents. Through these proceedings the United States grants valuable rights which may be exercised against others, including the United States itself. The granting of a patent is a matter of great public interest. . . . The United States is not only interested in the granting of a patent but also its interest in patents granted is a continuing one. It may, for example, bring suit to cancel patents obtained by fraud. . . .[67]

An unusual issue respecting the reach of the government's "interest" arose in *United States v. Olster*. It was there held that the United States was "interested" in certain claims and proceedings for purposes of Section 281, notwithstanding the fact that they were based on a statute that had been declared unconstitutional. Said the court:

The United States was still a party to the proceeding and interested therein notwithstanding the fact that the Agricultural Adjustment Act . . . was declared unconstitutional. Its interest did not immediately and finally cease when the act was declared unconstitutional. It was interested, for example, in retaining taxes that could not be lawfully returned, and in returning the taxes that were lawfully claimed, less proper charges for disbursement. The offense charged did not depend upon the validity of the pending proceeding; the gist of the crime is the wrong done to the people by corruption in public office, to wit, the receipt of money by an officer of the United States for services to any person in relation to any proceeding in which the United States is a party, or directly or indirectly interested. Certainly the corruptness of the defendants' acts and the wrong done the government and the people was not lessened by a subsequent determination that the processing taxes were invalid. . . .

Section [281] of the Criminal Code . . . requires only that the services rendered, for which money is received, be "in relation to" a proceeding in which the United States is interested, whether or not the pending matter is valid.[68]

Given so extensive a concept of governmental "interest," and so open-ended a word as "matter," what limits are there to the

[67] 41 Ops. Att'y Gen. No. 4, pp. 2–3 (1949).
[68] United States v. Olster, 15 F. Supp. 625, 626–27 (M.D. Pa. 1936).

scope of Section 281? Surely the most significant limitations are those relating to the forum in which the "matter" is being conducted, discussed in ¶ 1A–4.4. But there is another kind of limitation, vague though it may be, upon the term "matter."

The listing in Section 281 of "proceeding, contract, claim, controversy, charge, accusation, arrest" lends some atmosphere of particularity to the word "matter." The point is little discussed, but the cases in fact treat the statute almost as though it read "or other particular transaction in which . . ." Some such limitation is essential to lower the level of abstraction of the word "matter." For example, "economics" is surely a "matter" in which the United States is "interested"; but an indictment under Section 281 must do more than assert that the defendant provided compensated services "in relation to economics." The listing of concrete transactions in the section has led to a more or less conscious application of the notion of *eiusdem generis*, and correspondingly narrowed the potential breadth of the word "matter."[69]

Little further generalization can be offered regarding the scope of transactions covered by Section 281. Some guidance may be found by an empiric review of the following collected cases. The section does not make it necessary to distinguish in a particular case whether the facts at bar fall within one or another of the listed categories of transactions, and the courts have not usually attempted a classification. In some instances, however, the court has characterized a transaction as lying within one or more of the designated categories. Where this has occurred, the court's characterization is indicated in the footnotes.

The following transactions have been held to be within Section 281 so as to prohibit a government employee from provid-

[69] A grudging recognition of *eiusdem generis* appears in Burton v. United States, 131 Fed. 552, 555 (E.D. Mo. 1904). See note 88 *infra* for a case in which the court's opinion does not limit "matter" to a concrete transaction.

ing compensated services with regard thereto in an executive forum: mail fraud order inquiry;[70] application for tracts of public lands;[71] criminal prosecution;[72] eminent domain condemnation;[73] investigation regarding taxes;[74] patent application;[75] proceeding before War Department on behalf of officer convicted by a court martial;[76] government acquisition of land;[77] government procurement contracts;[78] claim for disability benefits from the Veterans' Administration;[79] Indian claim;[80] pension claim against the government;[81] certain tax and ad-

[70] Burton v. United States, 131 Fed. 552 (E.D. Mo. 1904), rev'd, 196 U.S. 283 (1905), aff'd, 202 U.S. 344 (1906) (proceeding or matter).

[71] United States v. Mitchell, 163 Fed. 1014 (C.C.D. Ore. 1908), aff'd, United States v. Dunne, 173 Fed. 254 (9th Cir. 1909) (applications, proceedings, claims, matters, and things); United States v. Long, 184 Fed. 184 (D. Ore. 1911) (a matter or thing). Until 1948, the predecessors to Section 281 included the words "or thing" after the word "matter." The deletion of these words in the 1948 Criminal Code is not thought to have affected the statute substantively; the point is mentioned only to explain the appearance of the words "matter or thing" in the older cases.

[72] Chudoff v. McGranery, 179 F.2d 869 (3d Cir. 1950); United States v. Quinn, 111 F. Supp. 870 (E.D.N.Y. 1953), 141 F. Supp. 622 (S.D.N.Y. 1956); Dahly v. United States, 50 F.2d 37 (8th Cir. 1931). Federal criminal prosecutions offer a clear instance of the appearance of the United States as a "party."

[73] Muschany v. United States, 324 U.S. 49 (1945); United States v. Adams, 115 F. Supp. 731 (D.N.D. 1953), appeal dismissed on stipulation, 209 F.2d 954 (8th Cir. 1954).

[74] United States v. Olster, 15 F. Supp. 625 (M.D. Pa. 1936) (proceedings, claims, matters, and things); United States v. Waldin, 122 F. Supp. 903 (E.D. Pa. 1954); United States v. Quinn, 111 F. Supp. 870 (E.D. N.Y. 1953), 116 F. Supp. 802 (E.D.N.Y. 1953) 141 F. Supp. 622 (S.D. N.Y. 1956); Morgenthau v. Barrett, 108 F.2d 481 (D.C. Cir. 1939).

[75] 40 Ops. Att'y Gen. 183 (1942); 41 Ops. Att'y Gen. No. 4 (1949).

[76] 14 Ops. Att'y Gen. 133 (1872).

[77] Muschany v. United States, 324 U.S. 49 (1945).

[78] Beavers v. Haubert, 198 U.S. 77 (1905); Opper v. United States 211 F.2d 719 (6th Cir. 1954), aff'd, 348 U.S. 84 (1954); McGregor v. United States, 134 Fed. 187 (4th Cir. 1904); United States v. Baneth, 155 F.2d 978 (2nd Cir. 1946); May v. United States, 175 F.2d 994 (D.C. Cir. 1949); United States v. Driggs, 125 Fed. 520 (C.C.E.D.N.Y. 1903).

[79] United States v. Reisley, 32 F. Supp. 432 (D.N.J. 1940), 35 F. Supp. 102 (D.N.J. 1940) (claim and matter).

[80] 18 Ops. Att'y Gen. 161 (1885) (claim).

[81] 28 Ops. Att'y Gen. 131 (1910) (claim).

miralty matters;[82] "claims" in general;[83] matters before Court of Claims;[84] matters before the Treasury Department;[85] enactment of excise tax;[86] "matters" in general;[87] status of public lands;[88] and Army commissions, transfers, promotions, and furloughs.[89]

As discussed in ¶ 1A–4.4, compensated services are not forbidden by Section 281 unless performed before an agency or other component of the executive branch of the government. But what "matter" is there pending before the executive branch that is not a "matter in which the United States is interested"? Expressed another way, is it possible that the limitation of forum makes it unnecessary to work out refined interpretations of what transactions are covered by the section? It may be plausibly argued that if the services are performed before the executive branch, they must relate to a matter in which the United States is interested. No case had gone quite this far in expanding the concept of transactions covered by the statute. But the language

[82] 40 Ops. Att'y Gen. 289 (1943).

[83] 40 Ops. Att'y Gen. 294 (1943).

[84] E.g., Captain Tyler's Motion, 18 Ct. Cl. 25 (1883); In re Winthrop, 31 Ct. Cl. 35 (1895); Simmons v. United States, 55 Ct. Cl. 56 (1920).

[85] Morgenthau v. Barrett, 108 F.2d 481 (D.C. Cir. 1939). The main issue in the case was the application of Section 281 to a reserve military officer. The matter is discussed in Appendix B infra. Overruled, or at least modified, as to reserve officers by subsequent amendment to Section 281, the decision remains good law in distinguishing between the ranges of transactions covered by Sections 281 and 283 respectively.

[86] McMullen v. United States, 96 F.2d 574 (D.C. Cir. 1938). Defendant arranged for a corporate officer to visit government officials to present the company's opposition to enactment of the tax.

[87] Finnegan v. United States, 204 F.2d 105 (8th Cir. 1953).

[88] United States v. Booth, 148 F.2d 112 (D. Ore. 1906). The court's decision calls for special comment. Defendant receiver in a United States Land Office received money for giving the payor advance information as to when certain lands were to become open to entry. The court found a violation of the predecessor of Section 281 since it considered the "status of the public lands" to be a "matter" in which the Government has an "interest." The opinion goes further than any other in generalizing the term "matter." See note 69 supra and accompanying text.

[89] May v. United States, 175 F.2d 994 (D.C. Cir. 1949).

of two decisions suggests this consequence.[90] And so far, no defendant has yet persuaded a court that the matter in which he assisted was not covered by the words "any proceeding, contract, claim, controversy, charge, accusation, arrest, or other matter in which the United States is a party or directly or indirectly interested."

1A–4.3b. SECTION 203 (1963)

The discussion at ¶ 1A–4.3a regarding transactions covered by Section 281 must be modified somewhat to make it applicable to Section 203.

Under the new section, the forbidden services must be performed "in relation to any proceeding, application, request for a ruling or other determination, contract, claim, controversy, charge, accusation, arrest, or other particular matter in which the United States is a party or has a direct and substantial interest . . ." Comparison with the language in Section 281 will show that "application" and "request for a ruling or other determination" have been added to the list of transactions covered. In all likelihood, these transactions were already included under the coverage of Section 281, but the new language was added "to make clear that the enumeration is comprehensive of all matters that come before a Federal department or agency."[91]

A second change made by Section 203 is considerably more important than initially appears. The new provision inserts the word "particular" before the language "other matter." It is noted in ¶ 1A–4.3a that the specific listing of "proceeding, con-

---

[90] Burton v. United States, 131 Fed. 552, 556 (E.D. Mo. 1904) ("Congress industriously specified the several subjects just mentioned, obviously intending to cover any and all matters and things that might be the subject of inquiry before a department in which the United States should be interested"); United States v. Cowart, 118 F. Supp. 903 (D.D.C. 1954) (government has an interest in investigations before government departments).

[91] H.R. REP. No. 748, 87th Cong., 1st Sess. 20 (1961).

tract, claim . . . etc." lends some atmosphere of particularity to the word "matter," and that a sensible interpretation of the restrictions contained in Section 281 requires that an indictment do more than assert, for example, that the defendant provided compensated services "in relation to economics." In recognition of this necessity, the new Section 203 is restricted to "particular matters" such as a particular contract, a particular case, a particular proceeding, or a particular claim. As the House report explains, the word "particular" is inserted in order "to emphasize that the restriction applies to a specific case or matter and not to a general area of activity."[92]

Finally there is the issue discussed in ¶ 1A–4.3a regarding the degree of governmental interest in a transaction required to bring it under Section 281. In a generalized way the government has some interest in virtually every transaction in the United States, and surely some interest in all transactions in a federal executive forum. Section 203 is intended not to reach this far, however. The new statute is limited to matters "in which the United States is a party or has a direct and substantial interest." This language has been substituted for the vague "directly or indirectly interested" standard contained in Section 281.

Except for these points, the discussion at ¶ 1A–4.3a regarding Section 281 has equal bearing on Section 203.

1A–4.4. Forum

1A–4.4a. SECTION 281

Since 1864, when the first predecessor of Section 281 was enacted, the statute has provided that criminal penalty attaches to a government employee's compensated services if, and only if, the services are performed in particular designated forums.

---

[92] *Ibid.* Compare the even more particularized language of subsection (c) of Section 203, discussed in ¶ 1A–4.6b.

Section 281 is not violated unless the services are performed before a "department, agency, court martial, officer, or any civil, military, or naval commission."

The bill that was originally introduced in 1863 forbade members of Congress from practicing before courts, with or without compensation. In debate, the bill was broadened to cover government employees in general, and narrowed to exclude uncompensated services and to exclude practice before courts. There was extended debate on the matter of excluding judicial proceedings, not only at the time of enactment but again in 1908 when an amendment to forbid practice before courts was proposed. Both times Congress explicitly chose to exclude matters before a court of law from the operation of the statute.[93]

It is settled that an indictment must allege specifically before what department, agency, officer, etc., services were rendered, in order to charge an offense under Section 281. Two recent District Court cases are illustrative.

In *United States v. Adams*,[94] the indictment charged the following facts. There was pending in the North Dakota District Court a condemnation proceeding for the Army Department brought under federal eminent domain laws. Certain parties appeared, claiming ownership in the lands and demanding compensation for their taking. The defendant, an employee of the Soil Conservation Service, allegedly agreed to receive compensation for services to be rendered by him for the claimants. He had agreed to appraise the lands of the claimants as a soil expert, and, as an expert witness on their behalf, to testify as to the value of the lands in the District Court action in which the amount of compensation was an issue. Defendant claimed that failure to allege that the proceedings were pending before an agency or department rendered the indictment fatally de-

[93] See Appendix E.
[94] 115 F. Supp. 731 (D.N.D. 1953), *appeal dismissed on stipulation*, 209 F.2d 954 (8th Cir. 1954).

fective. The government answered that even though the indictment referred to the proceeding as pending in the District Court only, the subject matter upon which the suits were based was also pending before the Army Department, and therefore defendant's conduct violated Section 281. Relying upon the legislative history of the statute, the court agreed with the defendant.

For this Court now to spell into the statute the idea that Congress intended to include proceedings before courts would be nothing more nor less than judicial legislation. Criminal statutes are to be strictly construed. . . . The Government's theory that the cases in which the defendant was employed by the former landowners were also pending before the Corps of Engineers, Department of the Army, cannot overcome the difficulty. The indictment itself refers to no proceeding pending before any department, but alleges only that the proceeding was before this Court. Furthermore, even if it be assumed that the proceeding was also necessarily pending before the Corps of Engineers, the indictment cannot stand because it is not alleged that the services were rendered or were to be rendered before such department. Nowhere in the indictment is the charge found, or even inferred, that the defendant *received* or agreed to receive "* * * *compensation for any services* * * *" in relation to any proceeding * * * *before any department* * * *," etc. (Emphasis supplied.) [Citation omitted.] It is alleged only that the defendant agreed to appraise the lands and to testify as an expert witness upon the trial in court. The Government's theory is not tenable.[95]

In *United States v. Waldin*,[96] the indictment charged that the defendant, a Zone Deputy Collector of the Office of the Collector of Internal Revenue, Treasury Department of the United States, received compensation for services to be rendered in relation to an investigation being conducted by the Treasury Department into alleged tax delinquencies of one Mogavero. Defendant moved to dismiss the indictment on the grounds that

[95] 115 F. Supp. 731, 735 (D.N.D. 1953).
[96] 122 F. Supp. 903 (E.D. Pa. 1954).

it failed to allege before what department or agency the services involved were to be rendered. The court interpreted the history of the statute to indicate an intent "to protect the right of members of Congress and Governmental officers and employees, if otherwise qualified, to appear as counsel before judicial tribunals as distinguished from executive departments, administrative agencies, and courts-martial."[97] The court then went further than the decision in the *Adams* case. There it was held than an indictment is defective if it shows on its face that services were rendered before a court rather than a department or agency, or if it fails to allege that the matter in question was pending before *some* department or agency. The court in the *Waldin* case added that even if it affirmatively appears that the proceeding was pending before, and the services were to be rendered before, a department rather than a court, the indictment is still insufficient if it does not contain an allegation of the specific department or agency before which the services are to be rendered. The court said:

The indictment does not allege what specific Government department or agency, if any, the services were to be rendered before. It is possible (at least as a matter of logic) that defendant's services were to be rendered before a judicial court. If they were, the defendant would have committed no crime under the Act in question. If defendant were a lawyer and had agreed to represent Mogavero in a judicial proceeding, perhaps his conduct would constitute an offense under some other statute and undoubtedly a violation of the civil service regulations, but his conduct would not constitute a crime under the statute involved in the present case.[98]

Inevitably there are problems where a matter is simultaneously pending before an administrative and a judicial tribunal, or where an administrative proceeding is in the process of ripening into a judicial proceeding. In *United States v.*

[97] *Id.* at 904.
[98] *Id.* at 904–05.

Quinn,[99] a former member of Congress and his law partners were indicted under Section 281. The charge was that they had received compensation for rendering services in connection with certain tax matters pending before the Bureau of Internal Revenue. Defendants moved for dismissal on the grounds that the services performed were legal services to clients in various stages of criminal proceedings and hence were not prohibited by the statute. The court agreed that the statute was not designed to cover cases or judicial proceedings, but stated:

Nowhere in the indictment does it appear that the acts charged to the defendant Quinn were steps or incidents in cases or judicial proceedings, whether then pending or not. In passing on the first ground stated in the defendants' notice of motion I am limited, so far as the facts are concerned, to consideration of the contents of the indictment, alone, and I find nothing therein to indicate that the matters involved were necessarily "cases or proceedings."[100]

Defendants then made another motion claiming that the indictment was defective in that it did not state that the "matters" involved in Quinn's appearances before the agencies or departments in question were not "cases or proceedings." The court rejected this argument, saying:

It . . . still is the Court's opinion that . . . the indictment sets forth with more than adequate particularity and clarity the "matters" pending in the Government agencies and departments in which the defendant Quinn is alleged to have appeared for compensation. . . . This Court's probably gratuitous observation that the statute does not prohibit the appearance by the defendant Quinn, a lawyer-congressman, in a "case or proceeding" is not inconsistent, as counsel intimates, with the opinion that the indictment is adequate, since there is nothing therein to indicate that the "matters" involved were in fact "cases or proceedings."[101]

[99] 111 F. Supp. 870 (E.D.N.Y. 1953), 116 F. Supp. 802 (E.D.N.Y. 1953), 141 F. Supp. 622 (S.D.N.Y. 1956).
[100] 111 F. Supp. 870, 872–73 (E.D.N.Y. 1953).
[101] 116 F. Supp. 802, 803 (E.D.N.Y. 1953).

The view taken by this court is more favorable to the prosecution than that indicated in the *Waldin* case, where the court bends over backwards to give the defendant the benefit of the doubt if there is even a theoretical possibility that the matters in question were judicial proceedings.

The *Adams* court implies that, if the defendant performs services before a department or agency in a matter also pending before a court, he violates Section 281. The *Quinn* case hints the contrary—that a government employee representing clients in a court proceeding may also perform certain services before departments or agencies if such services are incident to the court proceeding. The issue came close to decision in *Chudoff v. McGranery*.[102] There, a criminal proceeding against one Turner was pending in a federal District Court; Turner was represented by Chudoff, a lawyer and congressman. Chudoff appeared before Judge McGranery in the District Court and in-indicated that he would plead Turner not guilty and that he, Chudoff, intended to discuss the case with United States Postal Inspectors and with the United States Attorney. The judge answered that he believed that Chudoff would violate Section 281 if he went ahead with this plan. His theory was that while the statute did not forbid a congressman to try a court case in which the United States was a party, it did forbid him from communicating with an "agency" of the United States respecting the trial. The judge said: "[The statute] goes so far, Mr. Chudoff, that if you can try a case without talking to the Assistant United States Attorney you will be permitted to do so."[103] Chudoff later petitioned the Court of Appeals for the Third Circuit for a writ of mandamus or prohibition directing Judge McGranery to permit Chudoff to appear for Turner. The appellate could find no justiciable controversy, on the grounds that (1) at the time McGranery had refused to permit Chudoff

102 179 F.2d 869 (3d Cir. 1950).
103 *Id.* at 870.

to enter a plea Chudoff had not been admitted to the bar of the court, (2) in the interim a plea of guilty had been entered in the Turner matter, and (3) when the matter came up again it appeared that Judge McGranery had agreed to let Chudoff appear for Turner, adding only that if he did so he (the judge) would probably send the record to the Attorney General for such action as the Attorney General might see fit to take. The appellate court said:

we are of the opinion that this court could not impose any sanction that would prohibit a United States judge or any other person from making a complaint to the Attorney General of the United States if he believes that a federal statute is being violated. In so stating we do not determine the validity of the respective views expressed by Judge McGranery or by Mr. Chudoff in their colloquy in court or in their subsequent conferences.[104]

If Judge McGranery's view is adopted, any federal prosecution is also a matter before the Department of Justice, and, as a practical matter, no government employee may represent a defendant in a criminal proceeding in a federal court. It may be doubted that Section 281 was intended to reach so far, but as yet there is no decision on this important point.

In an even more unsatisfactory state are other questions raised by the language "department, agency, court martial, officer, or any civil, military, or naval commission . . ." appearing in Section 281. The Criminal Code contains definitions of both "department" and "agency." The definition of "agency" reads:

The term "agency" includes any department, independent establishment, commission, administration, authority, board or bureau of the United States or any corporation in which the United States has a proprietary interest.[105]

[104] *Id.* at 872.
[105] 18 U.S.C. § 6 (1958). The definition of "department" in the same section is less broad, since it refers to the ten Cabinet departments only. See ¶ 1A–3.1.

Since this definition includes "department" within "agency," the use of the word "department" in Section 281 is redundant. But what of the other words in the "forum" language of Section 281: what do they add to the scope of the section?

From the existing cases there is little to be learned about the forums before which services rendered will violate Section 281. In almost all the cases it has been obvious that a "department" or "agency" was involved, since the services were alleged to have been performed before one of the ten executive departments.[106] One case concerned an independent commission.[107] But the difficult problems of scope that bedevil the counseling lawyer have not yet come to litigation.

The most important unresolved question of this kind is

[106] *Defense Department:* Muschany v. United States, 324 U.S. 49 (1945); United States v. Baneth, 155 F.2d 978 (2d Cir. 1946); May v. United States, 175 F.2d 994 (D.C. Cir. 1949); United States v. Adams, 115 F. Supp. 731 (D.N.D. 1953), *appeal dismissed on stipulation,* 209 F.2d 954 (8th Cir. 1954); Opper v. United States, 211 F.2d 719 (6th Cir. 1954), *aff'd,* 348 U.S. 84 (1954); 14 Ops. Att'y Gen. 133 (1872).

Post Office Department: Beavers v. Haubert, 198 U.S. 77 (1905); Burton v. United States, 131 F.2d 552 (E.D. Mo. 1904), *rev'd,* 196 U.S. 283 (1905), *aff'd,* 202 U.S. 344 (1906); McGregor v. United States, 134 Fed. 187 (4th Cir. 1904).

Justice Department: Chudoff v. McGranery, 179 F.2d 869 (3d Cir. 1950).

Treasury Department: Morgenthau v. Barrett, 108 F.2d 481 (D.C. Cir. 1939); United States v. Waldin, 122 F. Supp. 903 (E.D. Pa. 1954); United States v. Olster, 15 F. Supp. 625 (M.D. Pa. 1936); United States v. Quinn, 111 F. Supp. 870 (E.D.N.Y. 1953), 116 F. Supp. 802 (E.D.N.Y. 1953), 141 F. Supp. 622 (S.D.N.Y. 1956).

Commerce Department: 40 Ops. Att'y Gen. 183 (1942); 41 Ops. Att'y Gen. No. 4 (1949).

Agriculture Department: United States v. Cowart, 118 F. Supp. 903 (D.D.C. 1954).

Interior Department: United States v. Booth, 148 Fed. 112 (D. Ore. 1906); United States v. Mitchell, 163 Fed. 1014 (D. Ore. 1908), *aff'd,* United States v. Dunne, 173 Fed. 254 (9th Cir. 1909); United States v. Long, 184 Fed. 184 (D. Ore. 1911).

McMullen v. United States, 96 F.2d 574 (D.C. Cir. 1938), involved services before the State Department, the War Department, and the Commerce Department.

[107] United States v. Reisley, 32 F. Supp. 432 (D.N.J. 1940), 35 F. Supp. 102 (D.N.J. 1940).

whether Section 281 forbids a government employee to render compensated services before Congress or a Congressional committee. Arguing against the statute's applicability are the absence of any supporting legislative history and the undeniably "executive" flavor of the forums listed in the section and in the definition of "agency" in the Criminal Code. Technical arguments are available to support such coverage, however; the definition of "agency" is by its terms inclusive and not exclusive; and, by general usage, Congress and its committees are "agencies" of the United States government. Moreover, for some purposes a member of Congress may be considered an "officer" of the United States, and services "before" an "officer" are expressly within the ambit of Section 281.[108] And then there is the policy argument. Congress could not have intended that its members, and officers and employees of the other branches, should be free to accept from private sources compensation for lobbying in favor of private-interest legislation and claims in the Congress —matters in which, by definition, the United States has a direct "interest." Yet there must also be taken into account the usual injunction about the need for specificity in a criminal statute. When all the arguments have been made, the result remains that there is no reliable basis for predicting whether services rendered before Congress or a Congressional committee violate Section 281.[109]

The broad words "board" and "commission" appearing in the

[108] In the opening clauses of Section 281, however, the express reference to members of Congress suggests that they are not to be considered as "officers of the United States" for purposes of coverage of the section. Yet the word "other" before "officer" looks the other way. For purposes of Section 283, it is clear that the term "officer of the United States" does not include members of Congress. See ¶ 1B–3.2.1.

[109] But see note 113 *infra* and accompanying text. What of other organs that are wholly or partly Congressional? Consider, for example, the Library of Congress; the United States Botanical Gardens; the General Accounting Office (surely this office must be included); and groups such as the Civil War Centennial Commission, made up in part of Members of Congress.

definition of "agency," the latter recurring in Section 281, probably blanket the dozens of *ad hoc*, part-time, and little-known
groups that are continually being created to meet special
needs.[110] But one encounters compounded uncertainty as he
moves into the international arena and weighs the applicability
of Section 281 to services before any of the increasing number
and variety of bi-nation and multi-nation boards, commissions,
and organizations.[111] The argument is obviously available that
these are not organs "of the United States." But there is no
authority, and counsel has nothing to go on except extrasensory
perception.

The possibility that a Congressman may be an "officer" for
purposes of the "forum" language of Section 281 has just been
mentioned. In ¶ 1A–3.2 appears a discussion of the scope of the
term "officer of the United States" for purposes of determining
who is covered by the section. It was pointed out there that
the section does not require nice distinctions between "officer"
and "employee" since it applies to both. In the "forum" language, however, the word "officer" appears alone, without
"employee," so that it might be thought that a distinction between the two was intended and must be sought for this purpose. As a practical matter, however, it strains the imagination
to think of an "employee" of the United States who is not an
employee of an "agency" of the United States, so that any services performed "before" such an employee would be services
performed "before" an agency and therefore covered by the
section. It continues to make no difference whether the person
before whom the services are performed is an "officer" or "employee." Services rendered before either will incriminate.

[110] A few examples would be the Smithsonian Institute, the Committee
on Purchases of Blind-Made Products, the American Battle Monuments
Commission, the Commission on Fine Arts, the Alexander Hamilton Bi-
centennial Commission, and other commemorative commissions.

[111] Omitting complicated instances like the United Nations and its
many relatives, what of organs such as the Caribbean Commission, the
Boundary and Water Commission (United States and Mexico), and the
Joint Brazil-United States Defense Commission?

The analysis just suggested can be used (though it has not been so used) to rationalize the case of the government employee who accepts compensation for the performance of services "before" himself. *United States v. Booth* was such a case.[112] There a United States land office receiver took money for giving out advance information regarding the time when certain tracts of public land were to become open to entry. He was indicted under the predecessor to Section 281. On the issue of service, the court chose to say that the section covered a government employee's services "before" himself rather than that such services were rendered "before" his employing agency. Situations involving services "before" oneself, incidentally, will often provide the elements for a bribery indictment as well.

Courts-martial are expressly covered by Section 281, and have been since the enactment of its original predecessor. In 1864 there was hot legislative dispute and debate over the inclusion of courts-martial. Since then there has been no mention of the matter and there have been no cases under the section that involved services rendered before a court-martial.

1A–4.4b. SECTION 203 (1963)

Section 203 makes no changes in the forum provisions of Section 281, discussed at ¶ 1A–4.4a. The House Committee report accompanying Law 87–849 makes the flat statement that neither the new Section 203 nor Section 281 prohibits services in court or before Congress or its committees.[113]

1A–4.5. Time of payment and of service

1A–4.5a. SECTION 281

Read literally, Section 281 hinges the offense upon the time of the payment for the services rather than upon the time of the services. The government employee is forbidden to receive

[112] 148 Fed. 112 (D. Ore. 1906).
[113] H.R. REP. No. 748, 87th Cong., 1st Sess. 20 (1961).

compensation while he is an employee if his services are of the character proscribed by the statute. So read, the statute would make it a crime to receive payment during the time of government service even though the services may have been performed years ago at a time when the recipient was not contemplating government service at all. At the other end of the line, an employee might, under a liberal construction of the statutory language, be compensated after he left government office for services performed while in office, and would thus escape the command of the statute if he could show that he had not agreed to receive such compensation while he was in office. No court has yet adopted either of these unfortunate interpretations, but the language of the section invites if it does not direct them.

1A–4.5b. Section 203 (1963)

The faulty drafting of Section 281 turns the offense on the time of the *payment* for the services rendered by the government employee. The resultant problems discussed at ¶ 1A–4.5a are resolved under Section 203, since the language of the new statute makes the time of receipt of the compensation immaterial. The critical point is that the employee is forbidden to perform the services while he is in office.[114]

1A–4.6. Restrictions on intermittent employee and Special Employee

1A–4.6a. Section 281

The application of Section 281 to intermittent employees raises some awkward problems.

The conclusion was reached in the discussion at ¶ 1A–3.2.2a that the intermittent employee is to be considered an "officer or employee" of the United States for the purposes of Section

[114] *Ibid.*

281. But this answer opens a second question: Does Section 281 apply to such an intermittent employee only during the periods when he is actually working for the government, or does it pursue him to restrict his activities also during the time he is not working for the government?

An extraordinarily well reasoned, creative, and recent opinion of the Attorney General addresses itself directly to this question. The Attorney General felt that it did not comport with the history and the purpose of Section 281 to apply it rigidly to all the activities of a person merely because he agrees to come to Washington for an occasional conference with government officials at their request. He said:

It is, as a general proposition, plain that the more time a consultant devotes to his Government employment within any given period the closer he moves to being in a position comparable to that of a regular Government official. An individual serving a day or two at widely separated intervals is far removed from that position. But service of two or three days a week over a period of time would no doubt place him within it. In other words, at the point at which a consultant is devoting a substantial portion of his time to the Government, he would appear to be within the spirit and purpose of the statute, and perhaps within its letter . . .

Accordingly I am of the view that such advisers and consultants are subject to the full impact of the section on all days when the Government is actually making use of their services. Furthermore, for the reasons already set forth, I conclude that section 281 applies also, on days when his services are not being so used, to an intermittent consultant or adviser whose Government employment during the period of his availability occupies a substantial portion of that period, or affords his principal means of livelihood. And for reasons which require no discussion, the section applies to him at all times he is carried as a consultant or adviser if he receives compensation for his service to a private party before a Government department or agency other than as an incidental part of his normal salary arrangement. While I believe it is possible that a court would hold the section in no case applicable to a Government consultant on days when he is not actually employed by the Government, I am not prepared to go so far in view of the general salutary purposes of the section.[115]

On the basis of this opinion the President issued a memorandum dated February 9, 1962 to the heads of all Executive Departments and agencies.[116] The memorandum reviewed the application of conflict of interest regulations to intermittent government employees. It adopted the general position of the Attorney General's opinion just quoted and further implemented it by declaring that an intermittent employee will be considered to devote a "substantial portion" of his time to the government if he spends 40 per cent or more of his time in actual government employment. By the terms of the Presidential memorandum, Section 281 applies to such a 40 per cent employee during the entire period of his availability for governmental service. For employees who devote less than 40 per cent of their time to governmental service, the regulation interprets the statute as applying only on the days on which they actually perform service.

Under the opinion of the Attorney General and the memorandum of the President, time is to be computed on a day-by-day basis. If the employee does any work at all for the government on a particular day, that day will be considered to be a day of government employment. Since this entire interpretation of Section 281 is an effort to arrive at a commonsense solution, the 40 per cent rule should also be viewed as a general criterion and rule of thumb, not a precisely graduated measuring tool for fussy arithmetic.

1A–4.6b. SECTION 203(c) (1963)

Intermittent or short-term government employees will be regulated under Section 203 differently from regular employees.

---

[115] 42 OPS. ATT'Y GEN. No. 6 (January 31, 1962).

[116] Preventing Conflicts of Interest on the part of Advisers and Consultants to the Government, The President's Memorandum of February 9, 1962, 27 Fed. Reg. 1341 (1962).

This differentiation marks a substantial change from Section 281.[117]

The special provisions under Section 203 apply only to those intermittent or short-term employees who qualify as Special Employees as defined under Section 202. The requirements for this qualification are discussed at ¶ 1A–3.2.2b.

The structure of Section 203 is to provide in subsection (a) for the general rule applicable to regular employees, and then to provide in subsection (c) that the rule under subsection (a) applies to Special Employees to a specified limited extent only. Finally, subsection (c) creates a subcategory of Special Employees as to whom the applicable restrictions are even more limited. The essence of the limitation introduced by subsection (c) for the benefit of Special Employees consists in the fact that its bar is limited to transactions in which the Special Employee has or is likely to have a special involvement in his governmental capacity. See Appendix A for the statutory text.

The relationship between subsection (c) and subsection (a) of Section 203 can most easily be illustrated by using a concrete example. Suppose a business corporation is negotiating with the Treasury on a claim for a tax refund. No regular government employee could, under subsection (a) of Section 203, accept compensation for services to the company in such a matter. An intermittent or short-term employee who qualifies as a "Special Employee" under Section 202 might lawfully receive compensation for assisting the company in the matter, depending upon his own proximity to the claim. As a Special Employee, he will not be barred by subsection (c) unless (1) his duties as a government employee have led him to participate in the matter, or unless (2) he is serving in the department or agency where the claim is pending. According to this standard set by subsection (c), any Special Employee of the Treasury Department would be barred by Clause (2) from rendering compensated assistance

[117] In addition to the statutory provisions discussed here, special regulations are applicable to advisers and consultants. See Appendix D.

to the company claiming the tax refund, while a Special Employee of the Defense Department would be so barred only by Clause (1), where, for example, the tax claim arose out of a dispute involving a contract between the Defense Department and the company, in which contract the Special Employee had had a hand in his governmental capacity.

Subsection (c) goes one step further, however. It recognizes that an intermittent employee who has had very short-term contact with a department need not be as closely restricted as an employee with longer and more continuous contact. Accordingly, subsection (c) provides that Special Employees who have served less than 60 days during a year are barred only from matters in which they *personally* participated. The short-term Special Employee (less than 60 days out of a year) of the Treasury Department could therefore receive pay for helping the company in its tax claim so long as his position as a government employee did not require him to participate in the same matter.

This is the general conception of subsection (c) of Section 203. Some details of its drafting call for further comment, however.

The Special Employee is restricted from providing compensated services only in respect of a particular matter "involving a specific party or parties." This language in subsection (c) goes even further than the "particular matter" phrase in subsection (a) to make it clear that the statute is concerned with discrete and isolatable transactions between identifiable parties, and is not aimed at excluding the Special Employee from broad ranges of activities. The Special Employee of the Defense Department who has worked on the establishment of contract procedures is not on that account forbidden to render paid assistance with respect to a particular contract. In a specific situation there will undoubtedly be lines to be drawn and judgments to be made in assessing the applicability of subsection (c), interpretation turn-

ing upon the strictness with which one views the phrase "particular matter involving a specific party or parties." But the
general import of the subsection is clear beyond question: "particular matter" is to be closely circumscribed and linked to
immediately identifiable and specific persons.

A second important point concerns the degree of participation in a particular matter that will evoke the bar of the statute.
This problem was foreseen by the draftsmen of the subsection,
and the statutory language in Clause (1) seeks to provide an
answer. It provides that the Special Employee is barred from
rendering compensated assistance in a matter if "he has at any
time participated personally and substantially as a government
employee or as a special government employee through decision, approval, disapproval, recommendation, the rendering of
advice, investigation or otherwise." Two points emerge. The
government employee must have taken some personal action in
the matter. Acts of others will not be "imputed" to the Special
Employee, whether performed by seniors or subordinates. The
statute requires that he have "participated personally." Second,
his personal involvement must be substantial. A casual inter-
change about the matter on an elevator is not enough. The
Special Employee will be barred under Clause (1) only if he
has significantly worked on the matter.

The rest of Clause (1) makes it clear, however, that the
form of the work done is irrelevant. The string of possible actions just quoted from the statute, including the "otherwise,"
are clearly intended to cover any kind of substantial working
involvement by the Special Employee.

Clause (2) bars the usual Special Employee from rendering
compensated assistance in respect of any matter which is pending in the "department or agency" of the government in which
he is serving. The use of both words is deliberate. It broadens
the scope of the restriction. The Bureau of Mines is an "agency"
of the government. But a Special Employee of the Bureau of

Mines will be barred from rendering compensated assistance in any matter pending anywhere in the Department of the Interior.

As a final technical point, it should be noted that the proviso to subsection (c) again lends importance to the manner in which the time of service is computed. In determining whether a Special Employee has served 60 days or more during the immediately preceding period of 365 days, the most probable interpretation of the section is that the employee should count as one day any day on which he did any work at all in his capacity as Special Employee. See ¶ 1A–4.6a. For those Special Employees who have served less than the 60-days standard, the only portion of Section 203 restricting their activities is that contained in Clause (1) of subsection (c).

The statutory solution reached by Section 203 in respect of the intermittent employee settles the questions discussed in ¶ 1A–4.6a regarding the applicability of Section 281 to the intermittent employee during periods when he is not working for the government. The special rules of subsection (c) of Section 203 clearly apply to the special employee continuously so long as he retains his status as a Special Employee.

1A–4.7. Restrictions on other persons: Section 203(b) (1963)

Section 281 deals only with the government employee who receives a payment, and does not create a payor's offense. Section 203, by contrast, provides in subsection (b) that if a government employee is forbidden to render certain compensated services under subsection (a), then anyone who promises or offers any compensation for such services commits a criminal offense of equal gravity.

It should be observed that there is no offense committed by the outsider unless he acted "knowingly." Undoubtedly this word will raise problems of interpretation, as all other efforts to express intention, motivation, and *scienter* have always raised problems of interpretation. But the general purpose behind the inclusion of the term "knowingly" is apparent. In some situations arising under Section 203, particularly those involving the application of subsection (c) to a Special Employee, the employee himself will be the only person who has the facts that permit him to judge whether certain services are illegal. For example, he is the only one who is apt to know how many days he has worked, and he may also be the only one who knows what items he has worked on in his official capacity. Without these facts, an innocent outsider could easily blunder into a violation of subsection (b) if the subsection did not protect him by prescribing knowledge as an element of the offense. How far the outsider may go in remaining deliberately ignorant, how much he has to know to invoke the statute, how much of an obligation he is under to inquire—these are all questions for judgment on the particular facts.

1A–5. APPLICABILITY TO EVENTS BEFORE AND AFTER JANUARY 21, 1963

Law 87–849, adopted October 23, 1962, and effective January 21, 1963, provides in section 2:

Sections 281 and 283 (except as they may apply to retired officers of the armed forces of the United States) . . . of title 18 of the United States Code are repealed and will, respectively, be supplanted by sections 203, [and] 205 . . . of title 18 of the United States Code as set forth in section 1 of this Act.

The background of Law 87–849 is reviewed in the Introduction to this volume.

By force of this provision, Section 203 superseded Section 281 on January 21, 1963, and governs the conduct of federal employees from and after that date. Events prior to January 21, 1963, continue to be governed and judged by Section 281.

Sections 281 and 283 contain special provisions governing the conduct of retired military officers. These portions of Sections 281 and 283 were not repealed and remain in effect. The conflict of interest law applicable to such retired officers is discussed in Appendix B.

PART B

SECTION 283 AND SECTION 205 (1963)

1B–1. General

18 U.S.C. § 283 and its successor Section 205, like their companions Sections 281 and 203, directly express the policy that a man should not serve two masters where their economic interests conflict. Section 283 in its first paragraph provides:

> Whoever, being an officer or employee of the United States or any department or agency thereof, or of the Senate or House of Representatives, acts as an agent or attorney for prosecuting any claim against the United States, or aids or assists in the prosecution or support of any such claim otherwise than in the proper discharge of his official duties, or receives any gratuity, or any share of or interest in any such claim in consideration of assistance in the prosecution of such claim, shall be fined not more than $10,000 or imprisoned not more than one year, or both.[1]

Similar in general thrust to Section 281, and overlapping in part, Section 283 differs from that section in vital respects. Unlike Section 281, Section 283 does not apply to members of Congress; it deals only with "claims" against the United States; it covers court proceedings as well as proceedings before an executive forum; and compensation is not a requisite element of the offense.

The text of the new Section 205 is set forth in Appendix A.

Section 205 has many paragraphs, but they are not lettered

---

[1] The second and third paragraphs of Section 283 provide limited exemptions for certain military personnel. They are discussed in Appendix B.

or numbered individually and citation to them is awkward. The statutory material under Section 205 may conveniently be broken into three categories. The section first sets forth the general substantive offense, generally similar to that of Section 283. It then provides a special rule for certain intermittent employees, Special Employees as defined under Section 202. Finally it lists a series of limited exemptions from the general restrictive rule of the section. Interpretation of Section 205 requires reference to Section 202, where certain definitions are contained, and to Sections 203 and 207, also set forth in Appendix A.

Law 87–849 provides that Section 283 is repealed and supplanted by the new Section 205 effective January 21, 1963. See ¶ 1B–5.

1B–2. BACKGROUND

Originally enacted in 1853, Section 283 antedates the other conflict of interest statutes. In 1850, 1851, and again in 1852, President Millard Fillmore requested Congress to improve procedures for handling claims against the government by creating a claims commission or tribunal and to provide protections against bribery and theft of public documents.[2] As a result of administration pressures, scandals, and a series of investigations and debates, Congress passed in 1853 an omnibus reform bill captioned "An Act to prevent Frauds upon the Treasury of the United States."[3] Of the eight sections of the 1853 omnibus bill, only Section 2 is reflected in Section 283. The other sections either have been repealed or dealt with matters other than conflicts of interest, such as bribery, assignment of claims against the United States, and purloining of public documents.

---

[2] 5 RICHARDSON, MESSAGES AND PAPERS OF THE PRESIDENTS 91–92, 178–79 (1897). The general historical background of the early conflict of interest statutes is reviewed in CONFLICT OF INTEREST AND FEDERAL SERVICE at 29–36.
[3] 10 Stat. 170 (1853).

Little debate attended Section 2 of the 1853 act. Most of the floor discussions related to the general purpose of the bill as a whole and to Section 3 (subsequently repealed), forbidding members of Congress to prosecute claims against the government for a fee. Except for the following quoted passage, there is little in the legislative history to show the purposes or intentions of the proponents of the section. Senator Badger of North Carolina, chairman of the committee that reported the bill and a chief proponent, outlined the purpose of Section 2 as follows:

It was confined to one or two specific purposes. It was intended for the benefit of a class of men who were entitled to the aid and assistance of the Government—for the benefit of the poor and ignorant, who have claims against the United States, and who are put under the necessity, as the law now exists, of submitting to the most grinding oppression—the most cruel and merciless oppression—for the purpose of getting their claim brought forward and sanctioned here in Congress, or before the Executive Departments.

It was intended, in the second place, to protect the United States, because, as the law stands at present, the largest inducements are held out to crafty or dishonest men to get up, by whatever means, maintain, and carry through before the Departments, or before Congress, claims that are really unfounded, or claims that are greatly exaggerated.

The next object was to protect the Government, by preventing the Executive officers of the Government from employing themselves, while they hold office under the Government of the United States, and are paid by the Government of the United States, from availing themselves of their opportunities to hunt up and to prosecute claims against the Government. It is needless for me to say to what crying abuses such a privilege has already led, and must continue to lead, unless it is put an end to.[4]

After its enactment, the statute underwent little change until repealed and superseded by its counterpart, Section 205 of Law 87–849, effective January 21, 1963. A detailed abstract of the history of Section 283 appears in Appendix E.

[4] CONG. GLOBE, 32nd Cong., 1st Sess. 1339 (1852).

The general background of Law 87–849 and of Section 205 thereof is discussed in the Introduction to this volume. A direct outgrowth of Section 283, Section 205 shares its substantive history and legislative intent. A technical abstract of the legislative development of Law 87–849 appears in Appendix E.

1B–3. Coverage

The classes of persons covered by Sections 283 and 205 are in some respects different from those subject to Sections 281 and 203.

1B–3.1. Federal employer

1B–3.1a. Section 283

The problems raised by the phrase "officer or employee of the United States, or any department or agency thereof" are common to Section 283 and Section 281. See ¶ 1A–3.1a.

Judiciary. There is no authority on the applicability of Section 283 to members of the judiciary and to employees of the judicial branch. It is likely that they would be held to be subject to the section, as was conjectured in the case of Section 281. The issue is blurred by the fact that Section 281 specifically refers to members of Congress without mentioning employees of the legislative branch, while Section 283 omits members of Congress but refers to legislative employees expressly. There appears no reason why employees of the judicial branch should enjoy special exemption from Section 283.

Legislative employees. Unlike Section 281, Section 283 applies by its terms to "an officer or employee of the . . . Senate or House of Representatives." A member of Congress is not, however, an "officer" for purposes of this phrase. See ¶ 1B–3.2.1a.

District of Columbia. The discussion at ¶ 1A–3.1a regarding District of Columbia employees under Section 281 is equally applicable to Section 283. The special statute exempting notaries public of the District of Columbia from Section 283 is discussed at the same place.

Government Corporations. See ¶ 1A–3.1a.

Non-appropriated fund agencies (PXs). See ¶ 1A–3.1a.

1B–3.1b. SECTION 205 (1963)

The basic coverage of Section 205 is set forth in its opening paragraph, applying the statute to any officer or employee "of the United States in the executive, legislative, or judicial branch of the government or in any agency of the United States, including the District of Columbia." This language is identical to that contained in subsection (a) (2) of Section 203. The discussion at ¶ 1A–3.1b with reference to the federal employers covered by Section 203 is therefore equally applicable to Section 205. See, however, ¶ 1B–3.2.1b.

1B–3.2. Officer or employee

Both Sections 283 and 205 apply to a federal "officer or employee." They thus yield problems and answers substantially identical to those raised by the same language in Sections 281 and 203. See ¶ 1A–3.2.

1B–3.2.1. Congressman

1B–3.2.1a. SECTION 283

It is quite clear that Section 283 does not apply to members of Congress. The 1853 act containing the predecessor of Section 283 also contained a separate section forbidding members of Congress to prosecute claims against the government for a fee. This provision was deleted in the codification of 1873, apparently on the basis that the 1864 predecessor of Section 281 had adequately taken care of the problem. Thus regardless of Sections 281 and 283, a member of Congress may lawfully prosecute a claim against the United States in any forum so long as he is not compensated for it, and may do so before a court even if he is compensated.

1B–3.2.1b. Section 205 (1963)

Like Section 283 (and unlike Sections 281 and 203) Section 205 does not apply to Congressmen. The language in subsection (a)(1) of Section 203 that sweeps Congressmen under that section is missing in Section 205.

1B–3.2.2. Intermittent employee; Special Employee
1B–3.2.2a. Section 283

¶ 1A–3.2.2a discusses the applicability of Section 281 to intermittent federal employees, WOCs and WAEs. The same considerations govern the applicability of Section 283.

1B–3.2.2b. Section 205 (1963)

The discussion at ¶ 1A–3.2.2b concerning intermittent federal employees under Section 203 is equally applicable to Section 205. Like Section 203, Section 205 contains special conflict of interest rules for those classified as Special Employees as defined in Section 202. See ¶ 1B–4.5.

1B–3.2.3. Non-employee; independent contractor
1B–3.2.3a. Section 283

See ¶ 1A–3.2.3a for discussion of the character of the federal employment relationship required to invoke Section 281, and of the position of the independent contractor. The discussion applies equally to Section 283.

1B–3.2.3b. Section 205 (1963)

See ¶ 1A–3.2.3b.

1B–3.3. Other persons

1B–3.3a. SECTION 283

While compensation is not a necessary component of a violation of Section 283, one facet of the section makes such compensation illegal when the other elements of the offense are present. In such a case, the payor of the compensation may be indictable as an aider or abettor, but Section 283 does not itself contain provisions reaching out to such a payor.

For the position of partners and associates of government employees under Section 283, see Appendix C.

1B–3.3b. SECTION 205 (1963)

Unlike Section 203, Section 205 is limited in its application to government employees. The offense proscribed by Section 203 requires that the government employee receive compensation for the services to the outsider, and subsection (b) of that section makes it an offense to pay such compensation. Section 205 does not contain a counterpart to subsection (b) of Section 203. See, however, ¶ 1B–4.4 discussing compensated assistance as an offense under Section 205.

See Appendix C for discussion of the position of partners and associates of government employees under Section 205.

1B–4. SUBSTANTIVE OFFENSE

1B–4a. SECTION 283

Essentially, Section 283 is aimed at preventing government employees from helping others in pressing claims against the government—regardless of the forum. It sets forth two offenses. The first may be committed even though the government employee receives no compensation for his help to the claimant; the second calls for compensation as an element of the crime.

Otherwise, the two offenses under Section 283 are the same.

A person covered by the statute commits a crime if he "acts as an agent or attorney for prosecuting any claim against the United States, or aids or assists in the prosecution or support of any such claim otherwise than in the proper discharge of his official duties . . ." Cases arising under Section 283 are collected in the margin.[5] Discussion of the separate elements of the offense follows.

1B–4b. SECTION 205 (1963)

The offense proscribed by Section 205 is substantially identical to that under Section 283. But a series of relatively minor changes in language have a considerable cumulative effect, and care must be used in drawing parallels between the two.

In two separately numbered clauses, Section 205 lays down one rule regarding prosecution of claims against the United States and a second rule with respect to acting as an agent or attorney in matters in which the United States is substantially involved. The relationship between these two clauses, and their joint relationship to the offense set forth in Section 203, are rather intricate.

Clause (1) of Section 205 applies only to claims against the United States. In respect of such claims, the government employee is forbidden to act as an agent or attorney, regardless of whether he is compensated. In addition, he is forbidden to receive a gratuity or any share of or interest in such claim in consideration of *assistance* in the prosecution of such claim.

---

[5] *Ex parte* Curtis, 106 U.S. 371 (1882); Morgenthau v. Barrett, 108 F.2d 481 (D.C. Cir. 1939) *cert. denied*, 309 U.S. 672 (1940); United States v. Adams, 115 F. Supp. 731 (D.N.D. 1953), *appeal dismissed on stipulation*, 209 F.2d 954 (8th Cir. 1954); Case v. Helwig, 65 F.2d 186 (D.C. Cir. 1933); Sierocinski v. E. I. Dupont de Nemours & Co., 25 F. Supp. 706 (E.D. Pa. 1938); Van Metre v. Nunn, 116 Minn. 444, 133 N.W. 1012 (1912); Ludwig v. Raydure, 25 Ohio App. 293, 157 N.E. 816, *cert. denied*, 275 U.S. 545 (1927); *In re* Winthrop, 31 Ct. Cl. 35 (1895); Captain Tyler's Motion, 18 Ct. Cl. 25 (1883); 34 OPS. ATT'Y GEN. 55 (1923); 23 OPS. ATT'Y GEN. 533 (1901); 16 OPS. ATT'Y GEN. 478 (1880).

Assistance in the prosecution of the claim does not invoke the statute unless the employee is compensated; but regardless of compensation, the employee may not act as agent or attorney. Where the employee is compensated and where the claim is being prosecuted before an executive rather than a judicial forum, the employee will violate both Section 203 and Clause (1) of Section 205.

Clause (2) of Section 205 may be viewed as an extension of, or perhaps a special exception to, Section 203. Like Section 203 (and unlike Clause (1) of Section 205), Clause (2) of Section 205 is applicable not only to claims but to any particular matter in which the United States is a party or has a direct and substantial interest. Unlike Section 203 (and in this respect similar to the first phrase of Clause (1) of Section 205), Clause (2) of Section 205 deals only with the employee who acts as an agent or attorney, and does not require as an element of the offense that the employee receive compensation. Thus, if the employee acts as agent or attorney in a claim against the United States, with or without compensation, he will violate both Clause (1) and Clause (2) of Section 205. If he acts as an agent or attorney without compensation in any matter in which the United States is a party or has a direct and substantial interest, he will violate Clause (2) of Section 205. If he acts in an executive forum as an agent or attorney for compensation in a matter other than a claim, he will violate both Section 203 and Clause (2) of Section 205, but not Clause (1) of Section 205. Clause (2) of Section 205 thus operates to suspend the compensation requirement of Section 203 where the employee's services take the form of acting as an agent or attorney where the other elements of the Section 203 offense are present; and it also extends the reach of Section 203 to include judicial proceedings.

An interesting side effect of this interlacing is that of all federal officers and employees, Congressmen—and only Congressmen—are left free to act as an agent or attorney, compensated or uncompensated, for outsiders in claims against and other dealings with the government—limited only by the prohibition in Section 203 against receiving compensation if the matter is in an executive forum.

1B–4.1. Acting as agent or attorney; assisting in prosecution

1B–4.1a. Section 283

The phrase "acts as an agent or attorney . . . or aids or assists in the prosecution or support" of a claim is comprehensive. It is not limited to formal representation or to matters ripened into judicial action, but includes extending legal or representative assistance of any kind in the initiation, prosecution, affirmance, or collection of a "claim," whether in an administrative or a judicial forum. In respect of forum, Section 283 is thus much broader than Section 281.

The difficulty with the phrase is not that it might not be broad enough, but rather that it may be too broad. Literally read, the words "assist . . . in the . . . support" of a claim would comprehend appearance as a witness or even providing information that the claimant needs to round out his claim. It would not be anticipated that the courts would interpret the statute so sweepingly, and perhaps "assists" implies conscious or knowing assistance in the process of the claim. Judicial authority on the limits of the phrase is nonexistent. The Attorney General has opined that representations made informally to a fellow employee on behalf of a potential claimant fall within the section.[6]

While Section 283 prohibits those covered from acting as agent or attorney for prosecuting, or assisting in prosecuting, "any" claim against the United States, this language is not held to prevent a government employee from prosecuting his own

[6] 34 Ops. Att'y Gen. 55 (1923).

claim, or acting as attorney *pro se*.[7] No available authority illuminates the extent of this exception where, for example, the government employee seeks to act for a corporation of which he owns all the stock, or for a family estate of which he is the executor, or for his wife or a ward. These and similar issues are most apt to arise in the context of tax disputes where the employee has *some* personal interest, and where it is virtually impossible for him not to assist to some extent in the prosecution of the claim, even if he does not appear as a formal attorney of record.

1B–4.1b. SECTION 205 (1963)

The new Section 205 clearly distinguishes between acting as an agent or attorney in the prosecution of a claim, on the one hand, and assisting in the prosecution of a claim, on the other. Section 283 forbids uncompensated assistance with respect to claims against the United States. See ¶ 1B–4.1a. In this respect Section 205 is much narrower where no compensation is involved, since the employee is not guilty of the offense unless he actually acts as agent or attorney. In contemplation of the statute, acting as agent or attorney is singled out as a peculiarly reprehensible kind of assistance to outsiders which the government employee is to avoid at all costs. The employee is thus free to engage in other kinds of assistance so long as he is not compensated.

As the House of Representatives Committee on the Judiciary stated in its report accompanying the 1962 legislation:

Section 205 would prohibit uncompensated activity when it involves acting as an attorney or agent for another . . . The reason

---

[7] 14 OPS. ATT'Y GEN. 482 (1874); 16 OPS. ATT'Y GEN. 478 (1880); 23 OPS. ATT'Y GEN. 533 (1901). The Court of Claims has gone so far as to suggest that the constitutional right of petition guarantees the right of each man to prosecute his own claim in person against the government. Captain Tyler's Motion, 18 Ct. Cl. 25 (1883).

for limiting the disqualification to acting as attorney or agent is that the inclusion of the term "aids or assists" would permit a broad construction embracing conduct not involving a real conflict of interest. However, acting as attorney or agent, which would afford the opportunity for the use of official influence, would continue to be prohibited.[8]

Assistance not constituting action as an agent or attorney does not offend Section 205 unless it is compensated and unless rendered to support a claim against the United States.

How far one may go in assisting another in the prosecution of a claim without acting as an agent or attorney cannot be easily foretold. The emphasis of Section 205 is upon action in a representative capacity, particularly in a situation involving direct confrontation between the government employee and other government employees. No guidance on the point can be found under Section 283, since the distinction between assistance and acting as agent or attorney does not appear in that section. Section 284, regulating certain conduct of former government employees, provides some precedent, since it deals only with prosecuting or acting as counsel, attorney, or agent for prosecuting claims, and omits the concept of "assistance" altogether. Unfortunately, the courts have not had occasion to develop this contrast between Sections 283 and 284. See ¶ 4A–4.1.3.

A few important exceptions are contained within Section 205. They are discussed in ¶ 1B–4.7.

1B–4.2. Claim against the United States; other transactions
1B–4.2a. Section 283

While Section 283 applies to all forums, and all the verbs in the section work to give it great reach, the single noun "claim" operates to restrict the force of the statute narrowly. By judicial

[8] H.R. Rep. No. 748, 87th Cong., 1st Sess. 21 (1961).

interpretation, the term "claim against the United States" refers solely to claims against the United States for money.

The Attorney General has tended toward a broader construction.

> While it may be that Congress, in enacting Section [283], was primarily concerned with the problem of protecting the United States against the exercise of improper influence in the prosecution of claims for money, I would be extremely reluctant, as chief prosecuting officer of the Government, to concede that Congress had no other type of claim in mind.[9]

But the courts have not agreed with him.

An early leading case is *Hobbs v. McLean*.[10] It arose under a statute forbidding the assignment of claims against the government. The statute was a sibling of Section 283, for both were originally contained in the 1853 "Act to prevent Frauds upon the Treasury." In the *Hobbs* case, the Supreme Court defined a claim against the United States as a "right to demand money from the United States."[11] In 1939 the Court of Appeals for the District of Columbia Circuit inferentially endorsed a similarly narrow construction of the term "claim" as used in Section 283.[12] And in 1954 a federal court held squarely that for purposes of 18 U.S.C. § 284, the criminal statute imposing conflict of interest restraints upon former government em-

[9] 40 OPS. ATT'Y GEN. 533, 534 (1947). The Attorney General felt that appearances before Army Retirement Boards would violate Section 283 because the Board's determination of retirement status would, in effect, lead to claims against the government. The same expanded approach was reflected in the position of the Department of Justice in the *Bergson* case, *infra* note 13.

[10] 117 U.S. 567 (1886).

[11] *Id.* at 575.

[12] Morgenthau v. Barrett, 108 F.2d 481 (D.C. Cir. 1939). The court did not define exactly what it would include within this category, but conceded that there were many matters before the Treasury Department in which one might perform representational services but which would not be barred by Section 283 because the matters were not "claims." The court distinguished the narrow coverage of Section 283 in this respect from the expanded range of Section 281.

ployees, the term "claim" should be strictly construed to mean monetary claims only.[13]

Under this view, the term "claim" is not considered to include a defense by a private party interposed against the United States. In *United States v. 679.19 Acres of Land,* the court held that the rights of a landowner in a condemnation proceeding are not claims against the United States, since the government, not the landowner, is plaintiff and claimant.[14] It is not difficult to see that this approach will produce some arbitrary consequences. It would suggest, for example, that a government employee may under Section 283 defend a taxpayer who is sued by the government for nonpayment of taxes, but may not act for the same taxpayer in the same matter if the taxpayer first pays the tax and then sues the United States for a refund.

Yet even the narrowest conception of "claim against the United States" may cause difficulties in some contexts. Is a government employee forbidden by Section 283 to assist a former employee in a proceeding for reinstatement that will lead to a claim for back pay? Does the section bar employees from participating in disciplinary or loyalty-security proceedings involving other employees—a drastic result, especially if the possibility mentioned earlier obtains, that the word "assist" includes the giving of testimony or affidavits. A similar problem in the interpretation of "claim" arises under the statutes restricting the activities of former government employees, Sections 284 and 99 discussed at ¶ 4A–4.1 and ¶ 4B–4–1.

[13] United States v. Bergson, 119 F. Supp. 459 (D.D.C. 1954). The case is discussed at ¶ 4A–4.1.1.

[14] 113 F. Supp. 590 (D.N.D. 1953). Before these federal cases were decided, a state court, acting in a different context under another of the conflict of interest statutes, REV. STAT. § 190 (1875), 5 U.S.C. § 99 (1958), implied that "claim against the United States" means in effect "any assertion against the United States that a claim of the United States is invalid." Day v. Laguna Land & Water Co., 115 Cal. App. 221, 1 P.2d 448 (Dist. Ct. App. 1931). See also another earlier case, Ludwig v. Raydure, 25 Ohio App. 293, 157 N.E. 816, *cert. denied,* 275 U.S. 545 (1927), looking in the same direction.

1B–4.2b. Section 205 (1963)

The bar of Section 283 is limited to "claims" against the United States. These have been interpreted narrowly as claims against the United States for money payments. See ¶ 1B–4.2a. In this respect, Clause (2) of Section 205 extends the scope of its predecessor. Under Clause (2) of the section, the government officer or employee (except a Congressman) is forbidden to act as agent or attorney in any matter before any forum, executive or judicial, if the United States is a party or has a direct and substantial interest in the matter. It is unimportant whether the matter is a claim or not and whether he is compensated or not.

In Clause (1) of Section 205, however, the more limited concept of "claim against the United States" is retained. Congress appears to have endorsed the narrow judicial interpretation of the word "claim" by using the single term in Clause (1) and by carefully using more extensive language in Clause (2) and in subsection (a) of Section 203 where it is intended that the statute should reach beyond "claims."

1B–4.3. Official duties

1B–4.3a. Section 283

By the terms of Section 283, no offense is committed if the aid given to the claimant is given by the government employee in the course of "the proper discharge of his official duties."[15] The exception is obviously necessary, but its scope is quite unclear.

There are no cases and no opinions of the Attorney General

[15] The section is somewhat unhappily punctuated for this purpose. A comma added between the word "claim" and "otherwise" would extend the "official duties" exception to the "agent or attorney" clause as well as to the "aid or assist" clause. It may be argued in answer that under *no* circumstances is a government employee ever required as part of his official duties to act as an agent or attorney for a claimant against the United States—but that is a dangerously flat and all-embracing statement.

on the point. But the Comptroller General has suggested that a government officer may be prohibited by Section 283 from notifying a private business of amounts due it by the government unless a formal claim has been filed.[16] Another opinion from the Comptroller General suggests a less rigid attitude on the point,[17] and periodically he is careful to point out that legal opinions are within the province of the Department of Justice, not the General Accounting Office.[18] But it is useful to note the problem and recognize that the range of "official duties" may be narrowly construed by a court. Section 283 stands as a caution to the employee who might be overzealous in his desire to have the government be helpful to its citizens.

1B–4.3b. SECTION 205 (1963)

Section 205 provides no additional guidance on the scope of the term "official duties." On the other hand, the problem raised by this term in Section 283, discussed at ¶ 1B.4.3a, is reduced under Section 205 for the reason that the new statute does not make it an offense to provide uncompensated assistance in a claim against the United States, but only forbids that form of assistance that constitutes acting as an agent or attorney. Where a government official under Section 283 provides uncompensated help to a claimant, his only defense is that the assistance was given as part of his official duties. So long as the government employee is not paid, he has the additional defense under Section 205 that his conduct did not constitute acting as agent or attorney.

1B–4.4. Compensated assistance

1B–4.4a. SECTION 283

The second offense under Section 283 differs from the first in that it requires compensation as an element of the crime. Per-

---

[16] 15 DECS. COMP. GEN. 683 (1936).
[17] 30 DECS. COMP. GEN. 266 (1951).
[18] *Ibid.* And see 20 DECS. COMP. GEN. 488 (1941).

sons covered by the section are forbidden to receive "any gratuity, or any share of or interest in any such claim in consideration of assistance in the prosecution of such claim . . ."[19]

Obviously the second offense under Section 283 overlaps the crime set forth in Section 281. A government employee who is not a member of Congress and who receives compensation for services before an executive forum in connection with a claim against the United States violates both statutes.

Under Section 283, a "gratuity . . . in consideration of assistance" (is that ever a "gratuity"?) may be in any form—money, property, or other emolument. A "share of" or "interest in" a claim is more particular and has given rise to litigation.

The leading decision is *Case v. Helwig.*[20] Plaintiff was an attorney whose law firm, at the time he entered service as an attorney for the government, was engaged in prosecuting a claim against the United States. In consideration of his disqualification from rendering further services on the case, he converted his 50 per cent share in the firm's contingent fee into a 40 per cent share, and assigned this share to his brother as security for advances made. The law firm paid the fee over to his brother. When the attorney sued the law firm, he was met by the defense that his interest in the claim violated the predecessor of Section 283. The court held against the plaintiff attorney. In the court's view, the section "contemplates the complete sever-

---

[19] The language raises technical difficulties typical of the conflict of interest statutes. "Gratuity" is an odd word to use where it is given "in consideration of" the assistance. And, for no apparent reason, the verbs in the clause defining the compensated crime are significantly narrower in scope than those defining the uncompensated offense. Moreover, the language defining the second offense invites the defendant to argue that there is no crime if the assistance has not already been rendered. Annoyingly, some support may be found for this literal reading in the fact that, until the 1948 Criminal Code was adopted, the section provided that the crime was complete if the compensation was received "with intent to aid or assist, or in consideration of having aided or assisted." REV. STAT. § 5498 (1874).

[20] 65 F.2d 186 (D.C. Cir. 1933).

ance of interest by one who, during the prosecution of any claim against the United States, becomes an officer of the United States."[21] Thus, even though the government attorney did not participate in bringing the claim after his government employment had commenced, he was barred from recovery of the claim because this would have constituted receiving a "share or interest" in such claim "in consideration of assistance in the prosecution of such claim." Mere retention of an interest in the claim was illegal.

1B–4.4b. Section 205 (1963)

In general, a government employee will not violate Section 205 unless he acts as an agent or attorney. But if he receives a gratuity, or any share of or interest in a claim against the government in consideration of assistance in the prosecution of that claim, he will violate Clause (1) of Section 205 even though the assistance rendered by him falls short of constituting action as an agent or attorney.

As Section 205 is constructed, this provision against compensated assistance in the case of claims against the United States has its greatest significance in that it applies to judicial proceedings. In so far as claims in an executive forum are concerned, compensated services are forbidden by Section 203 as well. But that section is limited to matters in an executive forum.

There is no reason to suppose that the language concerning "services" and "compensation" under Section 203 is to be distinguished from the references to "gratuity," "consideration," and "assistance" in Section 205.

Under Section 205 it must be recalled that the government employee is not forbidden to render assistance short of acting as agent or attorney, or to receive compensation for it, unless it is in connection with a claim against the government. Thus, in

[21] *Id.* at 188.

so far as Sections 203 and 205 are concerned, a government employee may render compensated assistance to an outside person who is litigating against the United States so long as the proceeding does not involve a "claim against the United States," and so long as his assistance does not reach the point of acting as agent or attorney for the outside litigant.

1B–4.5. Restrictions on intermittent employee and Special Employee

1B–4.5a. SECTION 283

The conclusion was reached in earlier discussion that the intermittent employee is to be considered an "officer or employee" of the United States for purposes of Section 283. See ¶ 1B–3.2a. But this leaves open a second question: Does Section 283 apply to such an intermittent employee only during the periods when he is actually working for the government, or does it pursue him to restrict his activities as well during the time he is not working for the government?

This subject is discussed in connection with Section 281 at ¶ 1A–4.6a. The conclusion reached in respect of Section 281 is however, different from that applicable to Section 283.

In the opinion of the Attorney General a consultant or other intermittent employee of the United States is barred by Section 283 from prosecuting claims against the United States not only on days on which he works for the United States but during the entire time he is carried as a consultant.[22] In addition, the post-employment restrictions of Section 284 and of Section 99 of Title 5, discussed in Chapter 4, bar him from prosecuting such claims for a period of two years after his last service. The reasoning of the Attorney General does not proceed entirely in terms of an interpretation of Section 283. His point is rather that the intermittent employee is at all times caught up in some combina-

---

[22] 42 OPS. ATT'Y GEN. No. 6 (January 31, 1962).

tion of Section 283, Section 284, and Section 99. If he works on Monday he will be barred from prosecuting claims on Tuesday either because Section 283 applies continuously or because he is in a post-employment phase during which time Section 284 and Section 99 apply to him.

This line of argument is plausible but not inevitable. A court might well hold that a consultant is not a "former employee" as long as his appointment remains in effect and as long as he holds himself available to perform consulting duties. He is a "current employee" and therefore not covered by Section 284 or 99. If this position were taken, it would then become necessary to arrive at an interpretation of Section 283 itself and to decide explicitly whether it bars the intermittent employee only on the days he works for the United States government, or whether it follows him and curtails his activities continuously throughout the period when he merely remains available for consultancy. The only authority available is the opinion of the Attorney General just referred to.

The issue under Section 283 will probably not be resolved, since the new legislation effective January 21, 1963, provides a clear statutory solution for the future.

1B–4.5b. Section 205 (1963)

Like Section 203, Section 205 contains a special rule applicable to some intermittent employees—those who qualify as Special Employees under Section 202, discussed at ¶ 1A–3.2.2b.

Section 205 handles the Special Employee in precisely the same manner as Section 203. The technique is to provide that the Special Employee is subject to the general rule of the Section, but only to a specified and limited extent. The paragraph in Section 205 specifying the extent to which the general rule under Section 205 is applicable to Special Employees is identical to the corresponding provision in Section 203. The discussion at ¶ 1A–4.6b of the regulation of Special Employees under Section 203 is therefore equally applicable to Section 205.

In general terms the position of the Special Employee—typically the intermittent consultant—under Section 205 may be summarized as follows. He may not act as attorney or agent for prosecuting a claim against the United States, and he may not receive compensation for assisting in prosecuting such a claim, and he may not act as agent or attorney in any matter in which the United States is a party or has a direct substantial interest, if either (1) he in any way participated in the claim or the matter in his capacity as a government employee; or (2) the claim or matter is pending in the agency in which he is serving. This statement is subject to the proviso that the clause numbered (2) does not apply to a Special Employee who has served with the government agency less than 60 days during the preceding 365 days. The details of the rule applicable to the Special Employee are technical and call for close reading. See ¶ 1A–4.6b.

1B–4.6. Restrictions on other persons

1B–4.6a. SECTION 283

Section 283 contains no provision for penalizing any person other than those government officers and employees who are subject to it. See ¶ 1B–3.3a.

1B–4.6b. SECTION 205 (1963)

Section 205 of the new statute, unlike Section 203, contains no special provisions with respect to the offense committed by the principal for whom the government employee illegally acts as attorney or agent. Presumably it was not considered necessary to include a provision on this point in Section 205, since in most circumstances compensation to the government employee is not a necessary element of the offense under Section 205. On the other hand, part of Clause (1) of the section contemplates the payment of some form of compensation, and to this extent the question could arise whether the payor was guilty of an offense under Section 205 as well as the payee. In the absence of a provision making the payor's act an offense under Section 205, the conclusion must be that he could not be indicted under that section. There remains the possibility of resorting to the statutes on aiding and abetting.

See Appendix D.

1B–4.7. Special exceptions under Section 205 (1963)

The final paragraphs under Section 205 list a number of qualifications or exceptions to the broad general rule of Section 205. In so doing, they also by cross-reference impose modifications and exceptions upon the general rule stated in Section 203.

Each of these exceptions represents an instance in which Congress felt that special circumstances justified a government employee in assisting or working for outsiders in their relations in the government. Four such statutory exceptions are listed.

The first exception provides that nothing in Section 205 prevents the government employee from acting without compensation as agent or attorney for any person who is a subject of disciplinary loyalty or other personnel administration proceedings. This exception is limited to participation in those proceedings, and may not be undertaken if such participation is inconsistent with the faithful performance of the employee's duties. The point of the exception is apparent. Primarily it means that, notwithstanding Clause (2) of Section 205, an employee may act as agent or attorney without compensation to help another employee in a loyalty or disciplinary proceeding unless the first employee is charged with an active role as the responsible governmental official in the conduct of the proceeding.

The second exception listed in Section 205 springs from a recognition that government employees will on occasion have family and other personal responsibilities that may be thoroughly proper but would, without special statutory recognition, be prohibited by the broad rules of Sections 203 and 205. This exception provides that notwithstanding Sections 203 and 205, a government employee may act, with or without compensation, as agent or attorney for his parents, spouse, child, or any person for whom, or any estate for which, he is serving as guardian, executor, administrator, trustee, or other personal fiduciary. This exception is hemmed in by two limitations. He may not act under this exception without the approval of the government official responsible for his appointment to his position. And the employee may not act under the exception in matters in which he has personally or substantially participated in his capacity as a government employee or in matters which are the subject of his official responsibility. The term "subject of his official responsibility" is a technical term of art defined especially in Section 202. See ¶ 4A–4.2.2.

The third exception appearing in Section 205 is born out of the government's modern need for consultants, particularly in technical areas. It provides that a Special Employee shall not be in violation of Sections 205 or 203 if he is acting as an agent or attorney for another person in the performance of work under a grant or contract with or for the benefit of the United States, provided that the head of the department or agency concerned with the grant or contract certifies in writing that the national interest requires that he act in these capacities. On this point, the report of the House of Representatives Committee on the Judiciary said the following:

This exception permits a special Government employee, with express written advance approval and certification as to the national interest, to assist a Government contractor in the performance of his work for the Government. In the case of a scientist employed by a private company and serving on a Government advisory board his responsibilities with his company may practically compel him to assist his company in the performance of work under a Government contract. And it is undoubtedly in the interest of the United States that he should so assist. In such a case, the permitted exception is needed and available. The protections surrounding the granting of an exception are sufficient to guarantee against abuse.[23]

The statute requires that the certification by the head of the department or agency be published in the *Federal Register*.

The final exception in Section 205 seeks to settle the legality under the section of sworn oaths and testimony made by government employees with regard to claims or other transactions against or with the government. Is a government employee illegally aiding or assisting a claimant if he gives testimony in connection with the claim—testimony that is favorable to the claimant? The conflict of interest laws must not be allowed to interfere with the administration of justice, and the exception for sworn testimony under Section 205 is well inspired. As a technical matter, however, the exception is not apt. The problem to which it is directed was a problem under Section 283 because that section forbids the government employee to give an outsider any aid or assistance in prosecuting a claim against the United States, even though uncompensated for such services. Under Section 205, there is no such provision; to violate the Section the employee must act as agent or attorney, or perform compensated services for a claimant. Giving testimony does not constitute the first of these; and compensated testimony (other than expert testimony) is both rare and inconsistent with the fact that the statutory exception in Section 205 is limited to testimony "required to be made." (The quoted phrase is itself more than usually ambiguous; does it mean that the employee cannot rely upon the exception unless he has been subpoenaed?) The exemption could come into play only where a "claim" is involved, where the testimony is compensated, and where it is "required" to be made. And unless the claim proceeding is a judicial one, the conditions that permit the invoca-

23 H.R. Rep. No. 748, 87th Cong., 1st Sess. 20 (1961).

tion of the exemption under Section 205 are conditions that precisely violate Section 203—but there is no testimony exemption from Section 203. The truth is that the testimony exception in Section 205 is a remembered solution to an extinct Section 283 problem.

1B–5. Applicability to events before and after January 21, 1963

The supersession of Section 283 by Section 205, effective January 21, 1963, is discussed in ¶ 1A–5.

PART C

SECTION 216

1C–1. General

18 U.S.C. § 216 is the third of the three old statutes curtailing the activities of government employees who would work for outsiders dealing with the government. The section reads:

> Whoever, being a Member of or Delegate to Congress, or a Resident Commissioner, either before or after he has qualified, or being an officer, employee or agent of the United States, directly or indirectly takes, receives, or agrees to receive, any money or thing of value, for giving, procuring or aiding to procure to or for any person, any contract from the United States or from any officer, department or agency thereof, or
>
> Whoever, directly or indirectly, offers, gives, or agrees to give any money or thing of value for procuring or aiding to procure, any such contract—
>
> Shall be fined not more than $10,000 or imprisoned not more than two years, or both; and be disqualified from holding any office of honor, profit, or trust under the United States.
>
> The President may declare void any such contract or agreement.

Section 216 is a hybrid statute—partly dealing with overt bribery, and partly with the less overt problem of conflict of interest. Where the government employee who receives compensation for procuring a contract is himself a contracting officer, the crime is bribery, for he is being paid to influence his official action; if the employee has no official connection with the contracting process, his offense is not bribery but is of the same order as that of the employee who violates Sections 281 and 283 by helping outsiders in matters in which his governmental employer has an adverse economic interest. Unlike Sections 281 and 283, Section 216 resembles a bribery statute in specifically subjecting the payor and offeror to criminal penalties. The section is similar to Section 283 (and dissimilar to Section 281) in the narrowness of its focus. As Section 283 is strictly limited to assisting outsiders in connection with "claims," so Section 216 is strictly limited to assistance in connection with "contracts."

Section 216 has long been criticized as redundant; offenses under it are also offenses either under Section 281 or under the general bribery statutes.[1] In recognition of this, Law 87–849 repeals Section 216 effective January 21, 1963. The new statute provides no successor provision, but the substance of Section 216 continues to be covered by Law 87–849 in Section 203, the successor to Section 281, and in Section 201, the new consolidated bribery provision.

1C–2. BACKGROUND

The predecessor of Section 216 was enacted after the predecessor of Section 283 and before that of Section 281. Like Section 281, it originated in the procurement scandals of the Civil War. Pressed by the states, public opinion, and its own concern, and after almost a year of continuous investigation and resolutions of alarm, Congress took action in June of 1862 to do

---

[1] Not all commentators have agreed that Section 216 has this hybrid character. It has been argued that the section should be construed strictly as a bribery statute violated only where the granting of the contract lies within the official duties of the government employee who receives the payment. McElwain & Vorenberg, *The Federal Conflict of Interest Statutes,* 65 HARV. L. REV. 955, 977–78 (1952).

something about government contracting practices. It passed a bill requiring each War, Navy, and Interior contract to be filed in a special office along with an affidavit of the contracting officer that he had made the contract "fairly without any benefit or advantage to [himself], or allowing any such benefit or advantage corruptly to the"[2] other party. This statute proved administratively unworkable for a nation engaged in a war, and on July 17, 1862, it was suspended.[3] One day earlier, a more general criminal act went into effect, entitled "An Act to Prevent Members of Congress and Officers of the Government of the United States from taking Consideration for procuring Contracts, Office or Place from the United States . . ."[4] This is the parent of modern Section 216. The provision had been altered little since its enactment until its repeal by Law 87–849, effective January 21, 1963.

A detailed abstract of the development of Section 216 appears in Appendix E.

1C–3. COVERAGE

The language in the first paragraph of Section 216 declaring who is covered by the section is almost identical to that of Section 281. The only substantive difference lies in the addition to Section 216 of the words "or agent" of the United States.

The coverage of the second paragraph of Section 216 is unlike Sections 281 and 283 since it is directed at outsiders having no employment relationship with the government.

1C–3.1. Federal employer

The discussion under ¶ 1A–3.1a regarding the coverage of Section 281 is equally applicable to Section 216.

----

[2] Ch. 93, § 2, 12 Stat. 412 (1862).
[3] CONG. GLOBE, 37th Cong., 2d Sess. 2915, 3404 (1862). See also Ch. 203, 12 Stat. 600 (1862).
[4] Ch. 180, 12 Stat. 577 (1862). See CONG. GLOBE, 37th Cong., 2d Sess. 3378 (1862).

1C–3.2. Officer, employee, or agent

Some significance must be given to the fact that Section 216 applies by its terms to an "agent" of the government as well as to an "officer" and "employee." The word "agent" was left in the statute in the 1948 Revision of the Criminal Code at the time the word "employee" was added, so presumably the section was intended to reach a broader segment of persons than either Sections 283 or 281. For example, employees of non-appropriated-fund agencies such as military Post Exchanges may well not be considered "employees" of the United States, but might be thought of as governmental "agents" responsible for carrying out an activity of considerable importance to the government.

Otherwise, the discussion at ¶ 1A–3.2a concerning the coverage of Section 281 is applicable to Section 216.

1C–3.2.1. Congressman

Congressmen occupy the same status under Section 216 as under Section 281. See ¶ 1A–3.2.1a.

1C–3.2.2. Intermittent employee

The discussion concerning the status of intermittent federal employees under Section 281 is applicable to Section 216 as well. See ¶ 1A–3.2.2a.

Should there be any doubt about the application of Section 216 to intermittent government employees, the term "agent" should help to resolve the question in favor of coverage. There are no cases on the point under Section 216, but a recent Supreme Court case arising under another of the conflict of interest statutes provides close support. In *United States v. Mississippi Valley Generating Co.*[5] the main issue was whether the government could, under 18 U.S.C. § 434, cancel a contract

[5] 364 U.S. 520 (1961).

that arose out of negotiations in which an intermittent government adviser participated on behalf of the government at the
same time that he allegedly had a personal economic interest
in the transaction. In substance Section 434 forbids self-dealing
by anyone who is "employed or acts as officer or agent of the
United States."[6] After a lengthy examination of the facts, the
Supreme Court concluded that the intermittent adviser was acting as an "agent" of the government and was therefore subject
to the statute.[7] There is every reason to think that the Supreme
Court would also have been willing to hold that the adviser was
"employed" by and therefore was an "employee" of the United
States, but it was not necessary to go so far. In the Court's
view, the range of the concept of "agent" was greater than that
of "employee," and the adviser was at least within the ambit of
the broader term.[8] The Court's analysis with respect to Section
434 is equally pertinent to Section 216. The case is discussed at
length in later pages. See ¶ 2–4.2a.

1C–3.2.3. Non-employee; independent contractor

See the discussion of independent contractor, and what is required to establish a federal employment relationship, at
¶ 1A–3.2.3a. It is possible that the word "agent" in Section 216
has a special impact in this area. Though there are no cases, a
court might find a person to be sufficiently an "independent
contractor" to place him outside the proscriptions of Sections
283 and 281, and yet sufficiently an "agent" of the government
to subject him to the ban of Section 216. Such a result would
not be a merely mechanical consequence of the appearance of
the word "agent" in the statute. It has a sound policy base as
well, springing from the hybrid-bribery character of Section

[6] See Chapter 2.

[7] 364 U.S. at 552.

[8] "This is undoubtedly why the statute applies not only to those who
are 'employed' by the Government, but also to '[w]hoever . . . acts' as an
agent for the Government." *Ibid.*

216. It is reasonable that an "agent" of the government might be left free to assist others in some of their relations with the government, yet be criminally liable if his work as an agent in some way involved government contracts and if he accepted compensation from an outside party to use his efforts to procure such a contract. This conception is not fully refined and worked out in Section 216, for the statute blurs the bribery situation and the conflict of interest situation and applies the same rules to both. Yet the bribery aspect of the section gives it an impulse toward a wider and more stringent application than that of Sections 283 and 281. It is interesting to note that the same underlying drive is reflected in the more drastic penalty provisions of Section 216.

1C–3.2.4. Other persons

Section 216 differs from Sections 283 and 281 in providing specifically in the second paragraph that the payor or offeror of compensation forbidden by the section is guilty of a crime. See ¶ 1C–4.2. See Appendix C for discussion of the application of Section 216 to partners and associates of government employees.

1C–4. SUBSTANTIVE OFFENSE

There is no useful judicial guidance directly bearing upon Section 216. Occasionally the government has included Section 216 as an element in a criminal indictment, but there is no instance in which an appellate court has been called upon to interpret the section where the defendant's conviction turned on the matter. All cases in which the section has been in issue at all appear in the margin.[9] We are left with the bare words

---

[9] McGregor v. United States, 134 Fed. 187 (4th Cir. 1904) (postal clerk convicted of receiving money for aiding to procure a contract to supply mail pouches to the Post Office Dept.); United States v. Dietrich, 126 Fed. 664 (C.C.D. Neb. 1904) (agreement by congressman to accept payment from another for aiding to procure an office for him held not a conspiracy to commit an offense against the United States under

of the statute and a sprawling background of common law and
statutory law of bribery.

1C–4.1. Recipient's offense

Any person who is employed by or is an agent of the United
States, as discussed in ¶ 1C–3, violates the first paragraph of the
section if he receives or agrees to receive anything of value for
giving, procuring, or aiding to procure any contract from the
United States.

Where the defendant government official deals with government contracts as part of his official duties, Section 216 simply
spells out in a straightforward manner the crime of bribery.
All the problems of interpretation associated with the criminal
law of bribery may arise under this section: What intent is
required?[10] Are multiple offenses committed where there is
both an agreement to receive and a receipt?[11] What is a thing of

---

Rev. Stat. § 5440 and Rev. Stat. § 1781, predecessor of Section 216, did
not prohibit a senator-elect from accepting payment for aiding to procure
an office for another); United States v. Driggs, 125 Fed. 520 (C.C.E.D.
N.Y. 1903) (nonnegotiable note given a congressman for assistance in
procuring a contract held not "property" or "other valuable consideration"
because the instrument was tainted and made worthless by the statute
itself; the statute of limitations ran, not from the date the note was given,
but from the date each individual payment was made). Cf. Atkinson v.
New Britain Mach. Co., 154 F.2d 895, 902 (7th Cir. 1946).

[10] See generally, Razete v. United States, 199 F.2d 44 (6th Cir.),
cert. denied, 344 U.S. 904 (1952); Bogileno v. United States, 38 F.2d
584 (10th Cir. 1930); Robinson v. United States, 32 F.2d 505 (8th Cir.
1928); Bradshaw v. United States, 15 F.2d 970 (9th Cir. 1926); Harris
v. United States, 8 F.2d 841 (5th Cir. 1925).

[11] Compare Wilson v. United States, 230 F.2d 521 (4th Cir.), cert.
denied, 351 U.S. 931 (1956) (defendant convicted of soliciting and accepting bribes and of conspiracy) and United States v. Michelson,
165 F.2d 732 (2d Cir.), aff'd, 335 U.S. 469 (1948) ("to 'offer' a bribe
and to 'give' a bribe are two distinct crimes even when parts of a single
transaction") with Krogmann v. United States, 225 F.2d 220, 227 (6th
Cir. 1955) ("The offense is the actual transfer of the money . . . Prepara-
tions for the commission of the crime are not parts of the crime.") and
United States v. Dietrich, 126 Fed. 664 (C.C.D. Neb. 1904) (agreement
to receive a bribe could not be made the basis for an indictment for conspiracy).

value?[12] Is it relevant that the recipient official would have acted the same way in any case,[13] or that the contract was to the benefit of the United States,[14] or that the official did not intend to carry out his part of the agreement?[15]

As noted earlier, however, Section 216 has a reach that extends beyond the simple prohibition of bribery. A government official who accepts money to help someone to obtain a government contract violates Section 216 even though the performance of the recipient's official duties is not influenced or intended to be influenced. For this situation, Section 216 needs its own jurisprudence; the body of case law on bribery is not a substitute. Section 216 raises problems of interpretation similar to those under Section 281. For example, what acts will be considered "aid" in the procuring of the contract? The law under Section 281 may be of some help in these areas. But there are no cases under Section 216.

Section 216 is both redundant and irrationally narrow. To the extent that it forbids bribery, it is overlapped by the general bribery statutes, and superfluous. For the rest, it is overlapped by the more extensive compass of Section 281.

[12] United States v. Green, 136 Fed. 618, 645–52 (N.D.N.Y.), aff'd, 199 U.S. 601 (1905); United States v. Driggs, 125 Fed. 520 (C.C.E.D.N.Y. 1903).

[13] United States v. Raff, 161 F. Supp. 276, 280 (M.D. Pa. 1958) (whether bribed officer was actually influenced is "immaterial").

[14] United States v. Mississippi Valley Generating Co., 364 U.S. 520, 548 (1961).

[15] Hurley v. United States, 192 F.2d 297 (4th Cir. 1951) (Army officer accepted money after informing F.B.I. of the offer); Patton v. United States, 42 F.2d 68 (8th Cir. 1930); Buckley v. United States, 33 F.2d 713, 718 (6th Cir. 1929).

For general treatment of the law of bribery, see PERKINS, CRIMINAL LAW 396–408 (1957); MODEL PENAL CODE §§ 208.10–18, comments (Tent. Draft No. 8, 1958); 11 C.J.S. BRIBERY §§ 1–20 (1938); 8 AM. JUR. BRIBERY §§1–35 (1937); annot., 69 A.L.R. 2d 1397 (1960) (discussion of entrapment); annot., 158 A.L.R. 323 (1945) (discussion of cases where the official had no duty to do or to refrain from doing the act which the bribe involved); annot., 52 A.L.R. 816 (1928) discussion of solicitation and attempt to bribe); Goldstein, Conspiracy to Defraud the United States, 68 YALE L.J. 405 (1959).

1C–4.2. Payor's offense

The second paragraph of Section 216 makes it a crime for anyone to offer, give, or agree to give anything of value for procuring or aiding to procure a government contract. There are no instances of indictment under this provision.

The paragraph makes it unnecessary to rely upon a theory of aider and abettor where it is desired to indict a payor. But it may do more than this. The scope of the second paragraph of Section 216 is broader than that of the first paragraph, and the crimes defined under the two paragraphs do not exactly match. A recipient commits a crime only if he is a member of Congress, or an officer, employee, or agent of the government; a payor or offeror under the wording of the second paragraph commits a crime if he pays or offers to pay *anyone* to get a government contract for him. In a criminal proceeding against a payor, a court might be receptive to the argument that the defendant is entitled to a narrow (not a literal) construction of the statute, and that the first paragraph should be read as a qualification upon the second. In that case, the payor would be guilty only in the case where he made the payment, or agreed to make it, to one of the government officials specified in the first paragraph. But this result, which reduces the second paragraph to an aider and abettor clause, cannot be predicted with confidence.

1C–5. Applicability to events before and after January 21, 1963

Law 87–849, adopted October 23, 1962, and effective January 21, 1963, provides in Section 1 (c) that "Sections 216 and 223 of Chapter 11 of title 18 of the United States Code are repealed. . . ." The background of Law 87–849 is reviewed in the Introduction to this volume.

Unlike the case of Sections 281 and 283 and other conflict of interest provisions, Section 216 has no successor named in Law 87–849. In fact, however, the conduct formerly forbidden by Section 216 continues to be forbidden under the new statute under Sections 201 and 203.

Events taking place prior to January 21, 1963, continue to be governed by Section 216 and, to the extent that they overlap Section 216, by Section 281 and the general bribery statutes in effect at the time of the relevant events.

CHAPTER 2. SELF-DEALING

SECTION 434 AND SECTION 208 (1963)

The simplest sort of conflict of interest arises when one man purports to act for both sides in a transaction between himself and another. The trustee who would buy for his own account property held in the trust; the tax auditor who would audit his own return; the mayor who would give a city contract to his own construction firm; each of these puts himself in a position of self-dealing which is likely to prejudice the other party, and which is certain to arouse criticism.

It is common to find state and local legislation against this kind of self-dealing in the case of government officials.[1] Federal law contains a number of narrowly focused laws aimed at particular offices and particular situations.[2] In confirmation proceedings, Senate committees and particularly the Armed Services Committee have been reluctant to confirm presidential appointees to offices where the character of the appointee's post might require him to deal on behalf of the government with firms in which he has a continuing interest.[3] In addition, since 1863 there has been on the federal statute books a provision of

---

[1] See CONFLICT OF INTEREST AND FEDERAL SERVICE, Appendix A.

[2] See Introduction to this volume, note 2, for illustrative examples.

[3] The experience in confirmation proceedings is reviewed in CONFLICT OF INTEREST AND FEDERAL SERVICE, ch. 5.

general application that implements the policy against self-dealing by federal officials.

Until January 21, 1963, the general provision against self-dealing was 18 U.S.C. § 434. Events since that date are governed by the new Section 208 of Law 87–849. These two provisions are the subject of this chapter. The new statute is a direct lineal descendant of the older one, and the family resemblance is great.

2–1. GENERAL

Section 434 reads:

Whoever, being an officer, agent or member of, or directly or indirectly interested in the pecuniary profits or contracts of any corporation, joint-stock company, or association, or of any firm or partnership, or other business entity, is employed or acts as an officer or agent of the United States for the transaction of business with such business entity, shall be fined not more than $2,000 or imprisoned not more than two years, or both.

The text of Section 208 is set forth in Appendix A.

These conflict of interest laws restrict official activities rather than private economic activities. They do not forbid the government official to acquire private interests; indeed, government officials may in general even go so far as to enter into private contracts with the government.[4] The effect of Sections 434 and

[4] 14 Ops. Att'y Gen. 482 (1874); 24 Ops. Att'y Gen. 557 (1903); 40 Ops. Att'y. Gen. 187 (1942). On the other hand, the Comptroller has tended to find a general public policy outside Section 434 against contracts between the government and its employees. 4 Decs. Comp. Gen. 116 (1924); 14 Decs. Comp. Gen. 403 (1934). See Rankin v. United States, 98 Ct. Cl. 357 (1943).

Members of Congress are forbidden to enter into contracts with the government. 18 U.S.C. §§ 431, 432 (1958). Even this restriction is drastically diluted, however. 18 U.S.C. § 433 (1958). A few narrow statutory provisions limit particular government contracts with particular officials. 18 U.S.C. §§ 437–39 (1958) (contract concerning Indians); 18 U.S.C. § 440 (1958) (postal employees and mail contracts); 18 U.S.C. § 442 (1958) (Government Printing Office employees and paper purchases).

208 is to disqualify the government employee from taking certain official actions if he holds certain related private interests.

2–2. BACKGROUND

Enacted in 1863, the ancestor to Section 434 sprang from the same environment of wartime procurement frauds as the ancestors of Section 216 and Section 281.[5] The record reveals almost no specific legislative history to Section 434. In 1863 Congress was again, or still, considering omnibus legislation to curb claims and contract abuses. It seems likely that instances had come to light of government employees' dealing in their official capacity with concerns in which they held a personal interest; indeed, in the same session of Congress a select committee had been appointed to "inquire whether any employees of the government are interested in the banks or Government contracts." To meet this matter of dual interests, Senator Howard of Michigan introduced a floor amendment that was agreed to without discussion and ultimately became Section 434.

A detailed abstract of the development of Section 434 appears in Appendix E.

As a redrafted outgrowth of Section 434, Section 208 shares the substantive history of the earlier provision. The legislative background of Law 87–849 is discussed in the Introduction. Appendix E contains an abstract of its legislative history.

2–3. COVERAGE

2–3a. SECTION 434

What government officials are covered by Section 434? The peculiar structure of the section puts a unique twist on this question. If one is "employed or acts as an officer or agent of the United States for" the transaction of business forbidden by the section, then he is subject to its penalties. The question of

[5] H.R. REP. Nos. 49 and 64, 37th Cong., 3d Sess. (1863).

who is covered by the section is thus merged with the substantive offense under it, and the discussion under this ¶ 2–3 must be read in the light of the discussion of the substantive offense at ¶ 2–4.

2–3b. SECTION 208 (1963)

In specifying its coverage, Section 208 does not follow the drafting model of Section 434. Instead it designates the persons covered by listing them in the same manner as the other sections of Law 87–849.

The specification of persons covered by Section 208 is identical to that in Section 207, which deals with certain disqualifications of former officers and employees of the government. See ¶ 4A–3.

2–3.1. Federal employer

2–3.1a. SECTION 434

To be subject to Section 434, one must be employed or act as an officer or agent "of the United States" for the transaction of business with an entity in which he has an economic interest. An initial question raised by this language is the scope of the term "the United States." The term is obviously broad, coterminous with any federal employing agency.

Judiciary. Members of the judiciary are officers of the United States and apparently subject to the restrictions of Section 434, but, as in the case of members of Congress, the issue is not apt to arise as a practical matter since their duties do not normally include transacting business for the government.

Employees of the judicial branch acting for the government in dealings with private firms are presumably covered, but there is no authority.

Legislative employees. Employees of the legislative branch are subject to the restrictions of Section 434 on the face of the statute.

Uniformed services. The position of the uniformed military services under the conflict of interest laws, including Section 434, is discussed in Appendix B.

District of Columbia. There is no authority either way on the application of Section 434 to employees of the District of Columbia. The likelihood is that they are subject to it. See ¶ 1A–3.1a.

Government corporations. In *United States v. Strang*[6] the Supreme Court held that an inspector of the Emergency Fleet Corporation, a government-owned corporation, was not an agent of the government within the meaning of the predecessor to Section 434. The Court said:

The Corporation was controlled and managed by its own officers and appointed its own servants and agents who became directly responsible to it. Notwithstanding all its stock was owned by the United States it must be regarded as a separate entity. Its inspectors were not appointed by the President, nor by any officer designated by Congress; they were subject to removal by the Corporation only and could contract only for it. In such circumstances we think they were not agents of the United States within the true intendment of § . . . [434].[7]

The holding has not been overruled, and the characterization of the corporation made in the *Strang* case has been relied upon subsequently in other contexts not involving conflict of interest issues.[8] Nonetheless, the weight that would today be given to the decision in litigation involving the application of Section 434 to any other federally owned corporation is questionable. The general definition of "agency" in the Criminal Code adopted in 1948 includes such corporations.[9] Though Section 434 refers to the United States only, and does not, like Section 281, add "or

[6] 254 U.S. 491 (1921).
[7] *Id.* at 493.
[8] Pierce v. United States, 314 U.S. 306, 313 (1941); United States *ex. rel.* Skinner & Eddy v. McCarl, 275 U.S. 1 (1927).
[9] 18 U.S.C. § 6 (1958). See ¶ 1A–3.1.

agency thereof," it would not be an unprecedentedly long step for a court so disposed to hold that the Criminal Code after 1948 expressly makes such a corporation an "agency," and that an employee of an agency of the United States "acts as an agent of the United States," as that phrase is used in Section 434.

The question is whether a court would be so disposed. It probably would be. Employees of federally owned corporations are clearly covered by some of the other conflict of interest laws, notably Sections 281, 283, and 284, and no reason is apparent for exempting them from the key conflict of interest principle embodied in Section 434. There is no reason to suppose that the legal form in which the federal corporation is set up in any way mitigates the risk to the public from self-dealing on the part of the corporation's employees.

Non-appropriated-fund agencies. It was suggested earlier that the use of the term "agent" in Section 216 makes it likely that the section would be held applicable to employees of non-appropriated-fund agencies (such as military post exchanges) even if they are not considered "officers or employees" of the United States.[10] The argument has equal force as applied to Section 434.

2–3.1b. SECTION 208 (1963)

Law 87–849 makes minor substantive changes in the coverage of the general federal statute on self-dealing.

The coverage of Section 208, while similar to that of Sections 207 and 209, differs substantially from that of Sections 203 and 205 in that the only persons subject to Section 208 are officers or employees "of the executive branch of the United States Government, of any independent agency of the United States, or of the District of Columbia." This language clearly excludes

[10] See ¶ 1C–3.1.

officers and employees of the legislative and judicial branches. It also explicitly answers several of the questions concerning the coverage of Section 434, just discussed.

Some areas of doubt remain, however. For example, there is the General Accounting Office, which is organizationally an arm of the Congress and not of the executive branch. As a matter of policy, employees of the General Accounting Office should clearly disqualify themselves from working on government matters in which they hold a personal interest. But the language of Section 208 does not seem to reach these employees.

A question exists, too, with respect to government corporations. The likelihood is that a government corporation would be held to be an "independent agency" of the United States, though the phrase is not particularly apt. The term "agency" of the United States is independently defined in the Criminal Code and includes government corporations. See 18 U.S.C. § 6 (1958), and ¶ 1A–3.1a. It might on this basis be thought that employees of government corporations would be brought under Section 208. The trouble is that this argument proves too much. Some force must be given to the word "independent" appearing in Section 208, implying that the phrase "independent agency" as used in the section has a narrower meaning than the full scope of the term "agency" as defined in 18 U.S.C. § 6. It may be doubtful, however, whether this technical imperfection of the drafting would prevent a court from applying the section broadly to all government employees who are not obviously employees of the legislative or judicial branches.

Section 208 provides no guidance with respect to non-appropriated agencies of the government such as post exchanges. See ¶ 1A–3.1a.

The position of the uniformed services under Section 208 is discussed in Appendix B.

Employees of the District of Columbia are specifically covered by Section 208.

2–3.2. Officer or employee

The discussion of the concept of "transaction of business" for the United States is inseparable from the question of who will be considered to be an officer or agent of the United States for purposes of Section 434. See ¶ 2–4. Some useful comment about the application of the section to particular classes of officers and employees can, however, be made.

Section 208 applies to anyone who is an "officer or employee" of a federal employer that is covered by the section. See ¶ 2–3.1.

2–3.2.1. Congressman

2–3.2.1a. SECTION 434

Members of Congress are not mentioned in Section 434, though they are generally "officers of the United States." It would be unusual to find a situation in which a Congressman would in the course of his official duty act for the United States for the transaction of business with a business entity. The issue has never been raised.

2–3.2.1b. SECTION 208 (1963)

Members of Congress are not subject to Section 208.

2–3.2.2. Intermittent employee; Special Employee

2–3.2.2a. SECTION 434

Section 434 clearly applies to intermittent employees of the government, whether or not compensated. If the individual "acts as an agent" of the United States for the transaction of business with the entity in question, he is covered by the language of the statute. Moreover, *United States v. Mississippi Valley Generating Co.* is square authority for the proposition that an unpaid consultant to the government is subject to the statute.[11] See ¶ 2–4.

[11] 364 U.S. 520 (1961). The case is reviewed at ¶ 2–4.2.

2–3.2.2b. SECTION 208 (1963)

Section 208 applies specifically to intermittent and temporary employees, including those defined as "Special Employees." The Special Employee under Law 87–849 is discussed at ¶ 1A–3.2.2b. See ¶ 2–4.

2–3.2.3. *Non-employee; independent contractor*
2–3.2.3a. SECTION 434

¶ 1A–3.2.3a discusses the inapplicability of Section 281 to those who are independent contractors with the government, or who have no formal employment relationship. Persons in this category may run somewhat greater risk of being subjected to the restrictions of Section 434, for that Section requires only that a person be employed *or* "act as an agent of the United States." On its face, therefore, Section 434 does not require a formal employment relationship in all cases. No authority on this point exists, however. A similar point is noted with respect to Section 216 in ¶ 1C–3.1.

2–3.2.2b. SECTION 208 (1963)

See ¶ 1A–3.2.2b.

2–3.3. Other persons

Neither Section 434 nor Section 208 (1963) provides for an offense by persons other than officers and employees of the government. The character of the offense does not give rise to an outsider's offense as in the case of the receipt of illegal payments.

See Appendix C for discussion of the application of these provisions to partners of government employees.

2–4. SUBSTANTIVE OFFENSE

Stated broadly, Sections 434 and 208 forbid a government employee who has an economic interest in an outside private entity to act for the federal government in dealings with that entity. Taken as a whole, Section 208 is broader than Section 434 and more sophisticated.

The restrictions of both sections apply equally to WOCs and intermittent employees and to regular employees.

The language of the sections is highly particular, and must be interpreted with some care. See the texts at Appendix A. Discussion of the sections here is grouped around the following four questions. (1) What type of private entity does the statute have reference to? (2) What kind and degree of financial interest in the private entity invokes the statute? (3) To what transactions does the statute apply? (4) What acts is the federal employee disqualified from taking on behalf of the government?

2–4.1. Type of entity

2–4.1a. SECTION 434

By its terms, Section 434 applies to the officer, agent, or member of "any corporation, joint-stock company, or association, or of any firm or partnership, *or other business entity*" (emphasis supplied). The term "business entity" appears again later in the section in the phrase "the transaction of business with such business entity." The question is whether this emphasis upon commercial enterprises means that the section does not apply to those who are officers, agents, or members of non-business entities—corporations not for profit, nonprofit organizations, universities, foundations and the like.

In recent years nonprofit foundations have become centers of great aggregates of wealth, universities have come to have the most intimate contractual relations with the federal government, and nonprofit corporations have become a major vehicle for the conduct of governmental research on a contract basis.[12] It is interesting to recall, too, that the practices of a nonprofit foundation were the immediate cause for the enactment of one of the conflict of interest statutes.[13] With increasing frequency it is important to know what legal restrictions are applicable, for instance, to a university official retained by the government as a consultant to advise on government contracts with universities, including his own.

Initially, it may be remarked that the term "entity" in Section 434 is itself hardly self-executing. A sole proprietorship, a labor union, a neighborhood association, an estate: all of these are said in a good many contexts not to be "legal entities" at all. Obviously, however, an "officer, agent, or member" of any one of these might be able, as government official, to shunt favors to it, and in many cases would have an economic incentive to do so. The likelihood is that in an actual case of criminal indictment of a paid official of a trade association or union, for example, a court would have little patience with the argument that these are not characterized as "entities" for many legal purposes. There is no authority either way.

Passing this point, the question of the statute's applicability to non-business entities is more troublesome, primarily because of the confusing legislative history behind the inclusion of the term "business entity" in Section 434.

The original predecessor of Section 434 applied to officers and agents of "any banking or other commercial corporation" and "any mercantile or trading firm."[14] In the 1909 Criminal Code the section was extended to include any officer or agent of "any corporation, joint stock company, or association," and

[12] See Ch. 1, part A, note 30 *supra,* and CONFLICT OF INTEREST AND FEDERAL SERVICE, ch. 7.
[13] 18 U.S.C. § 1914 (1958). See Chapter 3.
[14] Ch. 67 § 8, 12 Stat. 698 (1863); REV. STAT. § 1783 (1875).

any member of any firm.[15] Senator Heyburn explained the change as follows:

Now, there is no reason why the restrictions that were imposed against banking companies should not apply to all existing business organizations that are liable to be placed in the same relation to Government contracts as were banking corporations. So that the committee has merely enlarged the provisions of the statutes to cover existing conditions that have arisen largely since the enactment of the original statute.[16]

This statement could be used as the basis for an argument that the 1909 predecessor of Section 434 applied only to business entities and not to charitable or nonprofit organizations. The expansion in the wording of the section, however, seems to point to the contrary. The Senate report accompanying the 1909 bill makes no distinction between business and non-business entities.[17]

In 1948, the language of the section was changed to include "partnership" and to add "or other business entity." There was one other change made that bears on the issue. The 1909 predecessor to Section 434 forbade interested persons to act as government agents for "the transaction of business with such corporation, joint stock company, association, or firm." In 1948, this language was changed to its present form—" the transaction of business with *such business entity*" (emphasis supplied). The Revisor's notes explain that this change was made "[t]o remove all ambiguity as to scope of section."[18]

There is no other authority. The legislative history and the literal language certainly lean toward the exclusion of nonprofit enterprises after the 1948 revision. In a criminal proceeding, the court might be particularly inclined to give the defendant the

15 Ch. 321, § 41, 35 Stat. 1097 (1909).
16 42 Cong. Rec. 778 (1908).
17 S. Rep. No. 10, 60th Cong., 1st Sess. 15 (1908).
18 H.R. Rep. No. 304, 80th Cong., 1st Sess. A–32 (1947).

benefit of the doubt. Yet the degree of risk to the public arising out of the acts of the double agent does not turn on the business or non-business character of the private entity with which he is connected. The statute as drafted is defective, and the open, unresolvable question is whether a court would fill it in if the occasion should be presented.

2–4.1b. SECTION 208 (1963)

Under Section 208 it is not important whether the transaction involves a business entity or concerns some form of nonprofit entity. As the Senate Judiciary Committee commented:

A great number of universities, foundations, nonprofit research entities, and other similar organizations today are engaged in work for the Government. Conflicts of interest may arise in relation to them just as in the case of the ordinary business for profit. The committee therefore has deleted the word 'business' from the subsection to make clear that improper dealing by a Government employee in connection with nonprofit organizations is also prescribed [*sic*].[19]

2–4.2. Employee's economic interest

2–4.2a. SECTION 434

Section 434 is invoked by the presence of an economic nexus between the government official and a private entity. How much of a connection, and what kind of connection, must there be to bring the statute into operation? It is assumed here that the private entity in which the official has an interest is an entity comprehended by the statute. See ¶ 2–4.1a.

"*Officer, agent or member of.*" In the general simple case, the person acting for a private concern is being compensated for his efforts, and can be said to be an "officer, agent or member" of the concern. It is a little odd that the statutory language does not include the term "employee"; but "agent," while not co-

---

[19] S. REP. No. 2213, 87th Cong., 1st Sess. 14 (1962).

terminous with "employee," would normally fit any situation in which the employee is acting for his employer in the transaction of business.

But suppose the "officer, agent or member" of the entity is not paid, and has no other pecuniary interest in the entity? The bare words of the statute would lead to the conclusion that no economic interest is necessary. It speaks in the alternative, saying: "officer, agent or member of, *or* . . . interested in the . . . profits" (emphasis supplied). But judicial construction may have read into the statute the requirement that the officer, agent, or member have a pecuniary interest in the entity.

The case of *United States v. Chemical Foundation, Inc.* involved the sale and assignment after World War I of certain German chemical patents held by the Alien Property Custodian. Garvan was the Custodian. He was also the president of the Chemical Foundation, an organization set up by the government to purchase alien chemical patents seized by the Custodian and to hold them for the use of the American chemical industry. The sale of the German patents to the Foundation was authorized by President Wilson acting under the Trading with the Enemy Act. Later, the United States sued to set aside these transfers, and in the litigation the issue was raised whether the transfer was illegal under Section 434 as a result of Garvan's dual position. Garvan's defense rested in large part on section 7(e) of the Trading with the Enemy Act providing that "no person shall be held liable in any court for or in respect to anything done or omitted in pursuance of any order, rule, or regulation made by the President under the authority of this Act."[20]

The District Court held that Section 434 had been superseded by Section 7(e) of the Trading with the Enemy Act and was therefore irrelevant to the suit.[21] The Court of Appeals reached the same conclusion, but held in addition that the trans-

[20] Ch. 106, 40 Stat. 411 (1917).
[21] United States v. Chemical Foundation, Inc., 294 Fed. 300 (D. Del. 1924)

action was not covered by Section 434. The appellate court said:

In defining the offense the statute discloses that it has several elements; (a) that the offending person shall hold opposite and incompatible positions, in that (b) he shall be an officer or agent of the United States and (c) at the same time an officer or agent of a corporation engaged in a transaction with the United States, and (d) as such he shall be directly or indirectly interested in the pecuniary profits or contracts of such corporation . . .

[T]here was present the element of two official positions, and in these positions it is true he carried out the contract previously made, but there was lacking the element of a direct or indirect interest on his part in the pecuniary profits or contracts of The Foundation, for he agreed to serve as its president without compensation and he has kept his agreement . . .

It follows that the transaction was not consummated in violation of this criminal statute and therefore it is not invalid on this ground.[22]

Thus the Appellate Court took the view that the statute applied only to those officers or agents of an entity who hold a financial interest in it.

The Supreme Court affirmed the decision of the lower courts, and, in doing so, may have endorsed the substantive interpretation of the Court of Appeals.

The Trading with the Enemy Act is a war measure covering specifically, fully and exclusively the seizure and disposition of enemy properties. The authority of the President to authorize sales and to determine terms and conditions in lieu of those specified in the proviso, undoubtedly included the power to cause the Chemical Foundation to be incorporated to purchase and hold the patents, as specified, and to direct the selection of the directors, officers, and voting trustees. The President, and under him the Custodian, acting for the United States, the seller of the patents, caused the Foundation to be created to buy and hold them, and caused it to be controlled by officers or representatives of the United States acting exclusively in its interest. Neither Mr. Garvan nor any of the others who acted for the United States had any financial interest in the

[22] 5 F.2d 191, 209–10 (3d Cir. 1925).

Foundation, its profits or its contracts. All the corporate shares were subscribed and paid for by others—those interested in the chemical industries. . . . The Foundation is properly to be considered an instrumentality created under the direction of the President to effect that disposition and subsequent control of the patents which he determined to be in the public interest. The transactions complained of did not involve any of the evidence aimed at by § [434]. The Act will be construed and applied as not qualified or affected by that provision of the Criminal Code.[23]

One interpretation of the Supreme Court's language is that it holds merely that the Trading with the Enemy Act supersedes Section 434. Yet the language of the opinion appears to go further and to imply that Section 434 was not violated by this transaction. Whether it reaches still further and supports the Circuit Court's view that the section requires that an officer of a business be also interested financially is unclear. It appears to have been generally assumed that such is the case and that the Supreme Court adopted the lower court's position.

In a somewhat similar situation, the Comptroller General followed this line of reasoning to conclude that, in spite of Section 434, employees of the Resettlement Administration could act as unpaid officers and directors of a mutual aid corporation established by the government to assist in providing medical services to destitute families.[24]

It is difficult to assess the significance of these interpretations. In both instances, the outside organizations had been established by the government itself to carry out governmental policies considered to be in the public interest. Independently of the interpretation of Section 434, the courts may be expected to have been reluctant to tip over the arrangements openly arrived at between these organizations and the government. The *Chemical Foundation* case may mean no more than this, and the opin-

[23] 272 U.S. 1, 18–19 (1926).
[24] 16 DECS. COMP. GEN. 613 (1936). And see STAFF OF SUBCOMM. NO. 5, HOUSE COMM. ON THE JUDICIARY, 85TH CONG., 2D SESS., FEDERAL CONFLICT OF INTEREST LEGISLATION 19 (Comm. Print 1958).

ion itself may be adequately grounded upon the interpretation of the Trading with the Enemy Act.

On the other hand, however accurate this view may be as a matter of history, the opinion of the Supreme Court may well be used to help along a line of interpretation of Section 434 that is appealing—a restricting of the application of the statute to situations of pecuniary interest. Noneconomic conflicts of interest are everywhere; each man is a complex of loyalties and biases based on friendship, former employment relations, social and religious affiliations, and a lifetime of experiences peculiar to himself. But though the risks of favoritism inherent in these relationships are great, the tendency of legislatures and courts is to look at economic connections only—to say that regulation is needed only where the official stands to *profit* from the transaction. The unpaid officer of an entity who has no economic interest in the entity is not apt to appear to the courts as a source of major public risk.[25] There is therefore a considerable likelihood that Section 434 will be interpreted as requiring an economic interest in all cases, and the Supreme Court's *Chemical Foundation* opinion will be cited in support.

One further point should be mentioned in regard to the "officer, agent or member" language of the section. It is often relatively easy to say who is an "officer or member" of an entity, but determination of who is whose "agent" is often difficult and, indeed, may be the ultimate legal issue for decision. In blurred situations such as the *Chemical Foundation* case presented, an initial characterization must be made by the court: conceding that the defendant acted "as agent" for the government, did he, by so doing, cease to act "as agent" for the private entity? It may also be a question of legal characterization whether the individual was paid "by" the government or "by" the private party to the transaction. This was the formulation of the legal issue in *Muschany v. United States*, discussed earlier,

---

[25] This attitude is reflected as well in the doubt surrounding the application of the conflict of interest statutes to nonprofit entities.

and the Supreme Court's conclusion that the agent was paid
"by" the government and not by the private party led to the
conclusion that the agent had no adverse interest that would
invalidate the contract under section 434.[26]

*"Directly or indirectly interested in the pecuniary profits or
contracts of."* What kind of, and how much, economic interest
in an entity are required by this phrase in Section 434?

If the defendant is on the payroll of the entity, doing business with the government, there should be no question that the
statutory test is met. Authority is scant, however. The Attorney
General opined that a paid corporate officer could not be appointed to a government position where he would have to trans-
act business with his corporation: "To a degree his salary as an
officer of the corporation would be affected by whether his
advice leads the War Department to enter into a procurement
contract with his company."[27] And the Judge Advocate General
was of the view that Section 434 applies to a reserve officer on
active duty who is receiving an allowance from his previous corporate employer.[28]

Similarly, shareholdings in a corporation transacting business
with the government will constitute a disqualifying interest. In
the opinion just quoted, the Attorney General went on to say
of the officer who was also a shareholder in the corporation:
"To a larger degree his share in the earnings of the corporation

[26] 324 U.S. 49 (1945). The Muschany case is reviewed in ¶ 1A–4.1a.
The opinion of the court is not particularly satisfactory on the question
of the interpretation of Section 434. The government cited four conflict
of interest statutes, Sections 281, 283, 434, and 1914, in a shotgun argument intended to demonstrate a general public policy against commission
contracts. The court disposed of all the statutes as a package, saying that
their history showed no Congressional intent to outlaw commission contracts, and holding that the agent was really paid "by" the government
anyway. The question of who paid the compensation aside, the court
must have also meant that the agent's evident economic interest in the
contract price did not constitute a legal "interest" for the purposes of
Section 434, or that the private contracting parties were not "entities,"
but the point is implicit only.

[27] 40 Ops. Att'y Gen. 168, 169 (1942).

[28] 1 Bull. Army JAG 40 (1942).

as a stockholder would be affected by his advice."[29] And the
strenuous lengths to which the Senate Armed Services Committee has gone in confirmation proceedings has been largely
predicated upon its assumption that shareholdings will create
a disqualifying interest under Section 434.[30] (Whether the committee would take any different position on enforced divest-
ment of shareholdings even if there were no Section 434 is immaterial.)

A harder question is whether there is any rule of *de minimis*
interest in the case of shareholdings. Is a government official
barred from acting for the government in a transaction with
General Motors if he owns one share of General Motors? It is
doubtful whether the law should ever be silly, and commentators have tried to reassure themselves that Section 434 does not
come into play unless the official holds a "substantial" interest
in the entity in question.[31] Some tendril of support for this view
comes from the *Chemical Foundation* opinion, for the Supreme
Court there held that the holding of a few qualifying shares by
a director in the Foundation was not enough to constitute a
pecuniary interest for purposes of Section 434. The weight of
the authority is undermined, however, by the fact noted earlier,
that the Supreme Court put its opinion primarily upon an
interpretation of the Trading with the Enemy Act.[32] The actual

[29] 40 Ops. Att'y Gen. 168, 169 (1942).

[30] See Conflict of Interest and Federal Service, ch. 5.

[31] "The existence of a nominal or trivial interest, such as the possession
of a single qualifying share, or the possession of naked legal title to shares
in which the beneficial interest is held by others, probably would not be
enough. But a showing of an actual and beneficial interest of such magni-
tude as to demonstrate a probable influence upon the official actions of
the officer concerned would seem to be sufficient. The sufficiency of proof
of such influence necessarily presents a question to be determined from
all evidence presented in each individual case, and any endeavor to state
a generalization applicable to all cases would seem inadvisable." Office
of Senate Legislative Counsel, Compilation of Certain Legal Material Prepared on the Conflict of Interest Statutes 20 (Memorandum for Senator Saltonstall, Jan. 16, 1953).

[32] See discussion of the *Chemical Foundation* case in ¶ 2–4.1.

language of Section 434 holds out no support for a *de minimis* rule; the Armed Services Committee has repeatedly refused to accept an argument of *de minimis* interest;[33] and no one has yet developed satisfactory criteria for judging "reasonableness," though it has been tried.[34]

Apart from salary payments and shareholdings, other kinds of economic interest in a firm are common. There is little authority of any kind to help predict which of these would be considered to be within Section 434. One opinion of the Judge Advocate General has held that the section does not apply to reserve officers who are corporate officers on leave of absence without pay, and whose sole interest is an expectation of re-employment by the corporation.[35] Profit-sharing plans as such are clearly under the express language of the section, but what of other kinds of contingent interests such as options to buy shares, or participation in a company's retirement or insurance plan? The problems here are quite similar to those discussed later in connection with Section 1914.[36] It has been said that rights that have not "vested" under such plans will not constitute an "interest in pecuniary profits or contracts" of the entity, but there is nothing in publicly available authorities to support this conclusion.

[33] See CONFLICT OF INTEREST AND FEDERAL SERVICE, ch. 5, particularly the futile demonstration made by Dudley C. Sharp discussed at 104–5.

[34] The Special Committee of the Association of the Bar of the City of New York considered the feasibility of general standards for making this judgment, but the statute ultimately recommended by the Committee contains none. See CONFLICT OF INTEREST AND FEDERAL SERVICE at 200–202. In 1961, the Armed Services Committee itself tackled the problem with a subcommittee under the Chairmanship of Senator Henry Jackson of Washington. At this writing, no criteria have been made public by the subcommittee. The difficulty in setting such criteria is very great. Should the standard vary with the size of the individual's personal estate?—with the total assets of the company?—with the amount of government business done by the company?—with the amount of business the company expects to do with the government?—with the individual's degree of control of the company?—with the kind of government post held?

[35] 1 BULL. ARMY JAG 39 (1942).

[36] See ¶ 3–4.1.

It appears to be agreed tacitly that an economic interest held by a member of the official's family will not disqualify him under Section 434 from acting for the government. One can readily imagine circumstances, however, in which a court would be strongly inclined to impute a wife's interest to the husband, to find a constructive or vicarious interest, or to discover that the husband "in fact" had an economic interest in anything in which his wife had an economic interest.

What, if anything does the statutory word "indirectly" add to Section 434? In a widely publicized case turning on the section, the Supreme Court was recently called upon to interpret in a novel context the language "indirectly interested in . . . contracts." *United States v. Mississippi Valley Generating Co.*[37] arose out of the celebrated Dixon-Yates power contract of 1954. Wenzell, a shareholder and director of First Boston, an investment banking firm, was serving as an unpaid consultant to the Bureau of the Budget. An expert on public utility financing, he participated for the government in negotiations that ultimately led to a contract between the Atomic Energy Commission and a private power company for the construction of certain facilities to provide power to the Commission. The government subsequently canceled the contract, in part on the ground that it was tainted by the consultant's alleged violation of Section 434. The company sued in the Court of Claims for costs and damages. A central issue was whether the section had been violated, and this in turn raised the question whether the consultant was "interested" in the power contract.

First Boston had no contract with the government; the government's contract was with the power company. At the time the government contract was made, First Boston also had no contractual arrangement with the power company. After the government contract was made, however, the company entered into an agreement under which First Boston was to handle the

[37] 364 U.S. 520 (1961). See Annot., 5 L. Ed. 2d 954 (1961).

public financing required for the project. If there had been a prior contract between the power company and First Boston, it would have been clear to the entire Court that Wenzell had an "indirect interest"—that his position as a shareholder and director of the banking firm would have given him an economic interest in the financing contract, and, derivatively, in the underlying contract between the company and the Atomic Energy Commission. But in the absence of such a commitment by the power company, was it enough that the consultant anticipated and *hoped* that his firm would fall heir to the financing job? The company argued vigorously that the consultant was not "interested in the pecuniary profits or contracts" of the company, as the phrase is used in Section 434. Three justices agreed with this argument. But six did not. Writing for the majority, the Chief Justice found that under the facts there was more than a hope on Wenzell's part. There was a

substantial probability that, because of its prior experience in the area of private power financing, First Boston would be hired to secure the financing for the proposed Memphis project; if First Boston did receive the contract, it might not only profit directly from that contract, but it would also achieve great prestige and would thereby be likely to receive other business of the same kind in the future; therefore, Wenzell, as an officer and profit-sharer of First Boston, could expect to benefit from any agreement that might be made between the Government and the sponsors.

. . . First Boston had arranged the financing on the OVEC project and had acquired a reputation in the area of private power financing. Wenzell had also acquired a certain expertise in this area by virtue of his previous work for the Budget Bureau in preparing the TVA analysis. It was therefore probable that First Boston's services would again be utilized should the sponsors obtain a contract to construct a project similar to OVEC.

. . . The Court of Claims recognized that from the outset there was a "substantial possibility" that First Boston would be retained. It said:

". . . He [Wenzell] had an interest in First Boston which company, *by the logic of circumstances,* might be offered the work of arranging the financing of the project when and if a contract for the project should be made." 175 F. Supp., at 515. (Emphasis added.)

It was the "logic of circumstances" referred to by the Court of Claims that placed Wenzell in the ambivalent position at which the statute is aimed. Wenzell, as an agent of the Government, was entrusted with the responsibility of representing the Government's interest in the preliminary stages of a very important contract negotiation. However, because the sponsors were in a position to affect the fortunes of himself and his firm, he was, to say the least, subconsciously tempted to ingratiate himself with the sponsors and to accede to their demands, even though such concessions might have been adverse to the best interests of the Government. By thus placing himself in this ambiguous situation, Wenzell failed to honor the objective standard of conduct which the statute prescribes.[38]

The language of the Court is reproduced at some length to provide a flavor of the Court's reasoning, and to illustrate how closely the decision hinged upon the particular facts. The Court concluded that a contract did not have to be in existence at the time the agent acted in his dual capacity; but it was at some pains to show that the facts showed more than a mere hope or wishful expectation on Wenzell's part. The three dissenting justices would not have applied the statute in the absence of an existing contractual arrangement between First Boston and the sponsors of the power company.[39]

Considerable caution must be used in assessing the *Mississippi Valley Generating Co.* decision. The facts were complex; the opinion is long and detailed; the situation was charged with political overtones; the case did not involve a criminal proceeding against Wenzell; as the majority viewed the facts, there was

[38] *Id.* at 555–57.

[39] "Whether or not a prohibited interest exists must be determined as of the period during which an individual is acting for the Government. And when the asserted interest arises 'indirectly' by way of a subcontract, its existence can, in my opinion, only be found in some commitment, arrangement, or understanding obtaining at that time between the prime contractor, and subcontractor." (Dissenting opinion of Justice Harlan.) *Id.* at 569 (footnote omitted).

an overall atmosphere of uncomfortably close collaboration among all the parties and various government officials; and Wenzell had been advised by his own counsel to resign from his consultancy and had failed to do so.

Nevertheless, the Supreme Court's decision illuminates the concept of "interest" under Section 434. It demonstrates that the concept of an "indirect interest" has a real vitality. At the same time, the care of the majority opinion, and the vigor of the dissent, yield a clear reading that the Wenzell case was on the outer limits, and that a more speculative economic interest than his would not have been held to be within the section.

2–4.2b. Section 208 (1963)

Under Section 434, it has always been a question how much of an economic nexus there must be between the government employee and the outside entity to invoke the statute. See ¶ 2–4.2a. Section 208 seeks to clarify this question, and to some extent succeeds in doing so. See the statutory text at Appendix A.

Section 208 is brought into play if the government employee, or another person designated by the statute, "has a financial interest" in the transaction in question. Under this language in subsection (a) of the section, any financial interest will do; the statute does not stipulate that the interest must be a "substantial" interest. Indeed, the special provisions contained in subsection (b) of Section 208 makes it clear that subsection (a) is to be strictly construed to require the employee to disqualify himself even where his financial interest in the transaction is slender. Subsection (b) of Section 208 then proceeds in two ways to mitigate the harshness of a literal reading of subsection (a). Under subsection (b) the officer or employee may advise his superior of the nature and circumstances of the matter in question and make full disclosure of the financial interest he has in the matter. If the official to whom this disclosure is made determines in writing that the employee's financial interest is "not so substantial as to be deemed likely to affect the integrity of the services which a government may expect from" him, then the officer or employee may act for the government in the matter regardless of subsection (a). The second avenue under subsection (b) for permitting a government employee to act in cases where his financial interest is remote is through force of general rules or regulations published in the *Federal Register*. The regulations contemplated would not exempt particular persons or offices but would identify in advance certain financial interests as being too remote or too inconsequential to affect the integrity of government officers' or employees' services. Where there is such a regulation and where the financial interest in question is covered by it, the employee is free to act for the government in the transaction in question in spite of subsection (a) and without the necessity of the disclosure procedures set forth in clause (1) of subsection (b).

An interesting and important change made by Section 208 and unknown under Section 434 is the explicit extension of the disqualifying effect of the statute to interests of persons other than the government employee himself. Under Section 208, the government employee is required to disqualify himself from a transaction if he has a personal financial interest in it *or* if such a financial interest is held by "his spouse, minor child, partner, organization in which he is serving as an officer, director, trustee, partner or employee, or any person or organization with whom he is negotiating or has any arrangement." Section 208 thus substantially broadens the general rules on disqualification of government employees. The effect of this extension may well prove harsh and deleterious to the conduct of governmental operations, particularly in the recruitment of top executive personnel, who may be willing to dispose of their own personal holdings in order to work for the government but unwilling or unable to force other members of their family or their business associates to dispose of theirs.

Section 208 contains one other refinement not present in Section 434. The new statute requires as an element of the offense that the employee have personal knowledge of the disqualifying interest. If the employee does not know that he, or someone close to him, has a financial interest in a transaction, the risks of partisanship are not present. The necessity for including this element of knowledge in Section 208 is particularly apparent in the case of a disqualifying financial interest held by one other than the employee himself. The employee will have difficulty in showing that he does not know of his own financial interests (though such lack of knowledge might be understandable where, for example, the employee holds a beneficial but no controlling interest in a trust), but it would not be at all strange to find situations in which the employee is not familiar with the financial interests of the associates and associated entities listed in Section 208. The requirement of knowledge will raise some problems of interpretation in the future, but it is clear that the statute contemplates actual personal knowledge on the part of the employee, not merely constructive or imputed knowledge, as a precondition to disqualification.

With these exceptions, the discussion at ¶ 2–4.2a continues to have relevance to Section 208, particularly the review of the Supreme Court's decision in *United States v. Chemical Foundation, Inc.*, and *United States v. Mississippi Valley Generating Co.*

2–4.3. Transactions

2–4.3a. SECTION 434

There is no offense committed under Section 434 unless the person having an economic interest in an entity acts for the government in "the transaction of business" with the entity. This phrase has a limiting effect upon the disqualification principle imposed by the section.

Contracts for the procurement of goods form the simplest example of the government's transaction of business. But in the modern world the range of contacts between private companies and the federal government has expanded far beyond such simple relationships. Almost any company may find itself at almost any time engaged in dealings with the government involving taxes, or patents, or license applications, or regulatory proceedings, or loans, or subsidies, or operating agreements, or any of countless other matters. It is quite possible that if the issue were presented, a court might take a liberal view of the phrase "transaction of business" and apply it to situations in which the government's role in a matter is essentially regulatory —as in the issuance of an F.C.C. license. But neither the history nor the language of Section 434 seems to take account of such matters, and, consistently with its emphasis on business entities, the section seems to be focused on commercial transactions between the government and the outside entity.

2–4.3b. SECTION 208 (1963)

Unlike Section 434, the new Section 208 is not limited to dealings that can be described as the transaction of business. The government employee will under Section 208 be required to disqualify himself not only in business transactions but in any "judicial or other proceeding, application, request for a ruling or other determination, contract, claim, controversy, charge, accusation, arrest or other particular matter" in which he has a personal financial interest. This language, covering almost every kind of dealing between the executive branch and private citizens, matches the language contained in Section 203 discussed earlier, except that, for obvious reasons, Section 203 contains the additional requirement that the United States be a party or have a direct and substantial interest in the matter in question. See ¶ 1A–4.3b.

2–4.4. Employee's Participation

2–4.4a. SECTION 434

Where a government employee has an economic interest in an outside entity, how far must he remove himself from the government's dealings with it? Put the other way, what degree of contact with the government's transactions with that entity may the interested employee have without running afoul of Section 434?

Where the person with the outside private interest acts directly as a contracting or procurement officer for the United States, there is no difficulty in saying that he is the actor who is transacting the government's business. For example, the Comptroller General has disapproved as in contravention of Section 434 a contract for hospital facilities negotiated by a doctor for himself as proprietor of the hospital and for the government as a contracting officer.[40] He took a similar view of a contract made by a Census Bureau official with himself for the rental of typewriters by the Bureau.[41]

It is quite unclear, however, how far beyond direct execution of a contract Section 434 extends. Some light on the matter has been cast by the Supreme Court in the recent case of *United States v. Mississippi Valley Generating Co.*, other facets of which are discussed elsewhere.[42] One issue before the Court was whether participation by a consultant in early negotiations that ultimately led to a government contract was sufficient in itself to be considered "transaction of business" under Section 434. The Court held that it was, saying:

[40] 5 DECS. COMP. GEN. 93 (1925).
[41] 13 DECS. COMP. GEN. 281 (1934). See also 17 DECS. COMP. GEN. 123 (1937).
[42] 364 U.S. 520 (1961). See ¶ 2–4.2a.

Although it is true that Wenzell had no authority to sign a binding contract, and that he did not participate in the terminal negotiations which led to the final agreement, nevertheless, those facts do not support the respondent's conclusion that the negotiations in which Wenzell participated were too remote and tenuous to be considered "the transaction of business." Far from being tenuous, the negotiations in which he participated were the very foundation upon which the final contract was based. . . . Although Wenzell did not participate in the ultimate negotiations, those negotiations cannot be divorced from the events which led up to the submission of the second proposal. The final contract was not negotiated in a vacuum. . . .

Wenzell played a key role in the early stages of the negotiations, and it was quite likely that the contract would never have come into fruition had he not participated on behalf of the Government. . . . If the activities of a government agent have as decisive an effect upon the outcome of a transaction as . . . Wenzell's activities were said by the Court of Claims to have had in this case, then a refusal to characterize those activities as part of a business transaction merely because they occurred at an early stage of the negotiations is at war with the obvious purpose of the statute. To limit the application of the statute to government agents who participate only in the final formation of a contract would permit those who have a conflict of interest to engage in the preliminary, but often crucial stages of the transaction, and then to insulate themselves from prosecution under Section 434 by withdrawing from the negotiations at the final, and often perfunctory stage of the proceedings. Congress could not possibly have intended such an obvious evasion of the statute.[43]

Where a government contract is involved, it is evident that the government employee personally handling the contract is subject to Section 434, and the *Mississippi Valley Generating Co.* decision makes it clear that he is covered by it if he substantially participated in the negotiations. But there are innumerable degrees of lesser contact possible between the contract transaction and the government employee's acts. What of the employee who decided that the government should buy a

[43] 364 U.S. at 553–55.

particular item, but did not specifically select the supplier? Or the man who drew up the contract specifications? Or the individual who decided that another competing bidder should not be accepted as a qualified bidder? How far does Section 434 go in reaching beyond the personal execution and negotiation of contracts?

In 1942, the Attorney General opined that an army reserve officer should not be assigned to maintain liaison with a private corporation of which he was an officer and stockholder. The officer would not have had authority to purchase or procure supplies or services, but he would have given advice and recommendations to the War Department as to commercial services, facilities, and other matters that might have influenced procurement relations between the Department and the corporation. The Attorney General took the position that "transaction of business" was not confined to the approval, or direct negotiation or execution, of contracts. The term included, in his view, rendering of advice to the government which might lead to a business relation between the private concern and the government.

The advice of the officer would probably also materially influence the nature and extent of the contracts entered into with his company. Conflict between the interests of the United States, the interests of the corporation and the interests of the Army officer as an officer and stockholder of the corporation are more than likely to arise. Such conflicts and results were doubtless intended to be avoided by the statute. In this case, the officer would clearly be a person "directly or indirectly interested in the pecuniary profits" within the meaning of the statute. So too, the degree of relationship of the officer to the procurement process would be such as to constitute "the transaction of business with such corporation" as used in the statute. It was the obvious purpose of the statute to prevent an officer of the United States from transacting business with a corporation in such a way that his action might result in direct or indirect personal pecuniary benefit to the officer.[44]

[44] 40 Ops. Att'y Gen. 168, 169–70 (1942).

Drawing the line on the other side was *Ingalls v. Perkins*, a state court case in which the scope of Section 434 was at issue. It involved a physician who contracted with a private sanatorium to give medical service to hospitalized disabled veterans. The physician was also an examiner for the Public Health Service with authority to recommend that ex-servicemen be placed in contract hospitals if, in his opinion, such hospitalization was necessary. His recommendations to the government could indirectly affect the amount of work and returns under his private contract. The owner of the sanatorium refused payment to the physician under the contract, claiming that it was illegal because in contravention of Section 434. The New Mexico Supreme Court rejected this argument and upheld the physician's claim for payment. It found the trial court to be

in error in holding the contract illegal, as violative of . . . [Section 434]. These statutes are penal, hence to be strictly construed. So construed, we do not think they apply to this case.

The assignment of patients does not seem to have been within his province. He could only recommend generally that they be placed in contract hospitals. The private advantage likely to ensue upon [his] making such a recommendation is so remote and . . . indirect as to be hardly recognizable.[45]

The *Ingalls* case raised the issue of interpretation in a context highly favorable to the governmental adviser: a private con-

[45] Ingalls v. Perkins, 33 N.M. 269, 271, 273, 263 Pac. 761, 762–63 (1927).

The opinion in *Atkinson v. New Britain Mach. Co.*, 154 F.2d 895 (7th Cir. 1946) contains some discussion of Section 434. The context was parallel to that in the *Ingalls* case discussed in the text, the defendant company raising the statute as a defense to a suit for commissions brought by one who was serving as a consultant to the company and to the Army and Navy Munitions Board. The decision went off on the separate ground that there had been no "transaction of business" by the government at all. Further, the defense was not seriously pressed and no showing was made either that the consultant's Washington work related to the company's contracts, or that either the consultant or the company received any gain out of the plaintiff's governmental consultancy.

See OFFICE OF THE LEGISLATIVE COUNSEL, COMPILATION OF CERTAIN LEGAL MATERIAL PREPARED ON THE CONFLICT OF INTEREST STATUTES 9 (Memorandum for Senator Saltonstall, Jan. 16, 1953).

tracting party was seeking to use the federal statute as a device to avoid paying for services already performed for him by the adviser. By contrast, the Attorney General's opinion cited previously was delivered as counsel in advance of action, at which point the chief legal officer of the government has every incentive to be conservative; the opinion is an unreliable index as to whether he would have sought an indictment if the facts had been brought to him after the reserve officer had served as liaison man to his company.

Is it possible that Section 434 may even go so far as to apply to transactions in which the official has taken no personal part whatever, but over which he has an ultimate responsibility *ex officio*? Should a high policy-making official, such as a Departmental Secretary, who personally has nothing to do with the actual execution of contracts, be held to come within Section 434 because of his nondelegable responsibility for overall policy directives that ultimately have an effect upon a business entity in which he is interested?

This has been a key issue in confirmation hearings before the Senate Armed Services Committee.[46] The Committee's view has been that the Secretary of Defense may hold *no* interest in any company doing business with the Department. In the controversial hearings in 1952 on the appointment of Mr. Charles Wilson, president of General Motors, to be Secretary of Defense, Senator Byrd, for example, was of the view that Section 434 would be applicable to Mr. Wilson "so long as he was Secretary of Defense and so long as he owned a pecuniary financial interest in any company which transacts business with the Department of Defense," and that "he cannot, as Secretary of Defense, divest himself from the responsibility of making contracts or procurements or perform any other duty which would be assigned to him as Secretary of Defense."[47]

On the other hand, it is argued that negotiations for contracts

[46] CONFLICT OF INTEREST AND FEDERAL SERVICE, ch. 5.
[47] 99 CONG. REC. 565 (1953).

are carried on far below the Secretarial level, and that overall
procurement and production planning, policy-making, and recommendations of a general character are not contemplated by
Section 434.[48] The Armed Services Committee's interpretation
of the section has been particularly criticized because of its
alleged deterrent effect upon the Government's efforts to recruit
executives for government service.[49]

The very recent case of *Smith v. United States* bears directly
on this problem.[50] In Portland, Oregon, Corey was director of
the local office of the Commodity Stabilization Service of the
Department of Agriculture. The office was charged with the
local administration of the farm price control activities of the
Commodity Credit Corporation, including the storage of government-owned wheat. Corey became aware of the availability
of a warehouse, suitable for storing grain. He brought the
matter to the attention of Richards, the general manager of a
large grain cooperative, and the two of them then entered into
an oral agreement with Smith, who was experienced in grain
warehousing, for Smith to lease and operate warehouses while
Corey and Richards were to participate as "silent partners" in the
business, each supplying one-third of the required $90,000 cap-
ital and all sharing gains and losses equally. Having set up the
business, Smith applied for and received an agreement with the
Commodity Service for the storage of government-owned wheat.
Corey signed a promissory note for his one-third of the capital;
the note was paid off out of deductions from proceeds payable
to him out of the profits of the enterprise. Later the enterprise
was incorporated, and shortly thereafter Corey sold out his one-
third share of the enterprise to his partners for $30,000; at that

[48] Davis, *The Federal Conflict of Interest Laws,* 54 COLUM. L. REV.
893, 898 (1954).

[49] The deterrent effect of the conflict of interest laws and of the Senate
Committees' confirmation practices in the field is reviewed at length in
CONFLICT OF INTEREST AND FEDERAL SERVICE, ch. 6.

[50] Smith v. United States, 305 F.2d 197 (9th Cir. 1962).

time his economic interest in the matter had not yet come to light. When the facts became known, Smith was indicted for making false statements to the Service to the effect that he was the sole owner of the warehouses; Smith, Corey, and Richards were charged with conspiracy to make the false statements; Corey was charged with violating Section 434; and Corey, Smith, and Richards were charged with conspiracy to violate that section. Richards testified for the government and was not indicted. Smith and Corey were convicted on all counts and given concurrent two-year sentences on each count. The appeal of both to the Court of Appeals for the Ninth Circuit raised many issues, all of which were resolved against appellants, or deemed unnecessary to be decided. A key issue in Corey's appeal related to the degree of his personal participation in the execution of the storage contracts.

Prior to the creation of the partnership arrangement, Corey had, as authorized by regulation, redelegated to subordinates the authority vested in him to execute such contracts. The officers to whom this authority was redelegated exercised independent discretion in entering into the contracts without approval of or consultation with Corey or any other officer. As director, however, Corey was not freed of all duties that could affect the terms and conditions of warehouse contracts. For example, Corey participated in telephone conferences relating to the movement of grain in and out of the area, and assisted in the negotiation of warehouse rates. The trial court advised the jury that Corey could be convicted under Section 434 if he was employed as head of the office and knew that the company was doing business with the office. The jury was instructed that it was not necessary for the government to show that Corey physically executed one or more of the contracts between the Service and the warehouse company or that he engaged in negotiations looking toward the execution of these contracts. As stated by the appellate court, the issue was thus presented "whether an officer or agent of the United States who is the administrative head of an office which to his knowledge negotiates and enters into contracts with a particular business entity, but who does not personally participate in such negotiations or the execution of such contracts, and who does not give any particular instructions with regard to those dealings to his subordinates who carry on such dealings under blanket authority, may be found to have engaged in 'the transaction of business' with such entity," within the meaning of Section 434.[51] The court upheld the trial court's instruction and held that "the head of a Government office which, to his knowledge, does business with a business entity, may be found to have transacted business with that office [sic] without the necessity of showing his personal participation in the dealings. This is because, under these circumstances, the jury may conclude that he ordered, directed, authorized or consented to the dealings which his office subordinates carried on with the business entity."[52]

If the Smith opinion is read closely and in the context of its particular facts, the holding is quite supportable. Corey's behavior was egregious; his deliberate creation of the silent partnership for the purpose of dealing with his own office constituted the most flagrant violation imaginable of the policy expressed by Section 434. He deliberately participated in a series of false representations to his own office. He was the director of a relatively small government office operating locally and almost every act he took as director necessarily had some influence upon his own personal returns from the partnership. He disclosed to no one in his office that he had an interest in the warehouse partnership and made no special arrangements to exclude his participation from matters relating to the warehouses belonging to the partnership. Under all these circumstances a jury surely could find that, as a practical matter, Corey did participate in the office's transactions of business with the partner-

[51] *Id.* at 210.   [52] *Id.* at 213.

ship to which he belonged. It is relevant, too, that Corey had been found guilty on several counts and that his conviction and sentence would have been the same however the court held on the issue of the application of Section 434.

In a footnote to the opinion, however, the court at least suggests that it is not correct to view Section 434 as a disqualification statute—that it requires that the official do more than "step aside" where he knows that his office is engaged in business transactions with a private entity in which he has an interest.[53] The implications of this statement—unnecessary to the decision —would, if carried out to their logical extensions, be extremely serious. The effect would be to make it impossible for any government executive to hold any outside business interest that deals with the government, or at least with the agency in which he is employed. Although it cannot be said that the court placed much weight on this consideration, at least it recognized that there must be some limit to its statement in the *Smith* case. The court conceded that "under the facts of a particular case the connection which the head of an agency has with the dealings the agency carries on with a company may be so remote and tenuous that ultimate responsibility plus knowledge are not alone sufficient to warrant a finding that the official engaged in 'the transaction of business.' "[54]

Altogether, while the *Smith* case is a satisfactory decision as such, it is regrettable that the language of the opinion strikes the balance it does in its interpretation of the degree of personal participation required of an official under Section 434. The opinion seems to imply a general rule of imputed vicarious participation by responsible officers, with some exception for very high officials. In contrast, the statutory language, and all the other judicial authorities (including the Supreme Court in the *Mississippi Valley Generating Co.* case), contemplate that a significant degree of personal participation by the official is

[53] *Id.* at 211, n. 19.   [54] *Id.* at 211.

normally required to make out a violation of the Section, but with leeway left for a broad interpretation of what constitutes "participation" in exceptional local fact situations such as that presented in the *Smith* case.

Apart from the problem of the degree of the employee's participation, when does a "transaction" begin and when does it end? The *Mississippi Valley Generating Co.* case, for all its factual complexity, involved at heart a rather simple discrete transaction, a single isolatable contract between a private company and the government. But in the modern world of a mixed economy, private business entities and organizations have recurrent contacts and dealings with the federal government, many of which call for continuing relations, rather than one-shot deals. In these situations, what constitutes a "transaction" for purposes of Section 434? As an historical matter, Section 434 was aimed at the procurement contract, and it happened that something very close to that was at issue in the *Mississippi Valley Generating Co.* case. How the courts would break up a flow of events into "transactions" for purposes of the section is a matter of conjecture. A similar problem under Sections 281 and the new Section 203 is discussed at ¶ 1A–4.3.

2–4.4b. SECTION 208 (1963)

Section 208 is considerably clearer than the predecessor Section 434 in specifying the kind and degree of activity forbidden to a government employee who has a financial interest in a particular matter. While much of the discussion at ¶ 2–4.4a continues to bear upon Section 208, the new section will apply only where the government employee participates "personally and substantially as a Government officer or employee, through decision, approval, disapproval, recommendation, the rendering of advice, investigation or otherwise." The major effect of this redrafting of Section 434 is to make it clear that the government employee must refrain from personal action in matters where he has a financial interest, but will not be held vicariously responsible for the action of others, even his subordinates. Virtually all-inclusive in its listing of the *kinds* of activities comprehended, Section 208 is relatively narrow in its specification that the government employee himself must participate in the activity "personally and substantially as a Government officer or employee." Thus it clearly overrules the sweeping implications of the *Smith* opinion, discussed at ¶ 2–4.4a, though it is likely that the appalling facts in that case would still ground a conviction under Section 208.

2–5. APPLICABILITY TO EVENTS BEFORE AND AFTER JANUARY 21, 1963

Effective January 21, 1963, Section 2 of Law 87–849 repealed Section 434 and supplanted it by Section 208. Events prior to that date continue to be governed by Section 434.

CHAPTER 3. OUTSIDE COMPENSATION
SECTION 1914 AND SECTION 209 (1963)

Nothing in the conflict of interest statutes is intended to prevent, or discourage, government employees from having an outside income. Government employees may, and often do, have outside investments, holdings, and even jobs.

Since 1917, however, one sweeping criminal statute has regulated certain kinds of outside compensation to government employees. Section 209 of Law 87–849, effective January 21, 1963, and its predecessor, 18 U.S.C. § 1914, express in very general terms the idea that the government employee should not be paid by anyone except the government for doing his government job. The statutory objection is not to the outside income, but to the linkage between the income and the performance of official duties. The purpose is to prevent an outside source from diluting an official's loyalty by paying him on the side to do what the government has already hired him to do. Section 209 and the predecessor Section 1914 single out one overt technique for turning a government official into a private captive—not bribery, but perhaps a prelude to bribery.

In the words of the Attorney General, the underlying philosophy at work is "that no Government official or employee should serve two masters to the prejudice of his unbiased devotion to the interests of the United States."[1]

3–1. GENERAL

Section 1914 reads:

Whoever, being a Government official or employee, receives any salary in connection with his services as such an official or employee from any source other than the Government of the United States, except as may be contributed out of the treasury of any State, county or municipality; or

Whoever, whether a person, association, or corporation, makes any contribution to, or in any way supplements the salary of, any Government official or employee for the services performed by him for the Government of the United States—

Shall be fined not more than $1,000 or imprisoned not more than six months, or both.

The section thus provides for two separate offenses, one committed by the recipient, the other by the payor. The offenses are not, however, exactly parallel.

There are no reported prosecutions under Section 1914. Judicial interpretations are rare and have usually considered the section as a defense to the enforcement of a contract or of another statute. The principal sources of authority are opinions of the Attorney General and of the Comptroller General, and these tend to be elliptical in their treatment of the facts and issues. The Comptroller General has played an important role in the administration and interpretation of Section 1914: outside payments made to an official in violation of the section are considered illegal augmentations of the budget of the recipient's agency and therefore come under the budgetary scrutiny and supervision of the Comptroller General.

Section 209 of Law 87–849, effective January 21, 1963, is the child of and is closely similar to Section 1914. The text of Section 209 is set forth in Appendix A.

[1] 33 OPS. ATT'Y GEN. 273, 275 (1922).

The major differences between Section 209 and Section 1914 are that the new section does not apply to WOCs or so-called Special Employees (essentially short-term intermittent or temporary employees) and that it contains special exemptions with respect to certain pension and insurance benefits maintained by a former employer of the government employee.

3–2. BACKGROUND

All of the conflict of interest statutes except Section 1914 originated in abuses in the prosecution of government claims and in government contracting. Though Section 1914 dates from the year 1917, it did not arise out of World War I. It appears that the Bureau of Education of the Department of the Interior had entered into "cooperative relations" with certain private organizations, including the Rockefeller and Carnegie foundations, for the purpose of studying and promoting educational projects, such as Negro education and kindergarten programs. These outside organizations made no direct monetary contributions to the Bureau, but they did pay the real salaries of certain men who were employed by the Bureau at a dollar a year to perform Bureau tasks under the direct supervision and control of the Commission of Education. An additional number of persons throughout the United States who were employed in the universities and normal schools, or who held positions such as county school superintendents, were appointed to perform "occasional services" without pay for the Bureau of Education.[2] In some quarters these arrangements aroused fear that the foundations were wielding a new and noxious influence on national educational policy. A real, or ostensible, side issue in the debate over the foundation dollar-a-year men concerned the franking privilege.[3]

[2] 54 CONG. REC. 2039, 2045 (1917).

[3] Senator Chamberlain of Oregon, foremost proponent of legislation in the field, argued: "Some great educator of this country, who may be ever so highly respected by our people, writes a thesis on some great educational subject that may be very dear to the hearts of the American people,

Senator Chamberlain introduced a bill to curb dollar-a-year employees of the Bureau of Education. The bill was restricted in its application to that Bureau. Despite opposition from those who thought some good might derive from cooperative work between the government and private agencies, the bill passed the Senate. It failed in the House, apparently on the ground that it was too broad. Yet, as the bill emerged from Conference Committee, it assumed an even more sweeping form and, after two rejections, was adopted by both Houses in 1917. The statute remained unaltered until superseded by Section 209 in 1963.

A detailed abstract of the development of Section 1914 appears in Appendix E.

Section 209 shares with Section 1914 a common history and legislative purpose. The general background of Law 87–849 is described in the Introduction to this volume. An abstract of its legislative history appears in Appendix E.

3–3. COVERAGE

3–3a. SECTION 1914

Section 1914 applies by its terms to anyone who is "a Government official or employee." This precise phrase occurs in no other of the conflict of interest statutes, though it is similar to that of other sections. In most situations, no reason appears for distinguishing the reach of Section 1914 from other conflict of interest statutes, and interpretations of the other statutes offer persuasive analogies for the construction of Section 1914.

3–3b. SECTION 209 (1963)

Though the drafting is somewhat hind end to, Section 209 works out to apply to anyone who is "an officer or employee of

---

and yet he has no way of getting it before the people except that he may be able to pay to get his literature distributed, or in so far as he may be able to get the press to publish it; and yet one of these pets of the Bureau of Education, Mr. President, may get his answer to it, or his own view, before the American people through the franking privilege." *Id.* at 2039.

the executive branch of the United States Government, of any independent agency of the United States or of the District of Columbia." This language is identical to that appearing in Sections 208 and 207. See ¶ 2–3b and ¶ 4A–3b.

3–3.1. Federal employer

3–3.1a. SECTION 1914

As in the case of the other conflict of interest statutes, considerable question exists as to the coverage of Section 1914 where the employee's employing agency is something other than the executive branch, or where the employing agency is not clearly governmental in character.

Judiciary. There is no authority on the application of Section 1914 to members of the federal judiciary. On the face of it they would appear to be "Government officials" and subject to the restrictions of the section. One opinion of the Comptroller General applies the section to the secretary of a federal judge.[4]

Legislative employees. Though there is no authority respecting the application of Section 1914 to employees of the legislative branch, its application to employees of the executive branch and of the judiciary leaves little doubt that legislative employees are within its scope.

Uniformed services. The position of uniformed military personnel under the conflict of interest laws, including Section 1914, is discussed in Appendix B.

District of Columbia. There is no authority on the question whether employees of the District of Columbia are subject to Section 1914. But it seems virtually certain that they are. As a matter of public policy, there is more warrant for this conclusion in the case of Section 1914 than in the case of some of the other conflict of interest statutes. It may well be argued that there is little need or sense in requiring municipal employees

[4] 5 DECS. COMP. GEN. 650 (1926).

of the District of Columbia to curtail their relationships with the federal government in the manner required by, for example, Section 281. But this argument has no application to Section 1914. If it is a bad thing to be on a public and a private payroll simultaneously, the principle applies as well to the federal municipal government as on the national level.

It appears to have been generally assumed that Section 1914 applies to employees of the District of Columbia.

Government corporations. An employee of a governmentally owned corporation is in all probability a "Government employee" for purposes of Section 1914.[5]

Non-appropriated agencies. See ¶ 1A–3.1a.

3–3.1b. SECTION 209 (1963)

The discussion at ¶ 2–3.1b with regard to the scope of federal employment under Section 208 is equally applicable to Section 209.

3–3.2. Officer or employee

3–3.2a. SECTION 1914

The regular full-time worker in a government department or bureau is subject to Section 1914 as a "Government official or employee." For example, customs officials,[6] civilian employees of the Department of the Navy,[7] and accounting and auditing assistants of the Collector of Internal Revenue[8] have been considered to be subject to the section.

The question has been raised whether a regular government employee continues to be subject to the section while he is on leave of absence from his government job. The Attorney

[5] UNPUBLISHED DECS. COMP. GEN. A–76416 (July 25, 1936). The opinion is not a model of clarity, but on this point it seems correct.

[6] 3 DECS. COMP. GEN. 128 (1923).

[7] 32 DECS. COMP. GEN. 18 (1952).

[8] United States v. Gerdel, 103 F. Supp. 635 (E.D. Mo. 1952). (The court offers a suggestion, confessed to be "gratuitous.")

General opined in 1920 that it was not a violation of Section 1914 for the Chief Statistician for Vital Statistics of the Census Bureau to go on leave without pay from his regular job and receive compensation from the Red Cross in order to attend meetings of an international commission formed for the purpose of revising the nomenclature of diseases and causes of death.[9] More recently the Comptroller General arrived at a similar conclusion. An employee of the Department of the Interior was on leave of absence without pay at the request of a United States military mission. During this time he worked under the supervision of the mission but was carried on the payroll of a civilian contractor. The Comptroller General held that the arrangement did not violate Section 1914.[10]

Though these opinions have not been questioned, their doctrine cannot be carried very far. In an appropriate situation, a deciding authority might conclude that an employee who is on leave without pay from the government while on an outside payroll is in the same position as a government employee serving without compensation (a WOC) who is being paid from an outside private source. The instances just referred to must be viewed as rather special.

3–3.2b. SECTION 209 (1963)

Section 209 adds nothing to the meaning of the term "Government officer or employee." See ¶ 3–3.2a; ¶ 2–3.2b; ¶ 1A–3.2a and ¶ 1A–3.2b.

3–3.2.1. Congressman

3–3.2.1a. SECTION 1914

The history of Section 1914 shows a Congress suspicious and irate at the arrangement worked out between the executive

[9] 32 OPS. ATT'Y GEN. 309 (1920).

[10] 22 DECS. COMP. GEN. 178 (1942). To the same effect, where the employee was on "furlough," see 20 DECS. COMP. GEN. 488 (1941).

branch and private foundations under which the employees of the former were being paid by the latter. When Congress fired the shotgun of Section 1914 at this practice, no one on the floor noted that its gauge was sufficiently wide to cover members of Congress themselves. It could well be contended that a Congressman is not a "Government employee"; it is harder to contend that he is not a "Government official." But the only guidance is the bare language of the statute, coupled with the absence of discussion in the legislative debate.

3–3.2.1b. SECTION 209 (1963)

Members of Congress are not subject to Section 209.

3–3.2.2. Intermittent employee; Special Employee

3–3.2.2a. SECTION 1914

There is no doubt that Section 1914 applies to all those who work for the government, whether or not they are paid by the government and whether or not they perform only intermittent services for the government. The discussion of the point in connection with other conflict of interest statutes is equally applicable here.[11] Indeed, of all the conflict of interest statutes, Section 1914 is the only one which in its origins was deliberately pointed toward the dollar-a-year man. Thus the Attorney General considered it a violation of Section 1914 for the United States Geological Survey to employ a field representative at a dollar a year when his regular salary was to be paid by an association of coal operators.[12] Similarly, in 1943 the Attorney General rendered an opinion that it would violate Section 1914 if a manager of a railroad "donated" his services to the Office of Defense Transportation, his salary to be paid by the Western Association of Railway Executives.[13] And in 1955 the Comp-

[11] See ¶ 1A–3.2.2a.   [12] 31 OPS. ATT'Y GEN. 470 (1919).
[13] 40 OPS. ATT'Y GEN. 265 (1943).

troller General held that members of a labor mediating board
created by the Railway Labor Act could not arrange to continue
their private compensation "in lieu" of compensation from the
government as provided for the Act.[14] Though the authority
is slight, it is not now questioned that the intermittent employee
who works as a consultant or adviser, is covered by Section
1914.[15]

3–3.2.2b. SECTION 209 (1963)

Section 209 is unique among the provisions in the new legislation in that it does not apply at all to Special Employees. The
term "Special Employee" is defined in the statute and discussed
in ¶ 1A–3.2.2b. An intermittent compensated employee who
falls outside the definition of Special Employee is subject to
Section 209, but as a practical matter these will be few or
none.

By its own terms, Section 209 does not apply to an officer or
employee of the government serving without compensation,
whether or not he is a Special Employee. The irony of this aspect of Section 209 should not pass unnoted. In 1917 Congress
considered it necessary, in order to curb alleged abuses in the
practice of using WOCs, to enact in Section 1914 a sweeping
statute applicable to all governmental employees; in 1962 Congress unquestioningly accepted, or assumed, the need for continuing the broad rule of Section 1914 but, in translating it to
the modestly redrafted Section 209, included a blanket exemption for WOCs.

[14] 35 DECS. COMP. GEN. 354 (1955).
[15] 40 OPS. ATT'Y GEN. 168 (1942). The point is assumed, perhaps decided, by the Supreme Court in *United States v. Mississippi Valley Generating Co.*, 364 U.S. 520, 552 n.15. The Attorney General seems to have
made the same assumption in his ambiguous opinion at 39 OPS. ATT'Y
GEN. 501 (1940) discussed in ¶ 3–4.2a.

3–3.2.3. Non-employee; independent contractor
3–3.2.3a. SECTION 1914

By legal characterization, one who serves the federal government and who is not considered to be an "official or employee" is likely to be viewed as an "independent contractor." The independent contractor lies beyond the reach of Section 1914. See ¶ 1A–3.2.3a.

3–3.2.3b. SECTION 209 (1963)

See ¶ 1A–3.2.3b.

3–3.3. Other persons
3–3.3a. SECTION 1914

Some of the conflict of interest statutes, in declaring certain behavior of government employees to be criminal, leave open and unanswered the criminality of the behavior of other persons who participated in the conduct. See, for example, in connection with Section 281, ¶ 1A–3.3a.

Section 1914 does not have this deficiency. In its second paragraph the section defines a criminal offense committed by the outside payor of unlawful payments to the government employee. It is not necessary, therefore, under Section 1914 to resort to a theory classifying the payor as an aider or abettor. The section covers the payor by its own terms. See ¶ 3–4.5a.

See Appendix C regarding partners and associates of federal employees.

3–3.3b. SECTION 209 (1963)

Like its predecessor, Section 209 contains a special provision respecting the outside payor; see ¶ 3–4.5b.

See Appendix C for discussion of the position under Section 209 of partners and associates of federal employees.

3–4. Substantive offense

3–4a. Section 1914

Section 1914 is deceptive. Its two paragraphs appear simple and its objectives seem apparent. This simplicity and clarity prove, however, to be illusory.

The general policy of Section 1914 is described thus in *Conflict of Interest and Federal Service:*

> The rule is really a special case of the general injunction against serving two masters. Three basic concerns underlie this rule prohibiting two payrolls and two paymasters for the same employee on the same job. First, the outside payor has a hold on the employee deriving from his ability to cut off one of the employee's economic lifelines. Second, the employee may tend to favor his outside payor even though no direct pressure is put on him to do so. And, third, because of these real risks, the arrangement has a generally unwholesome appearance that breeds suspicion and bitterness among fellow employees and other observers. The public interpretation is apt to be that if an outside party is paying a government employee and is not paying him for past services, he must be paying him for some current services to the payor during a time when his services are supposed to be devoted to the government. In part the fear is that the government employee will not keep his nose to the grindstone; in part the fear is close to the fear of bribery; in part the fear is that outside forces will subvert the operation of regular policy-making procedures in the government (the historical source of Section 1914); and in part the rule is grounded in considerations of personnel administration.[16]

It must be emphasized that the statute forbids outside compensation even if the payor has no dealings or relations whatever with the government and no special interest in its policies. It is not limited in its application to compensation paid by a source in a sensitive relationship with the government employee's agency—a supply contractor dealing with the agency,

[16] Conflict of Interest and Federal Service at 211–12.

for example. The statute has often been criticized for its breadth
in this respect.

A second general noteworthy aspect of Section 1914 is its
relationship to the position of the government employee who
serves without compensation.

In general it is against the law to be an employee of the United
States Government without being paid by the United States.[*]
This statement must be distinguished from the rule of Section 1914,
just discussed, that if a person works for the United States, it is
illegal for another to pay him for that work. The relation, and the
distinction, between these two propositions require discussion.

The first rule requires that a United States employee be on the
government payroll. Whenever a period of special national emergency arises, or whenever specialized governmental programs cannot be staffed through regular sources, the issue arises whether
limited exceptions should be made to permit certain positions to be
filled by persons who will serve without compensation. Sometimes
such legislative exceptions are made. As has been noted, the persons who are appointed to the positions are given the tagname
WOCs from the phrase "without compensation."

The pros and cons of the WOC have been sharply debated since
World War I, and the issue is no nearer final resolution than ever.

On one side, all agree that in general government should be
staffed by government employees paid by and working primarily
for the United States. The government official participating in government action, but in office only temporarily and probably continuing to be paid by an outside source, is subject to incentives and
pressures that may influence his official decisions adversely to the
interests of the government. Without adopting a theory of history
as conspiracy, one can appreciate the risk that some companies or
organizations would be ready to use the WOC arrangement as a
device for planting agents in government positions for their own
ends. The WOC being paid by an outsider may be a conflict of
interest incarnate.

[*] See 33 Stat. 1257 (1906), 31 U.S.C. § 665(b) (1958); 27 DECS. COMP.
GEN. 194 (1947). A brief history of this statutory prohibition is contained
in ANTITRUST SUBCOMM., HOUSE COMM. ON THE JUDICIARY, 84TH CONG.,
2D SESS., INTERIM REPORT ON WOC's AND GOVERNMENT ADVISORY
GROUPS 4–7 (Comm. Print 1956).

Quite apart from arguments based on conflicts of interest, however, the practice of using WOCs can be questioned on grounds of sound personnel administration. The WOC is less subject to agency discipline and, with his outside income, may be a source of irritation to his fellow government workers.

Finally, the rule against the use of WOCs is a necessary safeguard to protect Congress' constitutional power over appropriations and expenditures. The use by an agency of a large and highly paid staff of public relations men whose salaries are paid by an interested outside organization, for example, could constitute a flagrant subversion of congressional control of the purse strings.

The arguments on the other side are equally apparent. WOCs and the organizations that pay them, if any, are generally acting out of patriotic motives. The WOC often brings to the particular job to which he is appointed special skills which the government desperately needs and which are not available elsewhere. Through the WOC device, the government succeeds in obtaining the services of men who would not have been willing to cut themselves off from their regular jobs and salaries to enter government service on a permanent basis.*

Congressional resolution of the WOC problem has been very much what might be anticipated. The general rule is that the United States is able to, and should, pay its own personnel, and that the use of WOCs is forbidden by Congress. This prohibition on the use of WOCs is addressed to the executive branch itself—not to the persons serving as WOCs. Where WOCs are permitted it is only by virtue of special statutory authorization and exception granted by Congress. When Congress makes an exception to its general rule it is nearly always because of a national emergency or quasi emergency. As the crisis recedes, Congress has historically cut back or abolished the special WOC authorization.† A measure of the nation's current

---

* See ANTITRUST SUBCOMM., HOUSE COMM. ON THE JUDICIARY, 84TH CONG., 2D SESS., INTERIM REPORT ON WOC's AND GOVERNMENT ADVISORY GROUPS 3 (Comm. Print 1956).

† See the discussion of the background of the WOC program in ANTITRUST SUBCOMM., HOUSE COMM. ON THE JUDICIARY, 84TH CONG., 2D SESS., INTERIM REPORT ON WOC's AND GOVERNMENT ADVISORY GROUPS 4–7 (Comm. Print 1956). See also the restrictive 1955 amendments to section 7 of the Defense Production Act at 69 Stat. 180, 583 (1955), 50 U.S.C. App. § 2160 (1958).

semibelligerent status is the fact that at the present time some critical defense agencies are permitted to use WOCs.*

The congressional ban on WOCs is thus not rooted solely in conflict of interest considerations. But whenever Congress does authorize the use of WOCs, it finds it collaterally necessary to write some
corresponding degree of exemption into the conflict of interest statutes. Section 1914, banning outside compensation, must always be
suspended in respect of the WOC to permit him to continue his
regular salary from nongovernmental sources; no one expects the
WOC to go off all payrolls, public and private. If the WOC will be
acting for the government in business transactions with his company, Congress may also give him a limited exemption from Section
434, the statute ordinarily requiring disqualification in situations of
conflicting interest. Such a situation could arise, for example, if a
company official should work for the government as a temporary
WOC expert to set up machinery regulating some activity of the
industry in which his own company was engaged. Other conflict
of interest rules may be collaterally relaxed by Congress when it
authorizes the use of the WOC, but the only statute from which he
must always be immunized is Section 1914.

Another category of government employment raises almost the
same problems under Section 1914 as the WOC. Part-time consultants to the government, if paid at all, are paid "when actually
employed." From this phrase comes, in the argot of Federalese, the
term WAE. Strictly speaking, there is less need to exempt WAEs from
Section 1914 than WOCs; but where Congress has authorized the
use of WAEs, it has often exempted them from Section 1914 to
make clear that their regular salaries from their private employers
will not be jeopardized by their work for the government as WAEs.

---

* See *Hearings Before the Antitrust Subcommittee of the House Committee on the Judiciary on WOC's and Government Advisory Groups*, 84th
Cong., 1st Sess. 642–44 (1955); ANTITRUST SUBCOMM., HOUSE COMM.
ON THE JUDICIARY, 84TH CONG., 2D SESS., INTERIM REPORT ON WOC's AND
GOVERNMENT ADVISORY GROUPS 114–17 (Comm. Print 1956) for figures
on the use of WOCs by the Defense Department and other government
agencies. On various dates in 1955, the Department of Defense reported
187 WOCs as employed; the Department of Commerce, 260; the Office
of Defense Mobilization, 108; and the Atomic Energy Commission, 33.
See *Id.* at 114–15.

As in the case of the WOC, Congress may, but need not, grant the WAE other exemptions from the conflict of interest statutes.[17]

These general observations should be kept in mind in dealing with Section 1914 and its successor.

3–4b. SECTION 209 (1963)

The offense under Section 209 is almost identical to that under its predecessor Section 1914, and the general discussion at ¶ 3–4a is applicable to Section 209. Only the most minor changes in drafting have been made. The only exception to this statement is ironic. In origins Section 1914 was aimed at the consultant and the WOC. See ¶ 3–2. Section 209 makes no substantial change in Section 1914 except to exempt most consultants and all WOCs.

3–4.1. Compensation

3–4.1a. SECTION 1914

The first paragraph of Section 1914 forbids the government employee to receive any "salary" in connection with his services as an employee from any source other than the government of the United States. In one sense, the word "salary" is a limiting conception; it clearly implies the receipt of a thing of value in consideration for or in payment for services rendered. The use of this term makes it clear that Section 1914 does not reach out to the receipt of gifts. And, in this interpretation, the word "salary" is reinforced by the later phrases in the statute "in connection with his services" and "for the services." These phrases are discussed below.

But in another sense the word "salary" appears by common agreement not to be narrow in its meaning. It would have been possible, perhaps, to interpret the word "salary" as a "fixed

[17] *Id.* at 57–59.

annual or periodical payment for services."[18] Wherever the issue has been passed upon, however, a much broader interpretation has been used; thus "salary" has been viewed as including tuition fees,[19] travel expenses,[20] professional expenses,[21] hotel or rental expenses,[22] overtime pay,[23] premium payment,[24] commission payments, and various honoraria.[25] The Comptroller General has stated that the "receiving . . . of additional pay, extra allowance, or compensation in any form whatever comes squarely within the provisions" of Section 1914.[26] And the Air Force Judge Advocate General has stated that the term "appears to mean any 'compensation' which increases an individual's 'net worth.' "[27]

[18] This was the narrow definition of "salary" adopted by the Supreme Court in the context of another statute. Benedict v. United States, 176 U.S. 357, 360 (1900). Cf. the language of the court in United States v. Gerdel, 103 F. Supp. 635, 639 (E.D. Mo. 1952), the only judicial expression on the use of "salary" in Section 1914, but not a particularly enlightening one.

[19] 36 DECS. COMP. GEN. 155 (1956). The Judge Advocate General of the Air Force has questioned whether this decision was appropriate in cases in which the government itself would be obliged to pay the tuition in question, and where any benefit thus would accrue to the government itself rather than to its employees. JUDGE ADVOCATE GENERAL OF THE AIR FORCE OPINION 87–11.1 (1957).

[20] E.g., 36 DECS. COMP. GEN. 155 (1956); 18 DECS. COMP. GEN. 460 (1938); 2 DECS. COMP. GEN. 634, 775 (1923); 26 DECS. COMP. TREAS. 43 (1919); UNPUBLISHED DECS. COMP. GEN. B-128527 (1956); UNPUBLISHED DECS. COMP. GEN. A-30685, p. 2 (1930). The opinions occasionally show a tendency to find a flexibility in this interpretation on travel expenses, and to permit reimbursements by an outside source where no actual conflict of interest is apparent and where the event giving rise to the expenses seems to have been in the government's interest. 33 OPS. ATT'Y GEN. 273 (1922); JUDGE ADVOCATE GENERAL OF THE AIR FORCE OPINION 57–85.77, p. 3 (1955); 37 DECS. COMP. GEN. 776 (1958).

[21] 36 DECS. COMP. GEN. 155 (1956).

[22] Ibid.; 30 DECS. COMP. GEN. 246 (1950).

[23] 3 DECS. COMP. GEN. 128 (1923); UNPUBLISHED DECS. COMP. GEN. A-30685 (1930). See International Railway Co. v. Davidson, 257 U.S. 506 (1922).

[24] UNPUBLISHED DECS. COMP. GEN. A-44017, p. 5 (1942).

[25] UNPUBLISHED DECS. COMP. GEN. A-51627 (1939). See also JUDGE ADVOCATE GENERAL OF THE AIR FORCE OPINION 57–85.77, p. 4 (1955).

[26] UNPUBLISHED DECS. COMP. GEN. A–30685, p. 4 (1930).

[27] JUDGE ADVOCATE GENERAL OF THE AIR FORCE OPINION 57–85.77, p.

Law practitioners have frequently been called upon to opine whether it violates Section 1914 for a company or other employer to continue an employee's medical, retirement, or insurance program while he is on government service. This problem has infinite variations. In an extreme case, the private source might make large cash payments into a retirement account for the benefit of the employee. Depending upon the motivations involved, the payments would look very much like direct salary payments. At another extreme, the government employee's former employer might do no more than permit the employee to retain his eligibility under the applicable plan, leaving all premiums and other payments into the plan to be made by the employee himself. In this case, while the continued eligibility as a member of the plan would clearly be of economic value to the government employee, it would be difficult to say that the former employer is continuing to make "salary" payments.[28] As discussed later, however, these questions have turned upon whether they were made "in connection with" the employee's government services. There has been little doubt that, given the requisite intention, the payments, credits, or other benefits under such plans would themselves be considered "salary." Mere continued eligibility or membership in the plan, without more, would likely not be considered so.

3–4.1b. SECTION 209 (1963)

The government officer or employee who is covered by Section 209 is forbidden to receive "any contribution to or supple-

---

1 (1955). It is immaterial that the compensation is to be donated to charity. 4 DIGEST OF OPINIONS OF THE JUDGE ADVOCATES GENERAL OF THE ARMED FORCES 408 (JAGA 1955/1294, 1955).

[28] A close reading of the statute may show problems even here, for under the second paragraph of Section 1914, the outsider may violate it if he simply "supplements the salary of" the government employee. So far at least, no authoritative source has sought to distinguish between the breadth of the first and second paragraphs.

mentation of salary" from private sources for his government services. This language from Section 209 differs in minor respects from that of the predecessor Section 1914, but no substantive change has been made. The discussion at ¶ 3–4.1a remains applicable to Section 209.

It was pointed out in that paragraph that in one sense the word "salary" is a limiting conception; it implies a receipt of a thing of value in consideration for or in payment for services rendered. This limitation of meaning is even clearer under Section 209 than under Section 1914. Section 209 does not prohibit gifts to government officers or employees. It may be debatable in a particular case whether a transfer of an item of value to the government employee was a gift or was a supplementation of the employee's salary "for" his services. But to make out the offense under Section 209, it is essential to establish the linkage between the transfer of the thing of value and the services rendered.

Section 209(b) modifies the discussion at ¶ 3–4.1a in one respect—it permits the continuation of certain private insurance and retirement plans in which the government employee participated before entering government service. See ¶ 3–4.2b.

3–4.2. Relation to governmental services; compensation for past services

3–4.2a. SECTION 1914

Section 1914 does not prohibit government employees from carrying on compensated outside activities, does not prohibit them from having an outside income, and does not prohibit gifts or gratuities to government employees. Both the first and second paragraphs of the section explicitly require that the payment bear some relationship to the employee's services to the federal government. Under the first paragraph, the payment must be "in connection with" those services; under the second paragraph the criminal act is the contribution to, or supplement to the salary of, the government employee "for" the services performed by him for the government.

This connective language is vague. It also appears to call for a judgment as to the subjective intention of the payor. As critics and commentators have pointed out, the connective has been difficult to apply and has prompted evasion.[29] But the "in connection with/for" language is at the same time the element that makes the statute administrable at all. Absent this restricting language, the statute would forbid all payments to government employees—an altogether impossible rule of conduct.

An unusually clear statement of the required connection between the payment and the services appears in a 1942 opinion of the Attorney General.

The statute clearly covers a salary received from a private person or source if it is paid or received as compensation or part compensation for the services rendered to the Government. It has also been held to apply if the officer or employee renders the same or similar services to both the Government and a private person (33 Op. A. G. 273). It does not, however, prohibit payment for services rendered exclusively to private persons or organizations and which have no connection with the services rendered to the Government.[30]

The preceding numbered paragraph stressed the fact that Section 1914 prohibits payments from any outside source to a government employee, not just payments from those who have a sensitive relationship to the employee's agency. While this is true, might not this consideration of sensitive relationship enter in, more or less consciously, wherever it is necessary to decide upon the kind of general intent with which the payments

[29] STAFF OF SUBCOMM. NO. 5, HOUSE COMM. ON THE JUDICIARY, 85TH CONG., 2D SESS. FEDERAL CONFLICT OF INTEREST LEGISLATION 44 (Comm. Print 1958); Davis, *The Federal Conflict of Interest Laws*, 54 COLUM. L. REV. 893, 903–06 (1954).
[30] 40 OPS. ATT'Y GEN. 187, 190 (1942).

to the employee were made? At least one opinion of the Attorney General seems to give weight to the presence or absence of dealings between the agency and the employee's payor. The Attorney General said:

I think I should also point out, however, that the determination of whether a particular payment is made "in connection with" the services of an individual as a Government official or employee is often a matter of ascertaining not only the intent with which the payment is made but also the intent of the employee in receiving payment. An important factor in determining intent is whether the individual rendering service to the Government is in a position by virtue of his Government service to assist his private employer.[31]

Some writers have suggested that this factor is crucial in assessing the applicability of Section 1914 in a given situation, in spite of the fact that it is often unstated and that the language of the statute itself contains no such restriction.[32] Probably this view goes too far. The various opinions and judgments of the deciding authorities cannot be rationalized entirely around this principle.[33] But the factor does on occasion intrude, as illustrated by the opinion of the Attorney General quoted above. It is probably true that if there is any substantial relationship or pattern of dealings between the employee's agency and the payor, the likelihood is substantially increased that a court or other deciding authority will find a violation.[34]

[31] 41 Ops. Att'y Gen. No. 45, p. 5 (1955).

[32] Dembling & Forest, *Government Service and Private Compensation,* 20 Geo. Wash. L. Rev. 174, 191–92 (1951); Davis, *The Federal Conflict of Interest Laws,* 54 Colum. L. Rev. 893, 904–05 (1954); McElwain & Vorenberg, *The Federal Conflict of Interest Statutes,* 65 Harv. L. Rev. 955 (1952).

[33] It is not easy to find the principle at work, for example, in 41 Ops. Att'y Gen. No. 45 (1955); 36 Decs. Comp. Gen. 155 (1955); 30 Decs. Comp. Gen. 246 (1950); 29 Decs. Comp. Gen. 163 (1949); or 16 Decs. Comp. Gen. 127 (1936).

[34] Compare 41 Ops. Att'y Gen. No. 45 (1955); 38 Ops. Att'y Gen. 294 (1935); 32 Ops. Att'y Gen. 309 (1920) *with* 40 Ops. Att'y Gen. 168 (1942); 31 Ops. Att'y Gen. 470 (1919); 26 Decs. Comp. Treas. 43 (1919).

Despite the uncertainty surrounding the interpretation of Section 1914, some recurrent situations are identifiable and more or less predictable.

The position of the government employee on leave of absence is discussed in ¶ 3–3.2a.

In the absence of specific statutory authorization, a government official or employee may not avoid the impact of Section 1914 by performing work connected with his government job after hours. If the services are the same or substantially the same or "connected with" his government services, it is immaterial that he performs them after hours.[35]

On occasion the government has seen fit to sponsor programs in cooperation with private groups which could, if strictly interpreted, have been held to violate the provisions of Section 1914. In most of these cases the deciding authorities have upheld the program, particularly where the devices used were designed to meet the exigencies of war.[36] Direct payment by private contractors to employees of the government for wartime services performed for and under the direction of the government was, however, held by the Comptroller General to be forbidden by Section 1914.[37]

Payments for past services. By its terms Section 1914 does not restrict payments for nongovernmental services or for services that are not "in connection with" governmental services. Thus payments made to a government employee "for" past services or, presumably, "for" future services are permissible so far as Section 1914 is concerned. It is a matter for determination on

[35] International Ry. v. Davidson, 257 U.S. 506 (1922); United States v. Myers, 320 U.S. 561 (1944); Pan American Airways, Inc. v. United States, 150 F. Supp. 569 (U.S. Customs Ct., 3d Div. 1957); 11 DECS. COMP. GEN. 10, 153 (1931); 2 DECS. COMP. GEN. 775 (1923); UNPUBLISHED DECS. COMP. GEN. A-93737 (1938) and A-30685 (1930).

[36] See Muschany v. United States, 324 U.S. 49 (1945); Johnson v. Sundstrand Mach. Tool Co., 204 F.2d 783 (7th Cir. 1953); Atkinson v. New Britain Mach. Co., 154 F.2d 895 (7th Cir. 1946).

[37] 32 DECS. COMP. GEN. 18 (1952) (alternative holding).

the facts of each situation whether the payments can be legitimately ascribed to prior or future work. Since payments for future work are rare, and since the future character of such services makes it difficult to demonstrate their actuality, there are no recorded instances of arrangements held or considered to be permissible under Section 1914 where the services were contemplated only. But it is common to find situations in which a government employee receives some form of economic benefit during his government service that he and the payor attribute to earlier services on his part.

The Attorney General has been ready to recognize that in many situations such payments are not "in connection with government services" and are therefore permissible under Section 1914. In one instance, for example, a professor from the Massachusetts Institute of Technology was granted a leave of absence to work as a consultant with the government on problems of protecting ships from magnetic mines. He continued to receive some payment from his regular employer. Under the circumstances, the Attorney General held that the payments were "made with respect to the former employment and incidental to the leave granted; they were not made 'in connection with' the services of the individual as an official or employee of the United States within the contemplation of the statute."[38]

The judgment in this particular opinion doubtless reflects to some extent the academic character of the consultant, the fact that his employer was an educational institution, and the obvious national need for his services. The principle underlying the opinion conforms to the language and objective of Section 1914, however.

It is easy to imagine hypothetical arrangements between government employees and outside sources that could take cover behind this interpretation of "in connection with" and seek to evade Section 1914 by attributing current payments to

[38] 39 Ops. Att'y Gen. 501, 503 (1940).

nonexistent former services. Some have said that Section 1914 can be and has been evaded through these arrangements.[39] In fact, however, there is no authority upholding arrangements that seem dubious or contrived; nor have instances raising the question been brought to the attention of the Attorney General or the Comptroller General or the courts. The issue really turns on the plausibility, in all the circumstances, of the former employer's payments to his former employee. Some obvious questions to be asked, and convincingly answered, would be: Was the employee adequately compensated at an earlier date? Is there anything in the employee's governmental duties that would tempt the former employer to wish for special favors in his dealings with the government and with the employee? Are the leave-of-absence payments the product of a pre-existing arrangement or suddenly invented for the occasion when the employee undertook the government assignment? Is it plausible that the employer would want to have this particular employee return after his period of government service? It is probably not as simple to construct a set of facts in real life that would put the employee safely beyond Section 1914 as it has been to imagine ways of achieving this result.

Stock options. Something should be said of the problem of stock options, a common device for corporate executive compensation in recent years. Such option arrangements have not been well understood in the context of the conflict of interest statutes. The difficult issue is not whether such options are compensation, but whether realization of profit by the government employee during his government service constitutes a receipt of compensation at that time.

Three or four different events usually occur at different times under an option contract and some confusion has been evident as to which of these events is the relevant one for purposes of Section 1914. A typical option arrangement involves

[39] *E.g.,* Davis, *supra* note 32, at 905; McElwain & Vorenberg, *supra* note 32, at 968.

the initial grant of the option right, periodic maturity of a power to exercise the option, the exercise itself, and the ultimate sale of the property (usually stock) acquired through exercise of the option. Under Section 1914, the date the option contract is irrevocably granted should be recognized as the critical date. As is observed in *Conflict of Interest and Federal Service:*

> This is the date on which economic value is effectively transferred. Like any convertible security or other convertible contract right, the value of the option contract, if it has any value, is dependent entirely upon the value of the property subject to purchase under it. If land is transferred to a government employee before he enters government service, neither a subsequent increase in the value of the land, nor a sale by him of the land, constitutes a new transfer of economic value to him. The situation is exactly the same where the employee receives an irrevocable option contract respecting the same land. His rights to the land are fixed on the date he receives the contract; the date he converts the contract right into the equivalent land sees no further transfer of economic value to him, nor does such a transfer take place on the day he ultimately sells the land.*

> * An option is a hedge. The distinction between the grant of the option and the grant of the land becomes important only if the market price of the land goes down. If the party holds the land he stands to lose when the market drops, but if he holds an option to purchase the land and the price drops below the option price, he simply does not exercise the option. The option holder does not get the land; neither does he lose on the transaction any more than the amount he paid for the option contract itself.[40]

Thus, if a government employee, before becoming such, was granted a bona fide irrevocable stock option exercisable in installments over a period of years, he should not be barred from exercising it in installments as they mature during his government employment. This statement might be abused, of course, and sought to be used to defend option grants, or any other kinds of contract granting benefits to the employee, based upon

[40] CONFLICT OF INTEREST AND FEDERAL SERVICE 214 (including footnote).

nonexistent prior services or vaguely contemplated future services. Where no commensurate past services can be shown, however, the inference will be virtually inescapable that the option rights accruing to the employee during his government service are "in connection with his government service."

Benefits under welfare plans. In ¶ 3–4.1a reference has been made to the question whether continued benefits and eligibility under retirement, health, and insurance programs constitutes "the receipt of salary" for purposes of Section 1914. It was concluded there that where the economic value of such arrangements to the employee is apparent, they are a form of "salary." But where the employer does not continue to pay money in to the fund, benefits under such plans would probably be considered to be "in connection with" prior services and not "in connection with government services." This statement assumes a general environment in which the employee had been a former qualified member under the plan and in which no sudden and drastic increase in benefits had attended his governmental employment. The archetypal situation is that where a permanent employee goes on leave of absence to take a government job for a period during which he maintains his eligibility under his private security plan but makes the payments himself. The greater deviation there is from this pattern, the more likely that the Attorney General or other deciding official would classify the arrangement as one made "in connection with government services." Again one is proceeding in this area largely without benefit of guidance from the Department of Justice or the General Accounting office, and totally without judicial guidance.

3–4.2b. SECTION 209 (1963)

With three exceptions, the problems of interpretation discussed at ¶ 3–4.2a continue to be equally pertinent to Section 209.

By a change of a few words, Section 209 helps to clarify the drafting of Section 1914. The troublesome problem of interpreting the phrase "in connection with" his government services is mitigated, for Section 209 forbids outside compensation to the government employee "for" his services as an officer or employee. The change from "in connection with" to "for" is a step toward further specifying that the outside salary payments are not illegal unless directly linked to the employee's governmental services.

The single substantial change of general application made in this regard by Section 209 concerns the continuation of benefits to the government employee under a welfare plan of a former employer. Subsection (b) of Section 209 provides that a government officer or employee who is subject to Section 209 is not prevented by the section from "continuing to participate in a bona fide pension, retirement, group life, health or accident insurance, profit-sharing, stock bonus or other employee welfare or benefit plan maintained by a former employer." Stress must be put upon the words "bona fide." Subsection (b) must not be interpreted as an invitation to rig up special compensation schemes for government employees in the form of retirement or insurance plans. To be entitled to the protection of subsection (b), the government employee must have been a participant in the bona fide retirement or insurance plan before he became a government employee, and the only plans in which he can continue to receive benefits while in government service are those maintained by a former employer. Granting these caveats, the scope of the immunity extended by subsection (b) remains broad, particularly since it specifically includes not only retirement and insurance plans but also profit-sharing and stock bonus and "other employee or welfare benefit plans." It should be noted that the exemption is not limited to plans where there is no continuing employer contribution.

Subsection (d) of Section 209 contains one other highly specialized exception for a highly specialized type of outside compensation. Under the Government Employees' Training Act,[41] and subject to certain limitations, government employees are permitted to accept grants and awards from private sources to advance their training for government service. Subsection (d) of Section 209 makes it clear that receipt of these stipends does not violate the section.

3–4.3. Source of payment

3–4.3a. SECTION 1914

Section 1914 permits a government employee to receive salary from "the Government of the United States," since manifestly the federal government must be in a position to pay its own employees. It also permits a government official or employee to receive salary from an outside source if it is "contributed out of the treasury of any State, county, or municipality." The exception for local governmental units was thought necessary by Congressmen from rural areas to preserve county and other agricultural extension programs;[42] doubtless too, the underlying policy of Section 1914 appears less threatened by the employee who receives part of his salary from two governmental units than by the government employee whose salary is supplemented by a private outside source. These plausible exceptions for governmental compensation have caused some problems in application.

How broadly should the term "Government of the United States" be construed as it is used in Section 1914? For example, the Judge Advocate General of the Air Force was called upon to opine whether the National Science Foundation could pay the tuition, travel, and other expenses of Air Force employees participating in its fellowship program. He concluded that it

[41] 5 U.S.C. §§ 2301–2319 (1958).
[42] See the legislative history of Section 1914 in Appendix E.

could make the payments despite the provisions of Section 1914, for in his opinion the purpose of that section

was to forbid payments and contributions from private sources. Payments and contributions from government funds would not violate the statute. As funds utilized by the National Science Foundation belong to the United States Government contributions and payments therefrom cannot be regarded as by a private corporation.[43]

What of governmentally owned corporations? One issue raised by these corporations is whether their employees will be considered to be "government employees" for purposes of one or more of the conflict of interest statutes. It is a separate question whether payments by such corporations to persons who are employees of another government agency will be considered to be exempted payments because considered payments "by the Government of the United States." The only case on the point concludes that though the Emergency Fleet Corporation was not exempt from liability except by virtue of special statutes, it "is in a substantial sense a governmental agency [whose] . . . property was transferred to the government."[44]

Section 1914 is unclear in its application to territories, protectorates, and other areas under United States administration. Is an employee of one of the nation's territories an "employee of the Government of the United States," and, on the other hand, are the territories permitted under the exemption language of Section 1914 to make supplementary salary payments to those who are federal employees? There is sufficient authority to establish the existence of this problem but not enough to permit close analysis or conclusions.[45] In the case of the territorial gov-

[43] JUDGE ADVOCATE GENERAL OF THE AIR FORCE OPINION 87–11.1 p. 2 (1957).

[44] United States v. Morse, 292 Fed. 273, 277 (S.D.N.Y. 1922), aff'd on other grounds, 267 U.S. 80 (1925). But cf. UNPUBLISHED DECS. COMP. GEN. A–76416 p. 5 (1936).

[45] 25 DECS. COMP. GEN. 912 (1946) (further obscured by the fact that the subject was a retired military officer); Wickersham v. Smith, 7 Alaska

ernments, it may be said either that they are part of the government of the United States or that they are to be viewed as "states" for purposes of Section 1914. Independence for the Philippines and statehood for Hawaii and Alaska have reduced the frequency of this problem.

Non-appropriated-fund instrumentalities, such as army post exchanges, probably would be viewed as outside sources rather than governmental sources, for their funds are handled independently from those of the federal government.[46]

A variant on the problem involves the United Nations and its agencies. An opinion of the Comptroller General relegates the UN to the classification of an outside source, and concludes that it would violate Section 1914 for the UN or any of its agencies to pay expenses or salary to an employee of the United States Government.[47] Foreign governments are viewed as outside sources.[48]

The language in Section 1914 "contributed out of the treasury of any state, county or municipality" appears to invite an arrangement under which an outside source would provide funds to a local governmental unit for distribution in turn out of the treasury of that governmental unit. In at least one instance, the Comptroller General has expressed the opinion that the section does authorize donations by private organizations to state, municipal, or county governments of funds that

---

522 (1927); 38 Ops. Att'y Gen. 294 (1935). An independent problem associated with these reported situations is the applicability of 47 Stat. 406 (1932), as amended, 5 U.S.C. § 59 (a)(1958) and 28 Stat. 205 (1894), as amended, 5 U.S.C. § 62 (1958), the so-called "dual compensation" statutes. These provisions in general prohibit anyone from being carried on two federal payrolls at once; their real concern, however, is not with conflict of interest, but with distribution of government employment.

[46] See ¶ 1A–3.1a. Employees of such exchanges have been considered "employees" of the government for purposes of Section 1914, however. Unpublished Decs. Comp. Gen. A–51624 (1942).

[47] 26 Decs. Comp. Gen. 15 (1946).

[48] 18 Decs. Comp. Gen. 460 (1938); Unpublished Decs. Comp. Gen. A–27765 (1929).

are earmarked to meet the expenses of federal officials engaged in projects involving joint efforts of local and federal agencies.[49] In assessing the weight to be given to this interpretation, it should be borne in mind that the case involved contributions toward a cooperative public health project, presented no real probability of an interest conflict, and was the kind of joint operation impliedly endorsed by the local government exception in Section 1914.

The first paragraph of Section 1914 prohibits the employee from receiving supplementary salary "from any source other than the Government of the United States," with certain exceptions already noted. The second paragraph, in defining the offense committed by a payor, uses different language beginning: "Whoever, whether a person, association, or corporation." Under the language of the first or second paragraph, or some combination of them not clearly specified, the following payors have been considered to be within the scope of Section 1914: trade associations,[50] charitable organizations,[51] colleges,[52] private contractors,[53] privately endowed hospitals,[54] commercial organizations,[55] and nongovernmental corporations.[56]

3–4.3b. Section 209 (1963)

Section 209 makes no changes from Section 1914 with respect to permitted and forbidden sources of salary payments to government employees who are subject to the Section. See ¶ 3–4.3a.

---

[49] 2 Decs. Comp. Gen. 634 (1923).
[50] 26 Decs. Comp. Treas. 43 (1919); 40 Ops. Att'y Gen. 265 (1943) (railway executives' association); 2 Decs. Comp. Gen. 775 (1923) (jewelers' protective association).
[51] 36 Decs. Comp. Gen. 155 (1956).
[52] 38 Ops. Att'y Gen. 294 (1935); 39 Ops. Att'y Gen. 501 (1940).
[53] Unpublished Decs. Comp. Gen. A–30685 (June 16, 1930).
[54] 29 Decs. Comp. Gen. 163 (1949).
[55] 26 Decs. Comp. Treas. 43 (1919).
[56] International Ry. v. Davidson, 257 U.S. 506 (1922).

3–4.4. Restrictions on intermittent employee and Special Employee

3–4.4a. SECTION 1914

Section 1914 applies to those who work for the government without compensation and those who are compensated for part-time services. See ¶ 3–3.2.2a. It is somewhat more difficult to say what restrictions are imposed by Section 1914 on such employees, or, to express it differently, to identify the offense when it occurs:

What does Section 1914 require of the government consultant who spends a day a month in Washington on the government's call? Should he have his employer dock him for a day's pay a month? Whose time was he on when he was in Washington? As an executive setting his own schedule, he could tave taken that day off to play golf. Does it make any difference that he worked at his regular office all the following Sunday, or that he took no vacation last year? What of *his* stock option, retirement and insurance plans? How can they be adjusted to take account of one day a month? Questions of this kind can be raised almost without end. They are further complicated by the fact that the adviser may in one week be called in for consultation five days running, then go three months without receiving another call.[57]

In view of the difficulty of applying Section 1914 to such situations, the tendency is to emphasize the element of subjective intent and to try to determine in each case whether it was intended by the parties that the payments be made "for" the government services. See ¶ 3–4.2a. Everything then hinges upon the standard of intent that is used. If the prosecution in an indictment under Section 1914 must show that the payor subjectively intended that the payment to the government employee was to be in consideration of, or for, the government services, there would be few situations in which the necessary

[57] CONFLICT OF INTEREST AND FEDERAL SERVICE 66.

evidentiary showing could be made. Very close to this position is the earlier cited opinion of the Attorney General permitting a consultant professor on temporary duty with the government while on leave of absence from his university to continue to receive payment from his regular employer.[58] A recent general opinion letter of the Attorney General appears to continue this interpretation of Section 1914 based largely upon the "intent" of the payment made.[59] Though there are no cases, a court might be tempted, in view of the problems of proof, to adopt a more objective standard of intent—one under which the continuing payment to the government employee would itself imply, in the absence of special circumstances, that the payment was "for" the employee's services to the government.

3–4.4b. SECTION 209 (1963)

The new Section 209 solves the problem discussed at ¶ 3–4.4a all but completely. Special Employees and WOCs are not subject to Section 209 at all. See ¶ 3–3.2.2b. The compensated intermittent employee who falls outside the statutory definition of Special Employee continues to be governed by Section 209, but there will probably be few of these.

3–4.5. Payor's offense

3–4.5a. SECTION 1914

The second paragraph of Section 1914 condemns the payor as well as the recipient of the illegal outside compensation. The drafting of this provision is hardly model. In subject, verb, and object the offense proscribed by the second paragraph differs in significant respects from that forbidden by the first paragraph. But it is doubtful whether any substantive difference was

---

[58] 39 OPS. ATT'Y GEN. 501 (1940).
[59] 42 OPS. ATT'Y GEN. No. 6 (January 31, 1962).

intended, and more doubtful that any court or other authority would distinguish between the two paragraphs. *Pari materia* would doubtless be used to homogenize the two provisions.

There has never been an indictment against a payor under Section 1914. But the second paragraph of the section provides the Department of Justice with a weapon against the payor more pointed than the aider and abettor statutes.

3–4.5b. SECTION 209 (1963)

Like Section 1914, subsection (a) of Section 209 forbids not only the receipt of illegal compensation by the government employee but also the payment to the government employee. Section 209 is markedly better drafted in specifying the payor's offense, for the new statute makes the two offenses coterminous. No substantive change in the payor's offense is made, however.

3–5. APPLICABILITY TO EVENTS BEFORE AND AFTER JANUARY 21, 1963

By force of section 2 of Law 87–849 Section 1914 was repealed and supplanted by Section 209, effective January 21, 1963. Events prior to that date continue to be governed by Section 1914.

CHAPTER 4. RESTRICTIONS ON POST-EMPLOYMENT ACTIVITIES

The restrictions imposed upon the federal employee by the conflict of interest laws do not end with the termination of his service with the government. For nearly a century, legislation has been on the books restricting the relations of former government employees with their agencies and with the government.

A consensus has long existed that some restrictions on the activities of former governmental employees are desirable. Beyond this, it has not been easy to find agreement on either the precise nature of the evil to be scotched, or the means to be used for the purpose. In the debates in 1872 attending the enactment of the first general statute on this subject three main themes appeared in the statements of the supporters.

Some were worried about the problem of inside information —in particular the possibility of fraudulent claims brought by a former employee with inside knowledge about a claim and its weaknesses. "The trouble in allowing these Departments to be open to everybody," argued Senator Edmunds of Vermont, "is not the disclosure of the facts that are there, but it is the disclosure of the facts that are not there, if I may use an Irishism; it is to enable people who are sharp and unscrupulous to see exactly what facts are wanting to make out a case, and then to find the witness who will swear to a lie to make up on the record, by affidavit or otherwise, what is wanting . . ."[1]

Others, exhibiting an essentially adversary concept of the claims process, were concerned to save money for the treasury and to prevent the treachery of switching sides. Senator Cragin of New Hampshire, for example, was worried at the financial success of a clerk in the Post Office Department who, having access to the files, discovered that many former postmasters were owed back pay by the government, though few of them knew it, and who circularized the potential claimants offering his collection services.[2] The adversary conception had a strong grip on the mind of Congress, preponderantly made up of lawyers. By analogy to the ethical ideas of the legal profession, many apparently saw an absolute immorality in the behavior of a former government employee who would switch sides.

Finally there were those who thought the question was one of continuing personal influence. Senator Edmunds put the hypothetical case of an official on a salary of $3,000 a year who had control of the conduct of the government's side of the controversy and was aware that particular clerks in the Department could be persuaded, either from ignorance or interest, to approve a claim. Often such an official, said the Senator, would quit his job and appear the very next day as attorney for the other side with a contingent fee of $10,000. Said the Senator, "[H]e goes right back into the Department, hunts up the proper clerk in that bureau, and uses his influence upon him; I do not say always corruptly in the sense of using money, but uses the influence which naturally could be exercised by a man of capacity upon people with whom he had been associated."[3]

These three arguments of policy have continued in the years

---

[1] CONG. GLOBE, 42d Cong., 2d Sess. 3133 (1872).
[2] *Id.* at 3112.
[3] *Id.* at 3109.

since to be the arguments supporting restrictive regulation of former government employees.

The statute enacted in 1872 became 5 U.S.C. § 99. A supplementary criminal statute regulating post-employment activities was passed in 1944 and became 18 U.S.C. § 284. On January 21, 1963, subsections (a) and (b) of Section 207 of Law 87–849, closely modeled on Section 284, superseded both the former provisions. Section 284 and the two relevant subsections of Section 207 are the subject of part A of this chapter. Section 99, deceased without issue after January 21, 1963, is treated briefly in part B.[4]

PART A

SECTION 284 AND SUBSECTIONS (a) AND (b) OF SECTION 207 (1963)

4A–1. GENERAL

4A–1a. SECTION 284

18 U.S.C. § 284 reads:

Whoever, having been employed in any agency of the United States, including commissioned officers assigned to duty in such agency, within two years after the time when such employment or service has ceased, prosecutes or acts as counsel, attorney, or agent for prosecuting, any claims against the United States involving any subject matter directly connected with which such person was so employed or performed duty, shall be fined not more than $10,000 or imprisoned not more than one year, or both.

The section applies to employees of all "agencies"; it operates where applicable to impose a bar for a two-year period;

---

[4] Because this statute has no criminal penalty, it is not part of the Criminal Code enacted into positive law in 1948. The proper technical reference to the legally operative section is Revised Statutes, Section 190 (1875). For ease and consistency, however, the section will be referred to here by its Code reference, Section 99 of Title 5.

and it is concerned only with "claims against the United States." The reach of the section is determined not by the time when the claim came into being but by the relationship between the claim and the employee's governmental duties.

4A–1b. Section 207 (1963)

Effective January 21, 1963, Section 284 of Title 18 and Section 99 of Title 5 were superseded by Subsections (a) and (b) of Section 207 of Law 87–849. The text is set forth in Appendix A.

The first two subsections of the new section are similar to Section 284 in that the scope of the disqualification imposed turns upon the particular job and responsibility of the former employee, not upon the time when a particular matter involving the government became "pending." Law 87–849 changes the predecessor Section 284 most notably by replacing the former two-year bar by a combination of a one-year bar on some activities and a permanent bar as to others.

See Appendix C for discussion of the unrelated subsection (c) of Section 207. In this chapter, references to Section 207 relate to subsections (a) and (b) only.

4A–2. Background

The history of Section 284, Section 207, and Section 99 is uniquely integrated. The story can best be told as a unity, beginning with the earliest, the predecessor to 5 U.S.C. § 99.

In 1853, and again in 1846, Congress had legislated against officials assisting outside claimants against the government (ultimately Sections 283 and 281, discussed in Chapter 1). It became clear, however, that many of the evils feared from this practice were equally present in the case of the claimant's attorney who until the day before had been a government official. In 1872 Congress enacted legislation on this problem that eventuated in Section 99.[5]

---

[5] 17 Stat. 202 (1872). The legislation was introduced by Representative James A. Garfield.

A striking feature of the 1872 statute on post-employment activities was that it provided no penalty for violation. In answer to those who wished to tack a criminal penalty onto the bill, Senator Bayard of Delaware argued that the real cure of the evils of improper claims prosecution must be found in the integrity and intelligence of the officers of the department. Asked what would be done if anyone violated the statute, Mr. Bayard replied that he could not imagine that a person would attempt to act in the face of an official pronouncement of illegality. "That," retorted Mr. Edmunds of Vermont, "is a very millennial argument."[6] Millennial or no, the bill went through in its non-criminal declaratory form and continued as the only one of the seven conflict of interest statutes not bearing a criminal penalty.

Under the original language of the 1874 act, though the drafting was not exemplary, it seems reasonably certain that the statute was intended to forbid participation by the ex-employee if, but only if, the claim involved was pending while he was in office and was pending before *his* department. When the general revision of the Federal statutes was made in 1873–74, however, the revisors, in pursuit of the goal of clarity, slightly altered the critical language defining the scope of the 1872 statute. As often occurs, the revised form was less clear than the original form. See ¶ 4B–4.2.

Section 99 was little heard from. It was never the subject of a reported federal case, and interpretive material is limited to a scattering of opinions of the Attorney General and oblique treatments in a handful of state court opinions.

A detailed abstract of the legislative history of Section 99 appears in Appendix E.

In 1919 the Secretary of War asked the Attorney General for an opinion on the applicability of Section 99 to officers of the Army. A wartime procurement crisis had again produced thousands of contract claims against the government, and former Army contracting officers had gone into business as

6 CONG. GLOBE, 42d Cong., 2d Sess. 3111 (1872).

attorneys and agents in the prosecution of these supply contract claims. The Secretary of War hoped to find a weapon of control in Section 99, but the Attorney General was not helpful. In his opinion, the Army was not a part of the War Department. It was a separate establishment supervised by the War Department. Army officers as such were not employees of a "Department" and were not, therefore, covered by Section 99.[7] Disappointed, the Secretary of War turned to Congress.[8]

After considerable debate and a snarl of amendments, and amendments to amendments, Congress responded in 1919 with a new statute designed to supplement Section 99.[9] Far more limited than the legislation requested by the Secretary of War, the 1919 act arguably did not even cover the very group that gave rise to the question—former Army officers. But attention had been called by these legislative events to the inadequacies of Section 99, and in 1921, 1923, and 1924 Congressional Committees were again at work on proposals to expand the prohibitions of the section. No legislation ensued from these efforts, however, and not until 1942, under pressure of a new war, did Congress move again in the field of post-employment restraints.

To make it possible during World War II to attract needed professional men into government service, a rider was added to the Renegotiation Act of 1942 exempting from the post-employment restrictions of Section 99 all employees appointed by the Secretaries of War, Navy, and the Treasury and by the Maritime Commission. This exemption provision, however, contained the counterproviso that no such employee should prosecute a claim against the United States arising from any matter with which he was directly connected while in office.[10] This was

7 "[A]n officer in the United States Army is not by virtue of that fact alone an officer in the Department of War within the meaning of" Section 99. 31 Ops. Att'y Gen. 471, 474–75 (1919). Military officers holding certain Defense posts may, however, be considered part of the Department.

8 58 Cong. Rec. 1735–36 (1919).   9 41 Stat. 131 (1919).

10 56 Stat. 982, 985 (1942).

an inconspicuous but important legislative step. What began as an exemption provision changed character radically through this counterproviso, for the counterproviso for the first time extended post-employment restrictions beyond a "Department," made certain restrictions permanent, and made the post-employment prohibition turn upon the existence of a direct nexus between the officer's work and the claim.

In 1944, in an unhappily garbled way, the conflict of interest provisions of the Renegotiation Act were twice amended to produce the direct predecessor to Section 284. Finally, out of the total revision of the federal criminal code adopted in 1948, Section 284 emerged. The section was a composite of the post–World War I statute passed in 1919 and the World War II restrictions and exemptions contained in the Renegotiation Act and the Contract Settlements Act, the language of Section 284 being taken almost entirely from the latter source.

A detailed abstract of the development of Section 284 appears in Appendix E.

The first two subsections of Law Section 207 of 87–849, effective January 21, 1963, are direct successors and products of Sections 284 and 99. Section 207 has no independent substantive history. The general background of Law 87–849 is discussed in the Introduction to this volume, and an abstract of its legislative history appears in Appendix E.

4A-3. COVERAGE

The draftsmen of Section 284 found a formulation different from all the other conflict of interest statutes to designate those covered by the section. The usual problems of interpretation of coverage remain, however.

Law 87–849 did much to lend consistency to the coverage of the conflict of interest laws. Section 207 applies to any person who has been an officer or employee of the executive branch of the United States Government, of any independent agency of the United States or of the District of Columbia, including a Special Employee. The coverage of Section 207 is thus identical to that of Section 208, discussed in Chapter 2.

4A–3.1. Federal employer

4A–3.1a. SECTION 284

Section 284 covers any person who has been employed by "any agency of the United States." See ¶ 1A–3.1a for discussion of the scope of this term and problems it has raised.

4A–3.1b. SECTION 207 (1963)

See the discussion at ¶ 2–3.1b.

4A–3.2. Officer or employee

4A–3.2a. SECTION 284

Although Section 284 does not make use of the usual term "officer or employee," nothing in the history or interpretative gloss put upon Section 284 supports any distinction in this regard between the section and Section 281. See ¶ 1A–3.2a.

4A–3.2b. SECTION 207 (1963)

Section 207, like the other sections of Law 87–849, applies to anyone who has been an "officer or employee" of a designated federal employer. This language is discussed at ¶ 2–3.2b.

4A–3.2.1. *Congressman*

4A–3.2.1a. SECTION 284

Members of Congress are not expressly included in the language of Section 284. Nor has any commentator or court suggested that they might be included under it. The language "employed in any agency of the United States" is not apt if the intention was to include members of the legislative branch.

4A–3.2.1b. Section 207 (1963)

Members of Congress are not subject to the restrictions of Section 207.

4A–3.2.2. Intermittent employee; Special Employee

4A–3.2.2a. Section 284

Former intermittent employees of the government are subject to the restrictions of Section 284. See ¶ 1A–3.2.2a.

4A–3.2.2b. Section 207 (1963)

Section 207 clearly applies to former intermittent employees, including Special Employees, defined in Section 202 of Law 87–849, and discussed at ¶ 1A–3.2.2b.

4A–3.2.3. Non-employee; independent contractor

4A–3.2.3a. Section 284

To be subject to Section 284, one must have been "employed" by an agency of the United States. See the discussion at ¶ 1A–3.2.3a for discussion of the limits of the concept of "employment."

4A–3.2.3b. Section 207 (1963)

The discussion at ¶ 2–3.2.3b regarding the concept of "employment" under Section 208 of Law 87–849 applies equally to Section 207.

4A–3.3. Other persons

4A–3.3a. Section 284

No authority indicates that a claimant who hires a former employee who is forbidden by Section 284 to assist with the claim is himself subject to criminal penalty under Section 284.

Technically one might conceive of the claimant who hires such a former employee as some sort of aider or abettor. But the criminality involved would be far-fetched. Section 284 is more analogous to a disqualification statute than to a bribery statute.

Partners and associates of former government employees are treated at Appendix C.

4A–3.3b. Section 207 (1963)

Section 207, like 284, contains no provision imposing criminal penalties on any person other than the former employee himself. See ¶ 4A–3.3a. See Appendix C for discussion of partners and associates of former employees.

4A–4. Substantive offense

The substantive offense specified by Section 284 for former employees is quite close to that reprehended in Section 283 for current employees. There are some differences in the drafting and the coverage of the two sections, but in each the emphasis is upon prohibitions against the employee's prosecution of "claims" against the United States. The greatest difference between the two sections is that the employee while in government service is barred from all claims against the United States, while the former employee is barred only with respect to those with which he had some connection while in government service.

The separate elements of the offense under Section 284 are regrettably vague.

Section 207 is more complex than the predecessor Section 284. Subsection (a) imposes a permanent criminal disqualification upon former government employees with respect to matters on which they worked in their governmental capacity. Subsection (b) imposes a more restricted and specific disqualification upon covered employees for a period of one year after the termination of their employment with respect to certain matters on which they worked or which were under their official responsibility. Section 207 then includes a special proviso applicable to subsections (a) and (b) with respect to certain scientific and technical personnel.

The structural and substantive differences between Section 284 and Section 207 make it impossible to discuss the subelements of the offenses in tandem. The offense under Section 284 is therefore reviewed at ¶ 4A–4.1; discussion of the Section 207 offense follows at ¶ 4A–4.2.

4A–4.1. Substantive offense under Section 284

The substantive offense under Section 284 is discussed here under four headings: Claim against the United States; Subject matter involved; Prosecuting or acting as attorney; and Time period of bar.

4A–4.1.1. Claim against the United States

Under Section 284 the former employee is forbidden to prosecute "any claim against the United States" involving matters with which he had the requisite statutory connections. As in the case of Section 283, a key question in the administration of Section 284 is to determine the scope of the word "claim." Should it be construed narrowly to include only a monetary claim? Or should it be construed broadly to cover any kind of argument or contention or difference between the government of the United States and another party? On this issue it happens that direct authority is available and, in general, harmonious. The courts have favored a narrow construction.

The major case is *United States v. Bergson.*[11] In this case, a former head of the Antitrust Division of the Department of Justice was indicted under Section 284. Within less than two years after leaving office, the official had on behalf of clients applied

[11] 119 F. Supp. 459 (D.D.C. 1954).

to the Division for a clearance letter to the effect that if a particular corporate merger were to proceed, the Department would not test its legality nor bring criminal prosecution under the anti-trust laws. The official was indicted on the theory that the application for the clearance letter constituted prosecution of a "claim against the United States." The Attorney General argued for a broad interpretation of the word "claim," insisting that it "encompasses all manner of demands made by one person or another (or the United States or any official thereof) to do some act or thing as a matter of duty, or even moral obligation. That the defendant's demand of the Department of Justice for an anti-trust clearance letter, pursuant to an established program of that Department, was a claim within the general meaning of that term cannot be doubted."[12] The Attorney General had taken a similar position in an earlier memorandum to United States Attorneys.[13] But the court concluded otherwise. It was "unable to find anything to indicate that it was the intention of Congress that the term 'claims against the United States' was intended to cover or embrace anything other than claims against the United States Government for money or for property."[14] Under this interpretation, the application for the anti-trust clearance papers did not constitute a "claim." The prosecution was dismissed.[15]

There are a handful of other cases arising under other statutes and in the state courts which, taken as a whole, tend to support a narrow construction of the term "claim." In *Hobbs v.*

[12] Justice Department Brief, p. 21, *United States v. Bergson.*

[13] MEM. No. 40 TO ALL UNITED STATES ATTORNEYS, p. 2 (August 27, 1953).

[14] 119 F. Supp. 459, 464 (1954). The court relied upon the legislative history of Section 284, and particularly its origin in the Army Appropriations Act of 1919. See ¶ 4A–2.

[15] The Department of Justice continued to press for its view in legislation offered to Congress to amend Section 284. Department of Justice, Press Release on Amendment to 18 U.S.C. Section 284, July 14, 1954. The bill was introduced as H.R. 10,000, 83d Cong., 2d Sess. (1954). 100 CONG. REC. 11496 (1954). It was not reported out of committee.

McLean,[16] in an opinion interpreting statutes relating to the assignment of claims against the United States, the Supreme Court stated that "What is a claim against the United States is well understood. It is a right to demand money from the United States."[17] Under 5 U.S.C. § 99, the civil post-employment conflict of interest statute, "claim" has been held to include a demand that the government pay for timber cut[18] and an application to the Treasury for a "special assessment."[19] The rights of landowners in condemnation proceedings had been held not to be "claims" in a case involving Section 283.[20] Two cases arising under Section 99 tend toward a broader view. In one of these the United States had filed a demand for back taxes and the question was whether the taxpayer's resistance to this demand would be considered a "claim against the United States"; the court held that it was.[21] The other holds that the term "claim" includes the formulation and presentation to the Treasury of a plan by which to measure the past and future depletion of oil wells.[22]

The opinion of the court in the Bergson case can be and has been criticized.[23] But, despite the resistance of the Department of Justice, that opinion remains the latest and most authoritative interpretation on the point.

See ¶ 1B–4.2.

[16] 117 U.S. 567 (1886).

[17] *Id.* at 575.

[18] Van Metre v. Nunn, 116 Minn. 444, 133 N.W. 1012 (1912).

[19] Day v. Gera Mills, 133 Misc. 220, 231 N.Y.S. 235 (1928).

[20] United States v. 679.19 Acres of Land, 113 F. Supp. 590 (D.N.D. 1953).

[21] Day v. Laguna Land & Water Co., 115 Cal. App. 221, 1 P.2d 448 (Dist. Ct. App. 1931).

[22] Ludwig v. Raydure, 25 Ohio App. 293, 157 N.E. 816, *cert. denied,* 275 U.S. 545 (1927).

[23] See CONFLICT OF INTEREST AND FEDERAL SERVICE 51; STAFF OF SUB-COMM. NO. 5, HOUSE COMM. ON THE JUDICIARY, 85TH CONG., 2D SESS., REPORT ON FEDERAL CONFLICT OF INTEREST LEGISLATION, pt. I, pp. 35, 37 (Comm. Print 1958); Davis, *The Federal Conflict of Interest Laws,* 54 COLUM. L. REV. 983, 910–11 (1954).

4A–4.1.2. Subject matter involved

The phrase "involving any subject matter directly connected with which" defines the kind of claims that the former government employee is forbidden to prosecute. Under 5 U.S.C. § 99, claims pending in any of the departments during the time of the former employee's service are prohibited to him for two years after he leaves the government. His personal knowledge of or connection with these claims is immaterial. Under Section 284, by contrast, some connection must exist between the former employee and the "subject matter" if he is to be barred by the statute.

Few statutes sport phrases of such obscurity. The basic problems are two. Does the clause cover only particular cases or does it cover entire fields of activities? And how intimately must the ex-employee have been involved for the statutory prohibition to be invoked? Literally, the clause covers the prosecution by a former procurement officer of an agency of any and all claims involving "procurement" anywhere in the government. This is because the claim "involves" procurement, and procurement was a "subject matter directly connected with which" the former officer was employed. The ridiculous extension is to say that no former legal officer could bring a claim involving law, and no former accounting officer a claim involving accounting, because law and accounting were the "subject matters directly connected with which" these persons were employed.

The opposite extreme would be to interpret "subject matter" as including no more than the specific contract, application, proceeding, negotiation, or similar specific transaction. The term "subject matter of employment" seems considerably broader than this conception of a particularized transaction. The prosecution against Mr. Bergson discussed in the preceding numbered paragraph failed because the court did not feel that he was representing a client in a "claim." But what of the other elements in the offense under Section 284? As former chief of the Antitrust Division, was Mr. Bergson to be barred from all antitrust matters—that being the "subject matter" of his former employment? The Department of Justice appeared to think so, since there was no indication that Bergson had during his time with the Division done any work directly with the particular client or the particular merger in question. This kind of approach would lead one to conclude that the lawyer who has worked with the internal revenue service could do no tax work for two years after terminating his employment—a result which can only be absurd and uncalled for by the policy objectives of Section 284.

If there were any substantial body of litigation, one could probably from the cases develop a feel for the critical breaking point of specificity under Section 284. But, aside from the *Bergson* case which went off on the meaning of the word "claim," there is no litigation and substantially no other authority.[24] One can only speculate about what a future court might do with the language. A reasonable guess would be that a court would attempt to preserve to the ex-employee of the government what might be called his professional skills—his generalized expertise; at the same time, it would seek to hold in check the particular advantage the former government em-

[24] The Attorney General's memorandum that fared badly on the "claim" issue in the Bergson case has something to say on the present topic. It offers the view that the statute covers "all matters . . . about which the former employee acquired knowledge or took action in connection with his official duties." MEM. NO. 40 TO ALL UNITED STATES ATTORNEYS 1 (August 27, 1953). The ring of the sentence suggests more a particularized transaction than a general topic such as "antitrust." One can spin a cobweb out of the tangled threads of the legislative history of Section 284. After the spinning, the exercise is found to tend either toward (a) a broad interpretation of the term "subject matter," or toward (b) a narrow interpretation of the term "subject matter." The structure is so fragile and in such equipoise that it does not justify the labor involved in building it. See Appendix E.

ployee might have gained through inside information or personal knowledge about a particular matter, transaction, or topic. The result would be apt to turn upon the extent to which this species of insider's advantage was present in the particular circumstances before the court. It is questionable that one can say more than this under the present circumstances.[25]

Assuming that we are clear, however, that only a "particular" matter is a "subject matter" under Section 284, the question remains regarding the degree of connection which the former employee had with that matter. This question becomes acute in upper echelons of executive authority and responsibility. Is the employment of the Secretary of Defense "directly connected with" each and every "subject matter" in the Department of Defense? Where the former employee personally works on a transaction, or even where he is sufficiently involved so that his signature or initials must go on one of the critical documents through which the government acts, there is not too much of a problem. He is fairly clearly "directly connected" with the transaction. But it is far from clear whether the top officials are to be held solely by virtue of their administrative responsibility to be "directly connected" for purposes of Section 284. On this vital issue of "imputed" responsibility there is no authority and no guidance whatsoever under Section 284.

One case has arisen, however, which, though it turned entirely on the lawyers' Canons of Professional Ethics, may suggest something about judicial response to this question.[26] The case arose as a by-product of litigation between the United

[25] Davis, *The Federal Conflict of Interest Laws,* 54 COLUM. L. REV. 893, 909 (1954); McElwain & Vorenberg, *The Federal Conflict of Interest Statutes,* 65 HARV. L. REV. 955, 970–71 (1952). Other commentators appear in general to agree with the view expressed here. In particular, see STAFF OF SUBCOMM. NO. 5, HOUSE COMM. ON THE JUDICIARY, 85TH CONG., 2D SESS., REPORT ON FEDERAL CONFLICT OF INTEREST LEGISLATION, pt. I, p. 36, n.197 (Comm. Print 1958).

[26] United States v. Standard Oil Co., 136 F. Supp. 345 (S.D.N.Y. 1955).

States and an oil company concerning certain alleged over-
charges on oil sold by the oil company under the Marshall
Plan in Europe at prices greater than legal prices set by the
Economic Cooperation Administration. The government was
entitled to recover damages if the prices were found illegal.
E.C.A. price regulation and administration work was carried
on entirely at its Washington office; its Paris office was engaged
solely in direct collaboration under the Marshall Plan. The two
offices worked independently of each other and had separate
functions. Among the lawyers working on the case for the law
firm representing the company was a non-partner employee who
had been an employee of the Paris Office of the E.C.A. Two
years after the termination of the lawyer's employment with
the E.C.A. (after the restricted post-employment period set by
Section 99 and Section 284) and while the litigation was in
progress, the lawyer was made a partner of the law firm. Many
months later, as the case came to trial, the government moved
that the court disqualify the law firm from representing the oil
company in the litigation on the ground that one of the firm's
partners working on the case had been serving as a lawyer for
E.C.A. at the time when the transactions involved in the litigation took place. The government based its motion for disqualification upon the American Bar Association's Canons of Professional Ethics, particularly Canon 36, reading in part: "A lawyer,
having once held public office or having been in the public
employ, should not after his retirement accept employment in
connection with any matter which he has investigated or
passed upon while in such office or employ." The evidence
showed that the lawyer had not in fact had any personal contact with the case while in government service, either in the
oil procurement or in setting the price regulations. The question raised by the motion therefore was whether the action and
knowledge of other employees of E.C.A. while the lawyer was
an employee would be imputed to him. (There was little doubt

in the judge's mind that if the lawyer was barred his firm was barred.) In an extended opinion the court concluded that the knowledge of employees of the Washington office would not automatically be imputed to employees of the Paris office, or vice versa, but that within one "office" the knowledge of subordinates would be imputed to higher officials. Whether the Paris and Washington operations worked so closely together as to constitute one "office" was held to be a question of "fact" for proof. The motion to disqualify was denied.

As an illustration of judicial attitude, the case may be helpful. The language of the canon in question is considerably more specific than the language of Section 284, for it requires that the lawyer have "investigated or passed upon" the matter during his time in government service. This language suggests a more direct personal involvement than the statutory language "directly connected with which such person was so employed." Nonetheless, the court was willing to talk easily about imputation; that is to say, the lawyer need not have "investigated or passed upon" the matter at all.[27] It is true that the word "directly" suggests that the former employee should have had more than a passing or vicarious concern with the matter, but this is small comfort in the sea of fog that is Section 284.

Under these circumstances, the counseling lawyer must take into account the possibility that a former high government official may well be in substantial jeopardy for a period of two years after he leaves his government employment if he seeks to act for others in transactions which might be regarded as "claims against the government." As one goes down the ladder of officialdom, the imputation risk correspondingly declines.

[27] It should be noted, though, that the *Standard Oil* case involved disqualification, not criminal indictment either of the former employee or of his partners.

But in *Smith v. United States*, discussed at length at ¶ 2–4.4a, the court responded in a similar way where an indictment under Section 434 was at bar.

The issue that was not reached in the *Bergson* case has been touched on once, but unfortunately not in a context that casts great illumination in other situations. The defendant in *Shaw v. United States* had served as assistant chief railroad dispatcher on a government-owned railroad. During the time of his employment, a person had been injured in an accident on the railroad. The dispatcher, having terminated his employment with the railroad, appeared for the injured party in a law suit against the United States Government representing the injured party in his damage claim. The suit was brought less than two years after the accident and less than two years after termination of the defendant's employment period. Thereupon the defendant was indicted under Section 284. In the trial and on appeal, a major issue was whether the subject matter of the damages suit arising out of the accident was "directly connected with" the defendant's employment at the time of the accident. The court thought it was, the defendant was convicted and the appellate court upheld the conviction.[28]

4A–4.1.3. Prosecuting or acting as attorney

Section 284 forbids the former employee to prosecute, or act as counsel, attorney, or agent for prosecuting, any claims against the United States where there is the necessary statutory connection and where the matter is brought within the two-year period. This language is much like the corresponding set of verbs in Section 283, but is not quite as broad since it omits the phrase "or aids or assists in the prosecution or support" of any such claims.

The clause covers the preparation and presentation of a damages action in court.[29] Dicta indicate that the statute would apply similarly in a contract action.[30] That the clause covers at

---

[28] Shaw v. United States, 244 F.2d 930 (9th Cir. 1957).   [29] *Ibid.*
[30] Empire Linotype School Inc. v. United States, 143 F. Supp. 627 (S.D.N.Y. 1956).

least judicial litigation is also indicated by construction of
similar language in Section 99[31] and in Section 283.[32] The
phrase "act as attorney for prosecuting" which appears in Section 283 has also been construed to cover appearances before
administrative tribunals[33] and appearances before claims commissions.[34] Similar language in Section 99 has been held applicable to claims presented to the Commissioner of Indian Affairs
and to Congress.[35]

It cannot be said with any certainty how far Section 284 goes
in condemning participation by the former employee in activities related to claims against the United States. Suppose, for
example, a former employee helps a land claimant by preparing
a map or geological survey for him to be used in connection
with the land claim. Or suppose the former employee provides
the claimant and his attorney with a substantial amount of information which the employee acquired during his government
service and which is helpful to the claimant. If Section 284
is to be interpreted to reach these situations, its language is not
particularly apt, for its emphasis is upon action as a counsel,
attorney, or agent for the claimant. Here, if anywhere, there
might be a difference between the range of activities forbidden
by Section 283 and those proscribed by Section 284, arising out
of the inclusion in the former of the clause forbidding the current government employee "to aid or assist in the prosecution
or support" of a claim. It would appear to conform to the objectives of the statutes if they were so differentiated in some circumstances. So construed, Section 283 would be the more
stringent of the two, and the ban imposed upon the former
employee would be somewhat more relaxed than that imposed
upon the current employee. This result seems quite sensible.

[31] Van Metre v. Nunn, 116 Minn. 444, 133 N.W. 1012 (1912).
[32] Captain Tyler's Motion, 18 Ct. Cl. 25 (1883).
[33] Morgenthau v. Barrett, 108 F.2d 481 (D.C. Cir. 1939), *cert. denied,*
309 U.S. 672 (1940); 16 Ops. Att'y Gen. 478 (1880).
[34] 23 Ops. Att'y Gen. 533 (1901).
[35] Van Metre v. Nunn, *supra* note 31.

This line of analysis cannot be pushed very far. If the ex-employee becomes too active in disposing of his information to the claimant, if he takes too active a role in locating a claimant, if he stands too often and too close at the shoulder of the person formally designated as the attorney—he will clearly invite a court to conclude that he, as a practical matter, "prosecuting" the claim in violation of Section 284.

May the former employee, under Section 284, prosecute claims of his own and on his own behalf? In most situations he may. The government employee should not be prohibited from pursuing his own claim for a tax refund on his own tax return; the Attorney General conceded this point in an early opinion under Section 283.[36] A *dictum* in a Court of Claims case goes so far as to say that the constitutional right of petition guarantees everyone the right to prosecute his own claim against the United States.[37]

But there must be some limit to this proposition. If prosecution *pro se* were permissible without further inquiry, the purpose of Section 284 could easily be defeated by a former government employee who, instead of representing claimants, buys up their claims and prosecutes them as his own. It is this possibility that leads to the provision in Section 283 that the current employee shall neither prosecute the claim nor have any share of or interest in the claim.[38] Section 284 has no such supplemental restriction in its language, but a court would be sure to find it present by implication if it were confronted in fact with a defendant who had sought to abuse the right to prosecute *pro se* by buying up claims.

What of the former employee's position if he undertakes to defend private parties against the government's assertion of a right or claim? Does the defensive action constitute the prosecution of a "claim" in such a case? This question was raised in

[36] 16 Ops. Att'y Gen. 478 (1880).
[37] Captain Tyler's Motion, 18 Ct. Cl. 25, 26 (1883).
[38] See ¶ 1B–4.4.

part in the *Bergson* case, but the issue was obscured by the fact that under the court's interpretation of the word "claim" neither the applicant party nor the government had a "claim." Suppose, however, the question is one of a tax refund or a tax deficiency. If the private party pays the tax and sues for a refund, he is clearly prosecuting a claim for money against the government, and a former employee who had worked on the matter could not, during the two-year period, prosecute the claim for him. If, as a procedural matter, the case arises the other way, with the taxpayer declining to pay and the government suing him for the tax deficiency, should the result be any different? Should the former employee be able to avoid the prohibition of Section 284 by arguing that he is merely "defending," not pressing, a claim against the United States? Perhaps the holding in the *Bergson* case tends toward this kind of paradox.

There is nothing definitive on this important point. One state court decision states, as *dicta,* that helping to defend against a claim by the United States is prosecution of a claim against the United States.[39] That case was decided under Section 99, however, where the issue was whether an attorney's fee could be collected. It is far more doubtful whether a court would so hold in a criminal proceeding brought under Section 284.

As in Section 283 but not in Section 281, compensation to the former employee is not an element of the offense under Section 284.

4A–4.1.4. Time period of bar

Whatever it is that former employees of the government are forbidden to do under Section 284, they are only forbidden to do it for two years "after the time when such employment or

[39] Day v. Laguna Land and Water Company, 115 Cal. App. 221, 1 P.2d 448 (Dist. Ct. App. 1931).

service has ceased." But when does the two-year period begin? Three interpretations are possible: that the two-year period runs from the time that the employee ceased to have a "direct connection" with the subject matter that the claim involves; that the two-year period runs from the time that the employee ceased to be employed by a particular agency; and that the two-year period runs from the time that the employee severed all employment with the government. There is also the related question of whether re-entry into government employment after an absence causes the period of limitation to run anew after former employment. With these questions added to the existing uncertainty about the meaning of "subject matter," the lot of the counseling lawyer under Section 284 is seen not to be a happy one.

There is no real authority on these questions. The Attorney General, without discussion, has stated that the prohibition extends "for a period of two years after leaving government service."[40] This is clearly the safest conclusion, and it is one that has been joined in by the Judge Advocate General and at least one published commentator.[41]

The position of the employee who works on an intermittent basis for the government, or who re-enters service after termination, is totally unresolved. The problem is illustrated by the case of an employee of department A who resigns and then after one and one half years takes a totally different kind of job with department B. At the end of a six-month period with department B, may he consider himself free from the restrictions of 284 in so far as they relate to his work at department A, or are those restrictions now to be considered applicable upon him until two years after he terminates his employment with department B? As an instructive parallel, suppose he had simply

[40] MEM. No. 40 TO ALL UNITED STATES ATTORNEYS 2 (August 27, 1953).

[41] Davis, *The Federal Conflict of Interest Statutes*, 54 COLUM. L. REV. 893, 909 (1954).

transferred from department A to department B without the intervening period out of government service. But these are not questions to be answered by logic and formal consistency. If re-entry into government service tolls the two-year period in any significant way, the result would be that the government would find it almost impossible to persuade lawyers, accountants, and other skilled personnel with government experience to return as part-time or intermittent employees. This is a loss the government cannot easily sustain, and it is likely that this argument would influence any court or other decision maker confronted with it. With hope, and with some confidence, it may be hazarded that Section 284 will be interpreted so that re-entry into government service will not affect the original two-year period which will continue to run after the prior service.

4A–4.2. Substantive offense under Section 207 (1963)

Section 207 provides for two separate restrictions on the post-employment conduct of former government employees, the first requiring permanent disqualification in certain circumstances, and the second continuing in a modified form the two year bar of Section 284.

4A–4.2.1. Permanent disqualification—Subsection (a)

Unlike Section 284 and 5 U.S.C. § 99, subsection (a) of Section 207 imposes a permanent bar upon former employees of the government with respect to certain limited matters. The rule of subsection (a) is in general similar to that imposed by the lawyers' canon forbidding the practitioner to switch sides or represent both sides.[42] If a government employee has personally worked on a matter for the government he is forever barred under subsection (a) from working on it later in a

---

[42] AMERICAN BAR ASSOCIATION, CANONS OF PROFESSIONAL ETHICS, Canon 36 (1958), quoted in ¶ 4A–4.1.2.

position adverse to the United States. This statement is, however, considerably oversimplified, for subsection (a) contains details of drafting that substantially qualify and modify its application.

First it is important to note that the former employee is not barred from participating in the matter by subsection (a) unless during his time as a government employee he "participated personally and substantially as an officer or an employee, through decision, approval, disapproval, recommendation, the rendering of advice, investigation or otherwise." This language is identical to that in subsection (a) of Section 208, to subsection (c) of Section 203, and to the third paragraph of Section 205. See ¶ 2–4.4b; ¶ 1A–4.6b; and ¶ 1B–4.5b.

Of first importance, as noted in the cited paragraphs, this statutory language clearly contemplates direct personal action by the officer or employee; the fact that an officer or employee had an overall supervisory responsibility with regard to a matter is not enough to invoke the prohibitions of subsection (a).

The next significant matter to be noted carefully about subsection (a) of Section 207 is the range of transactions to which it applies. Sections 284 and 99 deal only with exclusion of the former employee from "claims against the United States." In place of this narrowly conceived prohibition, subsection (a) of Section 207, where applicable, forbids the former employee to act as agent or attorney "in connection with any judicial or other proceeding, application, request for a ruling or other determination, contract, claim, controversy, charge, accusation, arrest, or other particular matter involving a specific party or parties in which the United States is a party or has a direct and substantial interest." In expanding the scope of post-employment restrictions beyond "claims" to virtually every possible kind of dealing with the United States government, Section 207 solves the problem of the *Bergson* case, discussed at ¶ 4A–4.1.1, and meets the most common criticism leveled at the predecessor Section 284. For discussion of the range of this universal catalog of dealings, see ¶ 1A–4.3b.

The new subsection (a) of Section 207, at the same time that it expands the horizontal scope of post-employment restrictions, adds a new degree of vertical focus by pinpointing its application to "particular" matters "involving a specific party or parties." The same restricting language appears in subsection (c) of Section 203 and in the third paragraph of Section 205. See ¶ 1A–4.6b. Where this language is used, it is clear that the statute is concerned with discrete and isolatable transactions between identifiable parties. Thus, the former employee of the Defense Department who worked on the establishment of contract procedures is not on that account forbidden by subsection (a) of Section 207 to act as an agent or attorney with respect to any particular Defense contract. A close standard of specificity is required in two different respects under subsection (a); for a matter to be swept under the subsection, it must involve a specific party or parties both at the time the government employee acted upon it in his official capacity and at the subsequent time when he undertakes to act as an agent or attorney following termination of his government service.

The significance of the phrase "involving a specific party or parties" must not be dismissed lightly or underestimated. Law 87–849 discriminates with great care in its use of this phrase. Wherever the phrase does appear in the new statute it will be found to reflect a deliberate effort to impose a more limited ban and to narrow the circumstances in which the ban is to operate. Thus the term appears in subsection (c) of Section 203 and in the third paragraph of Section 205 to make it clear that the rule to be applied to Special Employees is less stringent than that generally applicable to regular employees. Similarly, in view of the drastic rules of disqualification imposed upon the former employee by Section 207, both subsection (a) and subsection

(b) of Section 207 are deliberately narrowed in their application by the inclusion of the phrase.

One other feature of subsection (a) of Section 207 remains to be underscored. If a particular former employee is subject to the subsection and if the transaction involved complies with the requirements of the subsection, what is it that the former employee is forbidden to do with respect to that transaction? The statute says that he is forbidden to act "as agent or attorney for anyone other than the United States in connection with" the transaction. This language is identical to the restriction imposed upon the current employee by Clause (2) of the first paragraph of Section 205. See ¶ 1B–4.1b. Interpretation of this phrase calls for a somewhat refined analysis, however.

The problem is—what acts constitute acting as agent or attorney? Clause (1) of Section 205 makes it apparent that granting or providing *assistance* in the prosecution of a claim is a broader conception than acting as agent or attorney for the prosecution of the claim. The implication of this distinction is that one is acting as an agent or attorney in contemplation of the statute if he acts or appears personally on behalf of another person. That is probably about right. But subsection (b) of Section 207 distinguishes one who "appears personally before any court or department or agency of the Government as agent, or attorney for" anyone other than the United States. Taken together, these statutory uses indicate that "acting as agent or attorney" is less broad than providing assistance to another but broader than appearing for him personally in a decision-making forum. Yet there are problems in this interpretation. The language in Clause (2) of Section 205 clearly implies that one does not violate that clause unless he acts as an agent or attorney for another "before" a department, court, or other forum; the language of subsection (a) of Section 207 contains no reference to any forum or body "before" which one acts as agent or attorney. The implication is that the range of activity forbidden to the former employee by subsection (a) of Section 207 is broader than the range of activities denied to the current employee under Clause (2) of Section 205, and clearly broader than that prescribed by subsection (b) of Section 207.

As in the case of Clause (2) of Section 205 applicable to the current employee, subsection (a) of Section 207 draws no distinction among executive and judicial forums and does not distinguish between compensated and uncompensated services.

4A–4.2.2. *One year disqualification of former employee— Subsection (b)*

In addition to the permanent disqualification imposed by Section 207 upon former employees of the government, an independent disqualification with respect to some activities of former employees is imposed by subsection (b) of Section 207 for a period of one year after the employee's termination of governmental employment. Subsection (b) is relatively simple. Essentially it forbids the former employee to appear personally "before any court or department or agency of the Government as agent, or attorney for, anyone other than the United States" in connection with any particular matter involving a specific party or parties in which the United States is a party or is interested, if the matter was under the employee's former official responsibility at any time within a period of one year before he left government service. Subsection (b) is entirely new in several respects.

The range of transactions and matters covered by subsection (b) is identical to that covered by subsection (a) of Section 207. The prohibition of the subsection extends to substantially any kind of dealing between a private citizen and the United States government. The transaction involved must be an isolatable one, however—a particular matter involving specific parties. See ¶ 4A–4.2.1 on this point. The key difference between the permanent bar of subsection (a) and the one-year bar of subsection (b) lies in the fact that the first is applicable only where the former employee personally and substantially participated in the matter while in government service, while the second, more limited bar applies if the matter was under his official responsibility even though he had no personal hand in the matter. The distinction is a vital one, and forces close attention to be paid to the question of the meaning of "under his official responsibility as an officer or employee of the Government."

Law 87–849 seeks to provide some guidance for the interpretation of this phrase by providing a special definition in Section 202. Subsection (b) of Section 202 reads:

For the purposes of sections 205 and 207 of this title, the term "official responsibility" means the direct administrative or operating authority, whether intermediate or final, and either exercisable alone or with others, and either personally or through subordinates, to approve, disapprove, or otherwise direct Government action.

Neither the House of Representatives nor the Senate Committee Report contains any clarifying commentary interpreting this statutory language. The gist of the definition of Section 202 is, however, clear enough. It calls for a vicarious or imputed responsibility, but the imputation is to be closely contained. Responsibility is not to be imputed throughout an agency or department, with one employee responsible for the acts of all employees. The ban of subsection (b) of Section 207 applies only where the transaction in question was one which came under the line of authority of the former employee. As defined, it would appear that, for example, a consultant or adviser would seldom come under subsection (b) of Section 207 at all, since he usually has no "direct administrative or operating authority . . . to approve, disapprove or otherwise direct Government action," and thus would have no matters that were "under his official responsibility" within the meaning of Section 207. By contrast, the head of a department or agency would have "under his official responsibility" all matters in the department or agency.

As discussed in ¶ 4A–4.2.1, the type of activity forbidden by subsection (a) of Section 207 is broader than that forbidden by subsection (b). Subsection (a), where applicable, forbids the former employee to act "as agent or attorney"; subsection (b) merely forbids the former employee, for a period of one year after his employment has ceased, to appear personally before any court or department or agency of the government as agent or attorney in connection with the transaction. The one-year bar is thus cast explictly in terms of personal appearance. The reason for this is that, in the words of the Senate Committee on the Judiciary, there is a "distinct possibility of harm to the Government when a supervisory employee may sever his connection with it one day and come back the next seeking an advantage for a private interest in the very area where he has just had supervisory functions."[43]

It should be noted that the statute requires that the particular matter itself have been under the employee's responsibility. It is not enough that matters of that general character would come under his official responsibility. The former head of the Antitrust Division of the Department of Justice would be barred from appearing in an antitrust case only if that case itself was under his official responsibility while he was in office (assuming, of course, that he did not personally work on the matter and thereby become subject to the bar of subsection (a) of Section 207).

There are certain problems of timing raised by subsection (b) of Section 207. The former employee is barred by the subsection with respect to those matters which were under his official responsibility within the year preceding his termination of employment. But suppose the former employee changed his

[43] S. REP. No. 2213, 87th Cong., 2d Sess. 13 (1962).

job within the government before leaving office? In a general memorandum respecting the new conflict of interest statutes, the Attorney General has the following to say:

Where in the year prior to the end of his service, a former officer or employee has changed areas of responsibility by transferring from one agency to another, the period of his postemployment ineligibility as to matters in a particular matter ends 1 year after his responsibility for that area ends. For example, if an individual transfers from a supervisory position in the Internal Revenue Service to a supervisory position in the Post Office Department and leaves that department for private employment 9 month later, he will be free of the restriction of subsection (b) in 3 months insofar as Internal Revenue matters are concerned. He will of course be bound by it for a year in respect of Post Office Department matters.[44]

A somewhat peculiar facet of subsection (b) of Section 207 arises from the fact that it is geared to transactions that were under the former employee's official responsibility, whereas the rest of the provisions of the 1963 legislation calling for a link between the employee's work and a particular transaction are couched in terms of personal participation, not supervisory responsibility. In particular, the Special Employee, as defined by the statute, is limited by subsection (c) of Section 203 and by the third paragraph of Section 205 only with regard to matters in which he personally participates.[45] But when he terminates his employment, he finds himself restricted by force of subsection (b) of Section 207 as to matters that were under his official responsibility even though he did not participate in them. It is a bit odd that the restriction upon the intermittent

[44] *Memorandum of Department of Justice Regarding Conflict of Interest Provisions of Public Law 87–849,* 28 Fed. Reg. 985 (1963).

[45] The term "official responsibility" does appear in one minor subprovision of Section 205, and by extension in Section 203. The fifth paragraph of Section 205 permits a government employee to conduct certain family and fiduciary dealings with the government if he has not acted on them in his official capacity and if they are not "the subject of his official responsibility." See ¶ 1B–4.7.

employee should be broader after the termination of employment than during the time of employment. As noted above, however, in very few cases do Special Employees have "official responsibility" as that term is defined in Section 202, and therefore this anomaly will probably have little practical effect.

4A–4.2.3. Special proviso for technical scientific personnel

Section 207 contains a special proviso to subsections (a) and (b) setting out a procedure for granting a limited exemption from these subsections to former government employees who have outstanding scientific qualifications. Regarding this proviso, the Senate judiciary committee said:

> The committee received testimony at its hearings on the bill recommending the complete omission of . . . [Section 207] on the ground that it would certainly and adversely affect recruitment by the scientific agencies of the Government of top-flight personnel for regular service, especially in higher ranking supervisory positions, and their recruitment of intermittent personnel for work in broad areas of agency endeavor . . . [I]n order to make sure that a scientific agency is not cut off from the benefits which may accrue in an important situation from permitting the appearance of a former employee with outstanding scientific qualifications, the committee has added a proviso permitting such appearance, despite the provisions of subsection (a) or (b), upon an agency certification, published in the Federal Register, that the national interest would be served thereby.[46]

4A–5. APPLICABILITY TO EVENTS BEFORE AND AFTER JANUARY 21, 1963

Section 207 became effective on January 21, 1963. Section 3 of Law 87–849 provides for 5 U.S.C. § 99 to be repealed, and Section 2 provides that Section 284 is to be "supplanted" by Section 207 on that date. But how do the provisions restricting post-employment activities of former employees apply to gov-

---

[46] S. REP. No. 2213, 87th Cong., 2d Sess. 13 (1962).

ernment employees who terminated their government service before January 21, 1963? The question is whether an employee who resigned prior to the effective date of the new act continues to be subject to the restraints that Sections 284 and 99 imposed upon him at the time he terminated his service, or whether, on the other hand, he is, after January 21, 1963, subject to the restraints of subsection (a) and (b) of Section 207 of the new law.

Subsection (a) of Section 207 is particularly troublesome. The bar imposed by that subsection is a permanent bar forbidding the former employee forever from participating in certain matters. On its face, the section applies to any person who has ever been an officer or employee of the executive branch or of any independent agency of the United States, or of the District of Columbia. But if the language of subsection (a) is taken literally, the results are not appealing.

Two situations should be distinguished. Employee A resigned on January 1, 1950; he complied with the applicable post-employment restrictions of Sections 284 and 99 for the necessary two years; he then from 1953 to 1955 worked on a matter in private life from which the language of subsection (a) of Section 207 would bar him, if applicable. In this situation, it is unimaginable that—despite the scope of its language—subsection (a) of Section 207 would be held by a court to reach back retroactively to make criminal the work done by Employee A from 1953 to 1955.

But what should be the result in the case of Employee B? Employee B also resigned on January 1, 1950, and also complied with Sections 284 and 99 until their period of restraint ran out at the end of 1952. He then commenced work in 1953 on a matter from which he would have been barred by subsection (a) of Section 207 if it had been in effect at the time. In B's case, however, the work did not terminate in 1955, and he has continued for eight years to invest time and labor in the matter. Does subsection (a) of Section 207 require that on

January 21, 1963, B drop out of the matter or face criminal penalties for work done thereafter?

A variant on B's case would raise substantially the same question. If Employee C resigned on January 21, 1960, is he barred after January 21, 1963, from starting work on a matter covered by the language of subsection (a), despite the fact that he could have lawfully started work on the matter at any time between January 21, 1962, and January 21, 1963?

So far as the language of subsection (a) goes, both B and C would be caught up by the new Act on its effective date. As a practical matter, however, this is a harsh and erratic interpretation. There is no apparent way by which all former employees can be put on notice of this essentially retroactive change. And there is no reason to suppose that most former employees can even remember every official act they took as government employees ten, fifteen, or twenty years ago.

The situation under subsection (b), though analytically identical to that under subsection (a), is less serious. In the first place, present Sections 284 and 99 contain a two-year bar, whereas subsection (b) of Section 207 imposes a one-year bar. As a result, the effect of applying the new subsection (b) to those who left service before January 21, 1963, would in many cases operate to relax rather than to increase the statutory restraints put upon the former employee. This statement must be qualified to the extent that the bar of subsection (b) applies to more kinds of transactions than the "claims" to which Sections 284 and 99 are limited. In the second place, the problem under subsection (b) is a temporary one. By January 21, 1964, there will be no one who left government service before January 21, 1963, who would be restricted by subsection (b), even if it were held to be applicable to such former employees.

There is no evidence that any of these problems of retroactiveness were foreseen or discussed in the course of the legislative consideration of Section 207. Under these circumstances, and in view of the criminal character of the offense under the section, the section should be interpreted as entirely prospective—applicable only to employees who terminated service on or after January 21, 1963. At a minimum, it should not be interpreted as applicable to employees who terminated service before October 23, 1962, the date Law 87–849 was enacted. No alarming risks to the commonweal would arise from this statutory interpretation. We have lived a long time without the permanent statutory bar imposed by subsection (a) of the new Section 207. Though the rule of that subsection is probably salutary, it cannot be said to be critically necessary, to judge from past experience. Particularly is this seen to be true when it is recalled that the Canons of Ethics have long barred the lawyer permanently from participating in matters on which he worked while in government service—and it is mainly lawyers who professionally engage in the kinds of activities that are regulated by Section 207.

PART B

SECTION 99

4B–1. GENERAL

The oldest of the general statutes restricting post-employment activities of former government employees was enacted in 1872, ultimately becoming 5 U.S.C. § 99. Section 99 was repealed by force of Law 87–849, effective January 21, 1963. The section continues to have a relevance, however, to events that occurred before that date, and, in addition, the interpretative gloss put upon Section 99 provides some continuing guidance for other of the conflict of interest laws.

Section 99 reads:

It shall not be lawful for any person appointed as an officer, clerk, or employee in any of the departments, to act as counsel, attorney, or agent for prosecuting any claim against the United States which was pending in either of said departments, while he was such officer, clerk, or employee, nor in any manner, nor by any means, to aid in the prosecution of any such claim, within two years next after he shall have ceased to be such officer, clerk, or employee.

Unlike any other of the conflict of interest laws, Section 99 prescribes no penalties, criminal or other. It is similar to Section 284 in its focus upon prosecution of claims against the United States and in its two-year bar. It is radically different from Section 284 and Section 207 in its method of selecting those claims from which the former employee is to be barred; a tainted claim is identified by the time at which it was "pending," not by the relationship of the employee's job to the claim.

4B–2. BACKGROUND

The background of Section 99 is discussed earlier in connection with Sections 284 and 207. See ¶ 4A–2.

4B–3. COVERAGE

The coverage of Section 99 is very peculiar, quite unlike that of any other of the conflict of interest laws.

4B–3.1. Federal employer

Section 99 is unique among the conflict of interest statutes in referring to employees of "departments" only. There is no phrase such as "employees of the government" or "employees of the United States" or "employees of an agency of the United States government." It is not particularly surprising that the statute should refer to employees of "departments" only. In 1872, when the original version of Section 99 was enacted, the federal establishment consisted entirely of seven executive departments; the first of the independent agencies—the Civil Service Commission—was still eleven years in the future, and the second—the Interstate Commerce Commission—was fifteen

years ahead. When the question was raised in later years
whether Section 99 applied to employees of an independent
agency as well as of a "department," the Attorney General answered in the negative. To him the word "department" in the
statute meant what it said, and he concluded that employees of
executive Cabinet departments are the only persons covered
by the Section.[1]

This opinion of the Attorney General has not been contra-
vened or even seriously questioned. Thus Section 99 is considered to apply to former employees of the present ten executive cabinet departments, such as State or Agriculture, but to
have no application to employees of any of the dozens of federal
agencies, commissions, or other organizations of the government
that are not cabinet departments. Whatever may be said about
the rationality of that situation, it substantially simplifies the
problem of interpreting the coverage of the section. The other
conflict of interest statutes have raised serious interpretive
problems regarding their applicability to employees of a variety
of special employing agencies such as the judiciary, the District
of Columbia, and non-appropriated agencies. These problems
are solved under Section 99 by the peculiar limitation of the
section to former employees of the executive cabinet departments.

4B–3.2. Officer or employee

As to what constitutes an "officer, clerk or employee," there
is no authority peculiar to Section 99. See ¶ 1A–3.2a. The same
is true of the position of WOCs and intermittent employees
under Section 99. See ¶ 1A–3.2.2a.

Earlier discussion regarding the position of independent con-

[1] 25 Ops. Att'y Gen. 6 (1903). This opinion of the Attorney General
is considerably less mechanical and literal than appears at first reading. In
the 1873–74 Revision, the section had been quite specifically tied to a
separate statutory provision defining the term "department" and listing the
departments by name. See Rev. Stat. §§ 158, 159, 190 (1875).

tractors under the conflict of interest statutes applies as well in the case of Section 99. See ¶ 1A–3.2.3a. Congressmen are not subject to Section 99. The position of partners and associates of former government employees under Section 99 is discussed in Appendix C. Uniformed military personnel are discussed in Appendix B. The discussion in ¶ 4A–3.3a with respect to the application of Section 284 to other persons is equally applicable to Section 99.

4B–4. Substantive offense

Section 99 forbids an employee of an executive department to act as counsel, agent, or attorney, for a period of two years after leaving office, in the prosecution of claims pending in a department while he was in office.

4B–4.1. Claim against the United States

Like Section 283 and Section 284, Section 99 applies only to the prosecution of a "claim against the United States." The legislative history of Section 99 throws no significant light on the interpretation of this term, and the problem is identical with that discussed in ¶ 4A–4.1.1.

4B–4.2. Claim pending in a department

A claim is not barred to a former government employee under Section 99 unless it is a claim that was, while he was an employee, "pending in either of said departments." This phraseology is singular, to express it charitably. The section contains no specification of any departments to which the word "said" might refer; the word "either" suggests a selection between two departments, but in the context this is nonsense; and finally there is the question of what a "department" is.

The discussion at ¶ 4B–3.2 concludes that the restrictions of Section 99 apply to employees of the ten executive departments only, and that for purposes of determining the coverage of the section, the word "department" is to be taken literally. While there is no direct authority, the same conclusion is widely assumed to apply to the second appearance of the word "department," with the result that the section's ban is limited to claims pending before one of the ten cabinet departments and leaves all other claims against the United States government untouched. The use of the word "department" therefore cuts back upon the effect of Section 99 in two cumulative and different ways. It reduces the number of persons covered by the section, and it reduces the number of claims to which the statute applies.

A next question might be whether it makes any difference whether the claim was one pending before the former employee's own department. Perhaps the statute was so restricted in its original form. But despite the obscurity of the language added in 1874, it seems clear now that the former employee of a department must stay out of a claim if it was pending before his department or any other department while he was in federal service.[2] The significance of this point should not be missed. Section 99 does not attempt, as does Section 284, to keep the former employee out of matters in which he was formerly involved as an employee. Section 99 is a shotgun, not a rifle, and in the vast majority of situations to which it applies, no actual personal conflict of interest of any kind can be found.

This point is further underscored by the fact that the application of the statute to a particular claim depends upon the time when the claim was "pending" rather than any relationship between the claim and the former employee. But when does a claim become "pending"? Two different possibilities seem equally available. The claim might be said to be "pending" when it has been filed in some fashion, or it might be said to be "pending" when all of the elements for the claim are al-

[2] 20 Ops. Att'y Gen. 695 (1894).

ready in existence, even though not yet recognized and even though no proceedings of any sort have been instituted.

On this issue, there are no federal cases, and the state court opinions look in both directions. One court turned the question of pendency over to the jury. In that case, plaintiff contracted in 1907, within one year after leaving his job as head of an Indian Agency, to recover the value of timber cut by the government on his client's land in 1898. The jury held that the claim had been "pending" while the plaintiff was a government employee, and hence, because his contract of representation was illegal, he could not recover his fee.[3] In *Ludwig v. Raydure*[4] the plaintiffs had been employed as agents of the Internal Revenue Department and, within less than two years after leaving government service, had contracted to prepare and submit to the Treasury plans to measure and compute past and future depletion on oil wells. The court apparently assumed that some part of the past depletion constituted a matter that had been "pending" while the plaintiffs were working for the government, though no application in this regard had been filed. Again the plaintiffs were denied their fee and the defense of illegality of contract was upheld.

Two other cases look the other way. In *Day v. Gera Mills*[5] the plaintiff apparently had some contact with defendant's tax matters before resigning from the Treasury in 1923. In 1925 he filed a special assessment on behalf of the defendant for the year 1919. The court held that because the assessment was not filed until 1925, no "claim for a special assessment for the year 1919 was pending" when the plaintiff left the government. The implication is that the claim is not "pending" until some affirmative action such as filing is undertaken. The other case was *Day v. Laguna Land & Water Co.*[6] There the plaintiff had

[3] Van Metre v. Nunn, 116 Minn. 444, 133 N.W. 1012 (1912).
[4] 25 Ohio App. 293, 157 N.E. 816 (1927), *cert. denied,* 275 U.S. 545 (1927).
[5] 133 Misc. 220, 231 N.Y.S. 235 (1928).
[6] 115 Cal. App. 221, 1 P.2d 448 (Dist. Ct. App. 1931).

done some preliminary work in his investigations of defendant's tax return while working for the Treasury. He did not know whether or not the defendant owed the government any money. Subsequently the government asserted a claim for more taxes for the years plaintiff had investigated, and in this proceeding plaintiff represented the defendant. The court upheld the plaintiff in his suit for his fee, holding that the subsequently asserted claim had not been "pending" during the plaintiff's period of government service. This authority, already weak, is further diluted by the fact that the court apparently assumed that the former employee's personal contact with the claim while he was in service was a relevant fact under Section 99, an assumption clearly unsupported by the language of the section.

Each of these interpretations of "pending" offers its own difficulties. The first is difficult to administer and difficult to justify on any theory of actual conflict between personal economic interest and governmental duty; the second, on the other hand, would permit the former employee who had participated in a matter while in federal service to file a claim respecting that matter the day after he resigns, though he would be barred from acting in a claim about which he knew nothing and which was even before another department if it was filed the day before he resigned.

4B–4.3. Prosecuting or acting as attorney

If a particular claim and a particular person are covered by Section 99, then he is forbidden for two years after he leaves federal service "to act as counsel, attorney, or agent for prosecuting" the claim, and is also forbidden "by any means, to aid in the prosecution of" such claim. This language is substantially identical to that in Section 283.[7] See ¶ 1B–4.1a. It differs some-

---

[7] The services need not be performed in or before the department, however. Services before a court may also be a violation if the claim itself is pending in the department. Tomlinson v. Florida Iron and Metal Inc., 291 F.2d 333 (5th Cir. 1961).

what from the restrictions imposed by Section 284 on post-employment activities, in that Section 284 contains no reference to assisting or aiding in the prosecution of a claim. See ¶ 4A–4.1.3.

4B–4.4. Time period of bar

Section 99 requires that the former Government employee not undertake the forbidden conduct "within two years next after he shall have ceased to be such" employee. Problems of interpretation arise out of this apparently simple language, as they do under Section 284. See ¶ 4A–4.1.4. Theoretical problems of interpreting the application of Section 99 to the intermittent employee or the in-and-out employee are aggravated by the fact that the section is triggered off only by when he is working for a "department."

4B–5. APPLICABILITY TO EVENTS BEFORE AND AFTER JANUARY 21, 1963

Section 99 of U.S.C. Title 5 is repealed by Law 87–849, effective January 21, 1963, and superseded by the new Section 207, discussed in part A of this chapter. In most cases litigated under Section 99, however, the statute has been pleaded as a bar to collection of fees for services, and in this context the section may still be introduced in litigation arising out of events that took place before January 21, 1963.

APPENDIX A. TEXTS OF STATUTES

ASSISTING OUTSIDERS IN GOVERNMENTAL DEALINGS

Text of 18 U.S.C. § 281 (1958)

Whoever, being a Member of or Delegate to Congress, or a Resident Commissioner, either before or after he has qualified, or the head of a department, or other officer or employee of the United States or any department or agency thereof, directly or indirectly receives or agrees to receive, any compensation for any services rendered or to be rendered, either by himself or another, in relation to any proceeding, contract, claim, controversy, charge, accusation, arrest, or other matter in which the United States is a party or directly or indirectly interested, before any department, agency, court martial, officer, or any civil, military, or naval commission, shall be fined not more than $10,000 or imprisoned not more than two years, or both; and shall be incapable of holding any office of honor, trust, or profit under the United States.

Retired officers of the armed forces of the United States, while not on active duty, shall not by reason of their status as such be subject to the provisions of this section. Nothing herein shall be construed to allow any retired officer to represent any person in the sale of anything to the Government through the department in whose service he holds a retired status.

This section shall not apply to any person because of his membership in the National Guard of the District of Columbia nor to any person specially excepted by Act of Congress.

Section 203 (1963)

See Law 87–849 *infra*, this appendix.

Text of 18 U.S.C. § 283 (1958)

Whoever, being an officer or employee of the United States or any department or agency thereof, or of the Senate or House of Representatives, acts as an agent or attorney for prosecuting any claim against the United States, or aids or assists in the prosecution or support of any such claim otherwise than in the proper discharge of his official duties, or receives any gratuity, or any share of or interest in any such claim in consideration of assistance in the prosecution of such claim, shall be fined not more than $10,000 or imprisoned not more than one year, or both.

Retired officers of the armed forces of the United States, while not on active duty, shall not by reason of their status as such be subject to the provisions of this section. Nothing herein shall be construed to allow any such retired officer within two years next after his retirement to act as agent or attorney for prosecuting or assisting in the prosecution of any claim against the United States involving the department in whose service he holds a retired status, or to allow any such retired officer to act as agent or attorney for prosecuting or assisting in the prosecution of any claim against the United States involving any subject matter with which he was directly connected while he was in an active-duty status.

This section shall not apply to any person because of his membership in the National Guard of the District of Columbia nor to any person specially excepted by enactment of Congress.

Section 205 (1963)

See Law 87–849 *infra*, this appendix.

Text of 18 U.S.C. § 216 (1958)

Whoever, being a Member of or Delegate to Congress, or a Resident Commissioner, either before or after he has qualified, or being an officer, employee or agent of the United States, directly or indirectly takes, receives, or agrees to receive, any money or thing of value, for giving, procuring or aiding to procure to or for any person, any contract from the United States or from any officer, department or agency thereof; or

Whoever, directly or indirectly, offers, gives, or agrees to give any money or thing of value for procuring or aiding to procure any such contract—

Shall be fined not more than $10,000 or imprisoned not more than two years, or both; and be disqualified from holding any office of honor, profit, or trust under the United States.

The President may declare void any such contract or agreement.

SELF-DEALING

Text of 18 U.S.C. § 434 (1958)

Whoever, being an officer, agent or member of, or directly or indirectly interested in the pecuniary profits or contracts of any corporation, joint-stock company, or association, or of any firm or partnership, or other business entity, is employed or acts as an officer or agent of the United States for the transaction of business with such business entity, shall be fined not more than $2,000 or imprisoned not more than two years, or both.

Section 208 (1963)

See Law 87–849 *infra*, this appendix.

OUTSIDE COMPENSATION

Text of 18 U.S.C. § 1914 (1958)

Whoever, being a Government official or employee, receives any salary in connection with his services as such an official or employee from any source other than the Government of the United States, except as may be contributed out of the treasury of any State, county, or municipality; or

Whoever, whether a person, association, or corporation, makes any contribution to, or in any way supplements the salary of, any Government official or employee for the services performed by him for the Government of the United States—

Shall be fined not more than $1,000 or imprisoned not more than six months, or both.

Section 209 (1963)

See Law 87–849 *infra*, this appendix.

RESTRICTIONS ON POST-EMPLOYMENT ACTIVITIES

Text of 18 U.S.C. § 284 (1958)

Whoever, having been employed in any agency of the United States, including commissioned officers assigned to duty in such agency, within two years after the time when such employment or service has ceased, prosecutes or acts as counsel, attorney or agent for prosecuting, any claims against the United States involving any subject matter directly connected with which such person was so employed or performed duty, shall be fined not more than $10,000 or imprisoned not more than one year, or both.

Subsections (a) and (b) of Section 207 (1963)

See Law 87–849 *infra*, this appendix.

Text of 5 U.S.C. § 99 (1958)

It shall not be lawful for any person appointed as an officer, clerk, or employee in any of the departments, to act as counsel, attorney, or agent for prosecuting any claim against the United States which was pending in either of said departments, while he was such officer, clerk, or employee, nor in any manner, nor by any means, to aid in the prosecution of any such claim, within two years next after he shall have ceased to be such officer, clerk, or employee.

.   .   .   .   .

Text of Public Law 87–849

AN ACT

To strengthen the criminal laws relating to bribery, graft, and conflicts of interest, and for other purposes.

Be it enacted by the Senate and House of Representatives of the United States of America in Congress assembled, That (a) so much of chapter 11 of title 18 of the United States Code as precedes section 214 is amended to read as follows:

"Chapter 11—Bribery, Graft, and Conflicts of Interest

"§ 201. Bribery of public officials and witnesses

"(a) For the purpose of this section:

" 'public official' means Member of Congress, or Resident Commissioner, either before or after he has qualified, or an officer or employee or person acting for or on behalf of the United States, or any department, agency or branch of Government thereof, including the District of Columbia, in any official function, under or by authority of any such department, agency, or branch of Government, or a juror; and

" 'person who has been selected to be a public official' means any person who has been nominated or appointed to be a public official, or has been officially informed that he will be so nominated or appointed; and

" 'official act' means any decision or action on any question, matter, cause, suit, proceeding or controversy, which may at any time be pending, or which may by law be brought before any public official, in his official capacity, or in his place of trust or profit.

"(b) Whoever, directly or indirectly, corruptly gives, offers or promises anything of value to any public official or person who has been selected to be a public official, or offers or promises any public official or any person who has been selected to be a public official to give anything of value to any other person or entity, with intent—

"(1) to influence any official act; or

"(2) to influence such public official or person who has been selected to be a public official to commit or aid in committing, or collude in, or allow, any fraud, or make opportunity for the commission of any fraud, on the United States; or

"(3) to induce such public official or such person who has been selected to be a public official to do or omit to do any act in violation of his lawful duty, or

"(c) Whoever, being a public official or person selected to be a public official, directly or indirectly, corruptly asks, demands, exacts, solicits, seeks, accepts, receives, or agrees to receive anything of value for himself or for any other person or entity, in return for:

"(1) being influenced in his performance of any official act; or

"(2) being influenced to commit or aid in committing, or to collude in, or allow, any fraud, or make opportunity for the commission of any fraud, on the United States; or

"(3) being induced to do or omit to do any act in violation of his official duty; or

"(d) Whoever, directly or indirectly, corruptly gives, offers, or promises anything of value to any person, or offers or promises such person to give anything of value to any other person or entity, with intent to influence the testimony under oath or affirmation of such first-mentioned person as a witness upon a trial, hearing, or other proceeding, before any court, any committee of either House or both Houses of Congress, or any agency, commission, or officer authorized by the laws of the United States to hear evidence or take testimony, or with intent to influence such person to absent himself therefrom; or

"(e) Whoever, directly or indirectly, corruptly asks, demands, exacts, solicits, seeks, accepts, receives, or agrees to receive anything of value for himself or for any other person or entity in return for being influenced in his testimony under oath or affirmation as a witness upon any such trial, hearing, or other proceeding, or in return for absenting himself therefrom—

"Shall be fined not more than $20,000 or three times the monetary equivalent of the thing of value, whichever is greater, or imprisoned for not more than fifteen years, or both, and may be disqualified from holding any office of honor, trust, or profit under the United States.

"(f) Whoever, otherwise than as provided by law for the proper discharge of official duty, directly or indirectly gives, offers, or promises anything of value to any public official, former public official, or person selected to be a public official, for or because of any official act performed or to be performed by such public official, former public official, or person selected to be a public official; or

"(g) Whoever, being a public official, former public official, or person selected to be a public official, otherwise than as provided by law for the proper discharge of official duty, directly or indirectly asks, demands, exacts, solicits, seeks, accepts, receives, or agrees to receive anything of value for himself for or because of any official act performed or to be performed by him; or

"(h) Whoever, directly or indirectly, gives, offers, or promises anything of value to any person, for or because of the testimony under oath or affirmation given or to be given by such person as a witness upon a trial, hearing, or other proceeding, before any court, any committee of either House or both Houses of Congress, or any agency, commission, or officer authorized by the laws of the United States to hear evidence or take testimony, or for or because of his absence therefrom; or

"(i) Whoever, directly or indirectly, asks, demands, exacts, solicits, seeks, accepts, receives, or agrees to receive anything of value for himself for or because of the testimony under oath or affirmation given or to be given by him as a witness upon any such trial, hearing, or other proceeding, or for or because of his absence therefrom—

"Shall be fined not more than $10,000 or imprisoned for not more than two years, or both.

"(j) Subsections (d), (e), (h), and (i) shall not be construed to prohibit the payment or receipt of witness fees provided by law, or the payment, by the party upon whose behalf a witness is called and receipt by a witness, of the reasonable cost of travel and subsistence incurred and the reasonable value of time lost in attendance at any such trial, hearing, or proceeding, or, in the case of expert witnesses, involving a technical or professional opinion, a reasonable fee for time spent in the preparation of such opinion, and in appearing and testifying.

"(k) The offenses and penalties prescribed in this section are separate from and in addition to those prescribed in sections 1503, 1504, and 1505 of this title.

"§ 202. Definitions

"(a) For the purpose of sections 203, 205, 207, 208, and 209 of this title the term 'special Government employee' shall mean an officer or employee of the executive or legislative branch of the United States Government, of any independent agency of the United States or of the District of Columbia, who is retained, designated, appointed, or employed to perform, with or without compensation, for not to exceed one hundred and thirty days during any period of three hundred and sixty-five consecutive days, temporary duties either on a full-time or intermittent basis, or a part-time United States Commissioner. Notwithstanding the next preceding sentence, every person serving as a part-time local representative of a Member of Congress in the Member's home district or State shall be classified as a special Government employee. Notwithstanding section 29 (c) and (d) of the Act of August 10, 1956 (70A Stat. 632; 5 U.S.C. 30r (c) and (d)), a Reserve officer of the Armed Forces, or an officer of the National Guard of the United States, unless otherwise an officer or employee of the United States, shall be classified as a special Government employee while on active duty solely for training. A Reserve officer of the Armed Forces or an officer of the National Guard of the United States who is voluntarily serving a period of extended active duty in excess of one hundred and thirty days shall be classified as an officer of the United States within the meaning of section 203 and sections 205 through 209 and 218. A Reserve officer of the Armed Forces or an officer of the National Guard of the United States who is serving involuntarily shall be classified as a special Government employee. The terms 'officer or employee' and 'special Government employee' as used in sections 203, 205, 207 through 209, and 218, shall not include enlisted members of the Armed Forces.

"(b) For the purposes of sections 205 and 207 of this title, the term 'official responsibility' means the direct administrative or operating authority, whether intermediate or final, and either exercisable alone or with others, and either personally or through subordinates, to approve, disapprove, or otherwise direct Government action.

"§ 203. Compensation to Members of Congress, officers, and others in matters affecting the Government

"(a) Whoever, otherwise than as provided by law for the proper discharge of official duties, directly or indirectly receives or agrees to receive, or asks, demands, solicits, or seeks, any compensation for any services rendered or to be rendered either by himself or another—

"(1) at a time when he is a Member of Congress, Member of Congress Elect, Resident Commissioner, or Resident Commissioner Elect; or

"(2) at a time when he is an officer or employee of the United States in the executive, legislative, or judicial branch of the Government, or in any agency of the United States, including the District of Columbia,

in relation to any proceeding, application, request for a ruling or other determination, contract, claim, controversy, charge, accusation, arrest, or other particular matter in which the United States is a party or has a direct and substantial interest, before any department, agency, court-martial, officer, or any civil, military, or naval commission, or

"(b) Whoever, knowingly, otherwise than as provided by law for the proper discharge of official duties, directly or indirectly gives, promises, or offers any compensation for any such services rendered or to be rendered at a time when the person to whom the compensation is given, promised, or offered, is or was such a Member, Commissioner, officer, or employee—

"Shall be fined not more than $10,000 or imprisoned for not more than two years, or both; and shall be incapable of holding any office of honor, trust, or profit under the United States.

"(c) A special Government employee shall be subject to subsection (a) only in relation to a particular matter involving a specific party or parties (1) in which he has at any time participated personally and substantially as a Government employee or as a special Government employee through decision, approval, disapproval, recommendation, the rendering of advice, investigation or otherwise, or (2) which is pending in the department or agency of the Government in which he is serving: *Provided,* That clause (2) shall not apply in the case of a special Government employee who has served in such department or agency no more than sixty days during the immediately preceding period of three hundred and sixty-five consecutive days.

"§ 204. Practice in Court of Claims by Members of Congress

"Whoever, being a Member of Congress, Member of Congress Elect, Resident Commissioner, or Resident Commissioner Elect, practices in the Court of Claims, shall be fined not more than $10,000 or imprisoned for not more than two years, or both, and shall be incapable of holding any office of honor, trust, or profit under the United States.

"§ 205. Activities of officers and employees in claims against and other matters affecting the Government

"Whoever, being an officer or employee of the United States in the executive, legislative, or judicial branch of the Government or in any agency of the United States, including the District of Columbia, otherwise than in the proper discharge of his official duties—

"(1) acts as agent or attorney for prosecuting any claim against the United States, or receives any gratuity, or any share of or interest in any such claim in consideration of assistance in the prosecution of such claim, or

"(2) acts as agent or attorney for anyone before any department, agency, court, court-martial, officer, or any civil, military, or naval commission in connection with any proceeding, application, request for a ruling or other determination, contract, claim, controversy, charge, accusation, arrest, or other particular matter in which the United States is a party or has a direct and substantial interest—

"Shall be fined not more than $10,000 or imprisoned for not more than two years, or both.

"A special Government employee shall be subject to the preceding paragraphs only in relation to a particular matter involving a specific party or parties (1) in which he has at any time participated personally and substantially as a Government employee or as a special Government employee through decision, approval, disapproval, recommendation, the rendering of advice, investigation or otherwise, or (2) which is pending in the department or agency of the Government in which he is serving: *Provided,* That clause (2) shall not apply in the case of a special Government employee who has served in such department or agency no more than sixty days during the immediately preceding period of three hundred and sixty-five consecutive days.

"Nothing herein prevents an officer or employee, if not inconsistent with the faithful performance of his duties, from acting without compensation as agent or attorney for any person who is the subject of disciplinary, loyalty, or other personnel administration proceedings in connection with those proceedings.

"Nothing herein or in section 203 prevents an officer or employee, including a special Government employee, from acting, with or without compensation, as agent or attorney for his parents, spouse, child, or any person for whom, or for any estate for which, he is serving as guardian, executor, administrator, trustee, or other personal fiduciary except in those matters in which he has participated personally and substantially as a Government employee, through decision, approval, disapproval, recommendation, the rendering of advice, investigation, or otherwise, or which are the subject of his official responsibility, provided that the Government official responsible for appointment to his position approves.

"Nothing herein or in section 203 prevents a special Government employee from acting as agent or attorney for another person in the performance of work under a grant by, or a contract with or for the benefit of, the United States provided that the head of the department or agency concerned with the grant or contract shall certify in writing that the national interest so requires.

"Such certification shall be published in the Federal Register.

"Nothing herein prevents an officer or employee from giving testimony under oath or from making statements required to be made under penalty for perjury or contempt.

"§ 206. Exemption of retired officers of the uniformed services

"Sections 203 and 205 of this title shall not apply to a retired officer of the uniformed services of the United States while not on active duty and not otherwise an officer or employee of the United States, or to any person specially excepted by Act of Congress.

"§ 207. Disqualification of former officers and employees in matters connected with former duties or official responsibilities; disqualification of partners

"(a) Whoever, having been an officer or employee of the executive branch of the United States Government, of any independent agency of the United States, or of the District of Columbia, including a special Government employee, after his employment has ceased, knowingly acts as agent or attorney for anyone other than the United States in connection with any judicial or other proceeding, application, request for a ruling or other determination, contract, claim, controversy, charge, accusation, arrest, or other particular matter involving a specific party or parties in which the United States is a party or has a direct and substantial interest and in which he participated personally and substantially as an officer or employee, through decision, approval, disapproval, recommendation, the rendering of advice, investigation, or otherwise, while so employed, or

"(b) Whoever, having been so employed, within one year after his employment has ceased, appears personally before any court or department or agency of the Government as agent, or attorney for, anyone other than the United States in connection with any proceeding, application, request for a ruling or other determination, contract, claim, controversy, charge, accusation, arrest, or other particular matter involving a specific party or parties in which the United States is a party or directly and substantially interested, and which was under his official responsibility as an officer or employee of the Government at any time within a period of one year prior to the termination of such responsibility—

"Shall be fined not more than $10,000 or imprisoned for not more than two years, or both: *Provided,* That nothing in subsection (a) or (b) prevents a former officer or employee, including a former special Government employee, with outstanding scientific or technological qualifications from acting as attorney or agent or appearing personally in connection with a particular matter in a scientific or technological field if the head of the department or agency concerned with the matter shall make a certification in writing, published in the Federal Register, that the national interest would be served by such action or appearance by the former officer or employee.

"(c) Whoever, being a partner of an officer or employee of the executive branch of the United States Government, of any independent agency of the United States, or of the District of Columbia, including a special Government employee, acts as agent or attorney for anyone other than the United States, in connection with any judicial or other proceeding, application, request for a ruling or other determination, contract, claim, controversy, charge, accusation, arrest, or other particular matter in which the United States is a party or has a direct and substantial interest and in which such officer or employee of the Government or special Government employee participates or has participated personally and substantially as a Government employee through decision, approval, disapproval, recommendation, the rendering of advice, investigation or otherwise, or which is the subject of his official responsibility—

"Shall be fined not more than $5,000, or imprisoned not more than one year, or both.

"A partner of a present or former officer or employee of the executive branch of the United States Government, of any independent agency of the United States, or of the District of Columbia or of a present or former special Government employee shall as such be subject to the provisions of sections 203, 205, and 207 of this title only as expressly provided in subsection (c) of this section.

"§ 208. Acts affecting a personal financial interest

"(a) Except as permitted by subsection (b) hereof, whoever, being an officer or employee of the executive branch of the United States Government, of any independent agency of the United States, or of the District of Columbia, including a special Government employee, participates personally and substantially as a Government officer or employee, through decision, approval, disapproval, recommendation, the rendering of advice, investigation, or otherwise, in a judicial or other proceeding, application, request for a ruling or other determination, contract, claim, controversy, charge, accusation, arrest, or other particular matter in which, to his knowledge, he, his spouse, minor child, partner, organization in which he is serving as officer, director, trustee, partner or employee, or any person or organization with whom he is negotiating or has any arrangement concerning prospective employment, has a financial interest—

"Shall be fined not more than $10,000, or imprisoned not more than two years, or both.

"(b) Subsection (a) hereof shall not apply (1) if the officer or employee first advises the Government official responsible for appointment to his position of the nature and circumstances of the judicial or other proceeding, application, request for a ruling or other determination, contract, claim, controversy, charge, accusation, arrest, or other particular matter and makes full disclosure of the financial interest and receives in advance a written determination made by such official that the interest is not so substantial as to be deemed likely to affect the integrity of the services which the Government may expect from such officer or employee, or (2) if, by general rule or regulation published in the Federal Register, the financial interest has been exempted from the requirements of clause (1) hereof as being too remote or too inconsequential to affect the integrity of Government officers' or employees' services.

"§ 209. Salary of Government officials and employees payable only by United States

"(a) Whoever receives any salary, or any contribution to or supplementation of salary, as compensation for his services as an officer or employee of the executive branch of the United States Government, of any independent agency of the United States, or of the District of Columbia, from any source other than the Government of the United States, except as may be contributed out of the treasury of any State, county, or municipality; or

"Whoever, whether an individual, partnership, association, corporation, or other organization pays, or makes any contribution to, or in any way supplements the salary of, any such officer or employee under circumstances which would make its receipt a violation of this subsection—

"Shall be fined not more than $5,000 or imprisoned not more than one year, or both.

"(b) Nothing herein prevents an officer or employee of the executive branch of the United States Government, or of any independent agency of the United States, or of the District of Columbia, from continuing to participate in a bona fide pension, retirement, group life, health or accident insurance, profit-sharing, stock bonus, or other employee welfare or benefit plan maintained by a former employer.

"(c) This section does not apply to a special Government employee or to an officer or employee of the Government serving without compensation, whether or not he is a special Government employee, or to any person paying, contributing to, or supplementing his salary as such.

"(d) This section does not prohibit payment or acceptance of contributions, awards, or other expenses under the terms of the Government Employees Training Act (Public Law 85–507, 72 Stat. 327; 5 U.S.C. 2301–2319, July 7, 1958)."

(b) Sections 214 and 215 of chapter 11 of title 18 of the United States Code are respectively redesignated sections 210 and 211;

(c) Sections 216 and 223 of chapter 11 of title 18 of the United States Code are repealed:

(d) Sections 217, 218, 219, 220, 221, and 222 of chapter 11 of title 18 of the United States Code are respectively redesignated sections 212, 213, 214, 215, 216, and 217;

(e) Chapter 11 of title 18 of the United States Code is further amended by adding at the end thereof the following new section:

"§ 218. Voiding transactions in violation of chapter; recovery by the United States

"In addition to any other remedies provided by law the President or, under regulations prescribed by him, the head of any department or agency involved, may declare void and rescind any contract, loan, grant, subsidy, license, right, permit, franchise, use, authority, privilege, benefit, certificate, ruling, decision, opinion, or rate schedule awarded, granted, paid, furnished, or published, or the performance of any service or transfer or delivery of any thing to, by or for any agency of the United States or officer or employee of the United States or person acting on behalf thereof, in relation to which there has been a final conviction for any violation of this chapter, and the United States shall be entitled to recover in addition to any penalty prescribed by law or in a contract the amount expended or the thing transferred or delivered on its behalf, or the reasonable value thereof."

Sec. 2. Sections 281 and 283 (except as they may apply to retired officers of the armed forces of the United States), 282 and 284 of chapter 15 of title 18, section 434 of chapter 23 of title 18, and section 1914 of chapter 93 of title 18 of the United States Code are repealed and will, respectively, be supplanted by sections 203, 205, 204, 207, 208, and 209 of title 18 of the United States Code as set forth in section 1 of this Act. All exemptions from the provisions of sections 281, 282, 283, 284, 434, or 1914 of title 18 of the United States Code heretofore created or authorized by statute which are in force on the effective date of this Act shall, on and after that date, be deemed to be exemptions from sections 203, 204, 205, 207, 208, or 209, respectively, of title 18 of the United States Code except to the extent that they affect officers or employees of the executive branch of the United States Government, of any independent agency of the United States, or of the District of Columbia, as to whom they are no longer applicable.

Sec. 3. Section 190 of the Revised Statutes (5 U.S.C. 99) is repealed.

Sec. 4. This Act shall take effect ninety days after the date of its enactment.

Approved October 23, 1962.

APPENDIX B. THE UNIFORMED SERVICES UNDER THE CONFLICT OF INTEREST LAWS

The position of members of the uniformed services under the conflict of interest laws is peculiarly, and unnecessarily, vexed. The application of the earlier statutes to military personnel varies from statutory section to section and depends in large measure upon the particular status of the military personnel in question. This is true also of Law 87–849, effective January 21, 1963. Some questions are clarified by the new act; others are muddied.

It is worth taking special note of the important role played by military regulations in any consideration of conflict of interest restraints applicable to military personnel. Often the applicable service regulations are more stringent than the statutory restrictions discussed below.

A. REGULAR MILITARY PERSONNEL ON ACTIVE DUTY

First to be considered is the application of the conflict of interest laws to regular military personnel on active duty. Subsequent discussion will treat of retired service personnel, reservists, and the National Guard.

1. Officers

An officer in one of the armed forces, on active duty, is an "officer or employee" of the United States and is covered by 18 U.S.C. § 281. There are no square holdings or lengthy discussions of the issue.

The cases discussed later holding that a retired Army officer is subject to Section 281 take as an assumption that he would be covered
if he were still on active duty. Similarly 40 OPS. ATT'Y GEN. 183
(1942) assumes that the officer involved would have been subject
to the predecessor to Section 281 if there had been any actual conflict of interest situation at hand. Similarly, military officers on active
duty are subject to the restrictions of 18 U.S.C. §§ 283 and 216. See
Chapter 1 of this volume for discussion of these three sections.

18 U.S.C. § 434 by its language covers all active military officers
engaged in the transaction of business with private entities, for they
are clearly persons acting as "officers of the United States." See
Chapter 2 of this volume.

The Comptroller General (26 DECS. COMP. GEN. 15 (1946)) and
the Attorney General (40 OPS. ATT'Y GEN. 168 (1942)) have held
18 U.S.C. § 1914 to be applicable to regular Army officers on active
duty. See also H.R. REP. No. 884, 74th Cong., 1st Sess. 14–19
(1935). See Chapter 3 of this volume.

The applicability of the two general conflict of interest statutes
restricting post-employment activities of government employees is
related to, and blurred by, the special position of retired military
officers under Sections 281 and 283, discussed below. It is clear,
however, that the post-employment statute 18 U.S.C. § 284 applies
to regular military officers on active duty when they are "assigned to
duty in any agency of the United States." The term "agency of the
United States" is very broad and is statutorily defined in 18 U.S.C.
§ 6 (1958). The explicit coverage of commissioned officers in Section 284 was inserted to avoid an opinion of the Attorney General to
the effect that Army officers who have served on active duty are
not, by that fact alone, "officers of the United States" within REV.
STAT. § 190, the predecessor to 5 U.S.C. § 99 (1958). See 31 OPS.
ATT'Y GEN. 471 (1919), discussed in Chapter 4 of this volume. As
for 5 U.S.C. § 99 (1958) itself, the other general post-employment
restraint, it is probable that only military officers assigned to duty
in the Pentagon are covered by it, and, of these, only officers who
are assigned to the Department itself rather than to one of the armed
services. This is because Section 99 applies to officers and employees
of a "department" only, and the Attorney General has held that the
Army is not a part of the "Department of War" and Army officers
are not as such departmental officers. See 31 OPS. ATT'Y GEN. 471
(1919), cited with approval in 40 OPS. ATT'Y GEN. 168 (1942).
See Chapter 4.

2. Enlisted personnel

LAW PRIOR TO JANUARY 21, 1963

The position of regular enlisted personnel under the pre-1963 conflict of interest statutes was insolubly confused. A memorandum prepared within the Defense Department, and often referred to as informal authority, stated flatly that "all military personnel on active duty are covered by the term 'officer or employee.'" Brown, Scope and Applicability of the Conflict of Interest Statutes, p. 10, January 1952 (unpublished memorandum written for the Office of the General Counsel of the Department of Defense). Similarly, an opinion of the Navy Judge Advocate General asserted that "military personnel on active duty (both officers and enlisted men) and civilian employees are 'officers or employees' of the United States within the purview of Section 283, Title 18, U.S.C." 2 DIGEST OF OPINIONS OF THE JUDGE ADVOCATES GENERAL OF THE ARMED FORCES 546 (JAGN 1952/112, 1952). On the other hand, in the course of explaining an amendment to Section 281 with regard to military officers, the House of Representatives Committee on Military Affairs made the following statement about enlisted men:

> Section . . . [281] of the Criminal Code does not apply to enlisted men, and for that reason no amendment as to them is necessary. Former enlisted men who had commissioned service during the World War, and who were given commissioned rank on retirement, being within the inhibitions of the statute as construed by the court of appeals, would be exempted therefrom by the amendment proposed in this bill, and the same is true of warrant officers who have been retired with commissioned rank. [H.R. REP. No. 2330, 76th Cong., 3rd Sess., p. 2 (1940).]

One unpublished decision of the Comptroller General indicated that enlisted men on active duty were covered by 18 U.S.C. § 1914. UNPUBLISHED DECS. COMP. GEN. A–51624 (1942). In addition, it is relevant to note that Congress exempted from the operation of Section 1914 persons inducted into the armed services under the Selective Service and Training Act of 1940. This exemption appeared on its face to permit drafted military personnel to receive supplementations of their salary by former employers. 62 Stat. 608 (1940), 50 U.S.C. App. § 454(f) (1958). But the Attorney General took a narrow and restrictive view of the scope of this exemption in the case of a reserve officer, and interpreted it as merely declaratory of the existing law under Section 1914, permitting compensation to be paid during government service if the compensation is for past services. 40 Ops. Att'y Gen. 183 (1942); see also 29 Decs. Comp. Gen. 164, 167 (1949).

As for the post-employment restrictions, there was at least a suggestion in 18 U.S.C. § 284 that enlisted men were not subject to it. That sections begins: "Whoever having been employed in any agency of the United States, including commissioned officers assigned to duty in such agency . . ." The section, having chosen to refer to the problem of uniformed personnel, limited its reference to officers and thus, in some measure, suggested that enlisted personnel were not covered. 5 U.S.C. § 99, the other general statute restricting activities of former government employees, applies by its terms to any "officer, clerk or employee in any of the departments." As discussed earlier, if Section 99 applies to military personnel at all, it is limited to those who are assigned directly to the Department of Defense. But the section does not distinguish between officers and enlisted personnel.

Beyond these fragmentary straws in the legal wind, there was until 1963 no authority to guide judgment on the applicability to enlisted men of any of the conflict of interest laws. No enlisted man was ever indicted under any of these statutes. But it was recognized that some enlisted men are in a position where they would have an opportunity to favor their own economic interests over those of the government, that the literal language of several of the statutes was sufficiently broad to cover enlisted military personnel, and that there was little in the legislative history of any of the statutes to indicate that enlisted personnel were intended to be excluded—or included.

1963 LEGISLATION

Under Law 87–849, effective January 21, 1963, 18 U.S.C. § 202 specifically provides that "the terms 'officer or employee' and 'special Government employee' as used in" the substantive provisions of the 1963 legislation "shall not include enlisted members of the armed forces." Thus the troublesome question of the applicability of conflict of interest laws to enlisted men is resolved in the negative under the new statute.

B. RETIRED MILITARY PERSONNEL

1. Officers

The following discussion of retired officers under the older statutes is reproduced, with minor changes, from *Conflict of Interest and Federal Service*, Appendix B, pp. 319–325.

The conflict of interest problems of retired military officers have been the subject of special legislative attention.

18 U.S.C. § 281 (1958)

In 1940 the predecessor to Section 281 was amended to provide: "Retired officers of the armed forces of the United States, while not on active duty, shall not by reason of their status as such be subject to the provisions of this section. *Nothing herein shall be construed to allow any retired officer to represent any person in the sale of anything to the Government through the department in whose service he holds a retired status.*" (Emphasis supplied.)

The history of this amendment indicates that it was adopted in response to the court's holding in *Morgenthau v. Barrett*, 108 F.2d 481 (D.C. Cir. 1939), that a retired Army officer, not on active duty, was still an "officer" subject to the prohibitions and sanctions of Section 281. The court in the *Barrett* case felt compelled by the words of the statute and weight of authority to make this decision. But it expressed its opinion that the policy behind the law, and common sense, would dictate an opposite result. The Committee on Military Affairs agreed with the court's general view. In its report accompanying the 1940 amendment the Committee stated:

> The only effect of this bill will be to extend to retired officers not on active duty the same exemptions from the operation of Section . . . [281] as were extended to Reserve officers by the Act of July 1, 1930 (46 Stat. 841). . . .
>
> . . . Though a part of the Military Establishment, retired officers not on active duty—the only class to which this bill applies—are more nearly in a civil than a military status. They have no military duties to perform, and though in time of war they may be called to duty without their consent, this is a contingency to which every citizen is subject. In time of peace their status is no different from that of citizens, generally. [*sic*] and, as said by the court of

appeals, their "activities are wholly separated from official life."
It is absurd, therefore to think that retired officers, particularly
while not on active duty, as such, can exert any undue influence in
the departments or bureaus, or with commissions, agencies, or
instrumentalities of the Government, or with any officers there-
with connected. The time of retired officers not on active duty
is their own. There is no loss of time to the Government, through
their employment by private interests, as there is in the case of
officers and employees on active duty whose whole time belongs
to the Government. As the primary purposes of the statute seem
to be to discourage the use of undue or sinister influence by those
in a position to exert it, and to prevent the loss to the Government of time for which officers and employees are paid by the
Government, and neither of these reasons can have any application to retired officers not on active duty, there appears to be no
good reason why they should not be exempted from the provisions
of Section [281] . . . as proposed in this bill. [H.R. Rep. No. 2330,
76th Cong., 3d Sess. 1–2 (1940).]

Thus retired officers are in general exempted from the prohibitions
of Section 281. But the built-in exception to this exemption is broad
and has caused trouble. The force of the exception is to forbid a
retired officer to "represent any person in the sale of anything to
the Government through the department in whose service he holds
a retired status."

The Navy Judge Advocate General has pointed out some of the
ambiguities of this language:

The statute most frequently referenced in this field is 18 U.S.C.
281. The Preparedness Investigating Subcommittee of the Senate
Committee on Armed Services has recently stated that this section
"prohibits retired officers * * * from representing—'any person
in the sale of anything to the Government through the department
in whose service he holds a retired status.'" Under this interpretation, the phrase "to represent any person in the sale of anything" is
sufficiently comprehensive to include not only the sale of materials
and supplies but also the sale of various types of services. The
phrase "to represent any person" seems adequate to include situations where a retired officer sells for himself as well as those where
he sells for or on behalf of another person or organization. The
"department in whose service" a retired Navy or Marine Corps

officer holds his retired status is the Department of the Navy, not the Department of Defense. Accordingly, this law does not prohibit a retired Navy or Marine Corps officer from selling to the Army, to the Air Force, or to other Government agencies.

The Government viewpoint is well expressed by the quotation from the Senate Committee. A careful reading of Section 281, however, raises some doubt about the validity of that interpretation. Notice that the first sentence of the second paragraph in Section 281 in general terms exempts retired officers (not on active duty) from the prohibitory provisions of the first paragraph of Section 281. The second sentence of the second paragraph does not specifically prohibit retired Navy and Marine Corps officers from selling to the Navy. Rather it states that "nothing herein shall be construed to allow" any retired Navy or Marine Corps officer to sell to the Navy Department. Because of the awkward and somewhat vague manner in which this exception has been written, it is arguable that the second sentence in the second paragraph of Section 281 is not intended to subject a retired naval officer to criminal prosecution if he sells to the Navy Department but is designed only to make certain that the exception contained in the prior sentence is not construed as a defense to criminal charges (or a loss of pay) under other laws. Admittedly, a retired officer who acts on this assumption would be taking a calculated risk in regard to criminal prosecution, particularly in the present conflict of interest climate. [Navy Judge Advocate General Journal, November 1957, pp. 8–9.]

A recent case touching on the point is United States v. Gillilan, 288 F.2d 796 (2d Cir. 1961).

18 U.S.C. § 283 (1958)

In 1949 retired officers were exempted by amendment from the conflict of interest prohibitions of 18 U.S.C. § 283 respecting prosecution of claims. Thus after nine years of inconsistency, Section 283 was harmonized in this respect with Section 281. Again, however, a substantial exception was carved out of the exemption. The exception reads: "Nothing herein shall be construed to allow any such retired officer within two years next after his retirement to act as agent or attorney for prosecuting or assisting in the prosecution of any claim against the United States involving the department in

whose service he hold a retired status, or to allow any such retired
officer to act as agent or attorney for prosecuting or assisting in the
prosecution of any claim against the United States involving any
subject matter with which he was directly connected while he was
in an active duty status." The two year limitation period does not
carry over to the phrase following the comma, and the statutory language therefore imposes upon retired officers a lifetime disqualification from prosecuting claims involving any "subject matter" with
which they were connected while on active duty. Except for the
permanence of the bar, the language of the second clause obviously
parallels that of the general post-employment statute, 18 U.S.C.
§ 284.

The Navy Judge Advocate General Journal has stated: "The emphasis of this section in relation to retired Navy and Marine Corps
officers is a prohibition (1) upon acting 'as agent or attorney for prosecuting or assisting in the prosecution of any claim against the
United States involving' the Department of the Navy and (2) upon
the prosecution of any claim against the United States involving any
subject matter with which the retired officer was directly connected
while on active duty. A retired Navy or Marine Corps officer is restricted for only two years in regard to claims involving the Department of the Navy; he is forever restricted in regard to matters with
which he was directly connected while on active duty." Navy Judge
Advocate General Journal, November 1957, p. 9.

OTHER CRIMINAL STATUTES

The prohibitions of 18 U.S.C. §§ 434 and 1914 by their nature
have no application to retired personnel. 18 U.S.C. § 216 probably
does not apply to retired personnel, though the contrary opinion
was apparently formerly held by the Judge Advocate General.

Whether general conflict of interest statutes on post-employment
conduct apply to retired personnel is a special problem, since by
definition retired employees are already in a post-employment stage.
18 U.S.C. § 284, the general criminal conflicts statute on post-
employment, is applicable to military personnel in active service.
Thus, by its provisions, such persons are forbidden for two years
after termination to prosecute or act "as counsel, attorney, or agent
for prosecuting, any claims against the United States involving any
subject matter directly connected with which such person was so
employed or performed duty." But retired military personnel are
probably not considered as such to be "officers" under Section 284,

and the statute therefore does not in all likelihood continue to apply to them indefinitely past the two-year period. The net result is that in the case of retired military personnel, Section 284 runs as a concurrent bar with the special two-year post-employment provision in Section 283.

22 U.S.C. § 1764 prohibits any Government employee for two years subsequent to the termination of his government service from receiving any pecuniary reward in connection with the procurement of goods or services under the Mutual Security Act as amended in 1958. Retired military officers are not infrequently involved in the procurement of supplies and services for the Western allies, and may to this extent find themselves subject to this statute.

5 U.S.C. § 99 (1958) (CIVIL STATUTE)

5 U.S.C. § 99, the civil statute dealing with post-employment activities of former employees of the government, applies to employees of a "department" only, and the Attorney General has taken the view that it does not automatically apply to retired military officers by virtue of their status as such, since they are not members of a "department." Military officers who held certain posts in the Defense Department might fall within the scope of the section, however. 31 Ops. Att'y Gen. 471 (1919). Compare, however, the special exemptive provisions contained in Section 113 of the Renegotiation Act of 1951, as amended, 65 Stat. 22 (1951), as amended, 70 Stat. 792, 50 U.S.C. § 1223 (1958); cf. 40 Ops. Att'y Gen. 289 (1943).

STATUTES RESTRICTING RETIREMENT PAY

Three conflict of interest statutes, instead of imposing criminal sanctions, call for forfeiture of the retired officer's retirement pay. These statutes are 5 U.S.C. § 59c, 10 U.S.C. § 6112(b), and 5 U.S.C. § 740c.

The first two of these statutes prohibit the sale by former military personnel of various supplies and war materials; Section 740c is more general. It provides that anyone convicted under certain bribery or conflict of interest sections will be precluded from receiving federal retirement pay.

67 Stat. 437 (1953), 5 U.S.C. § 59c (1958), and
70A Stat. 381 (1956), 10 U.S.C. § 6112(b) (1958)

5 U.S.C. § 59c provides: "No payment shall be made from appropriations in any Act to any officer on the retired lists of the Regular

Army, Regular Navy, Regular Marine Corps, Regular Air Force, Regular Coast Guard, Coast and Geodetic Survey, and Public Health Service for a period of two years after retirement who for himself or for others is engaged in the selling of or contracting for the sale of or negotiating for the sale of to an agency of the Department of Defense, the Coast Guard and Geodetic Survey, and the Public Health Service any supplies or war materials." Significant aspects of this section include coverage of all retired military personnel, a two-year limitation, its limited coverage prohibiting only "sales" or contracting or negotiating for "sales" of "supplies or war materials," and application of the bar throughout the entire Defense Department.

10 U.S.C. § 6112(b), applicable to retired naval and marine officers only, provides: "If a retired officer of the Regular Navy or the Regular Marine Corps is engaged for himself or others in selling, or contracting or negotiating to sell, naval supplies or war materials to the Department of the Navy he is not entitled to any payment from the United States while he is so engaged." Important features of this section include the limitation of its coverage to naval and marine officers, a perpetual bar, limitation to "selling, or contracting or negotiating to sell, naval supplies or war materials," and its limited scope in prohibiting sales to the Department of the Navy only.

A general comment on the scope of these two sections has been supplied by the Navy Judge Advocate General:

> The distinction between these two statutes should be carefully noted. [10 U.S.C. § 6112(b)] . . . applies (a) only to retired officers of the Regular Navy and Regular Marine Corps, (b) as long as they hold their retired status, (c) who, for themselves or others, sell, contract or negotiate for the sale of naval supplies or war materials to the Navy Department. [5 U.S.C. § 59c] . . . applies (a) to retired regular officers of all Armed Forces (and other listed government departments), (b) only for a period of two years after retirement, (c) who, for themselves or others, sell, contract or negotiate for the sale of any supplies or war materials to the specified government departments (including the Department of Defense). Neither statute applies to reserve officers; and it appears that neither statute applies to retired permanent enlisted personnel, advanced to commissioned rank on the retired list under the provisions of 10 U.S.C. 6151 (1956). (Comp. Gen. dec. B–129273 of 12 October 1956) . . .

What activities constitute "selling, contracting for sale or negotiating for sale"? The quoted terms have been interpreted to include virtually all activities surrounding the selling process. The signing of a government contract by the President of a Corporation, although that is his only relationship to a particular transaction, has been held "contracting for sale" within these laws. (JAG:II:2:JAC:sh of 13 August 1956.) Preliminary negotiations preceding a contract or sale constitute "negotiating for sale." [See 38 Decs. Comp. Gen. 470, 472–73 (1959).] The precise extent to which activities related to a sale to the government are within the quoted phrase cannot always be delineated with any degree of certainty. However, wherever possible and where all relevant facts are available, the Office of the Judge Advocate General will supply an advisory opinion to retired personnel concerning their proposed activities. As noted in the introduction, any such opinions will not bind the government.

What are "naval supplies or war materials"? The words "naval supplies or war material" have been interpreted to include almost any conceivable [property] item. Pocket combs and soft drinks are naval supplies within the quoted statute. (JAG:II:2:JAC:mks of 5 March 1956; JAG:II: :mmt of 15 September 1949, pub. in CMO 3–1950, 98.) [The Comptroller General has sanctioned this broad construction of the phrase "naval supplies and war materials." See Comp. Gen. Dec. B–140581 (1959), reported in 28 U.S.L. Week 2234 (Nov. 9, 1959). 38 Decs. Comp. Gen. 470, 474–75 (1959) also interprets broadly this phrase and other ambiguous portions of 5 U.S.C. § 59c and 10 U.S.C. § 6112(b).] There is, however, an important exception to this term. Persons or firms who "are commonly understood as being engaged in the furnishing of professional services . . . [such as plans, specifications, designs, or drawings]" are not engaged in selling "naval supplies or war material" to the government, since "clearly professional services are not "naval supplies or war materials" within the accepted meaning of that term." (Comp. Gen. Dec. B–12238 of November 7, 1940) The term "supplies or war materials" . . . should be similarly interpreted.

What is the "Navy Department"? This term . . . has been construed to include not only the Navy itself, but Agencies and instrumentalities, such as Navy Exchanges, ships' stores and commissaries of the Navy. (JAG:II:2:JAC:mks of 5 March 1956; see

CMO 3–1950, 98; JAG:II:JWB:mmt of 31 March 1950) [See 38
DECS. COMP. GEN. 470, 475–76 (1959).] This is an indication of
the construction which will be placed upon the comparable phrase,
listing various government departments, in [5 U.S.C. 59c). . . .

*What is the effect of engaging in the activities listed in the
quoted statutes?* The quoted statutes are not criminal and do not
purport to make illegal the selling, contracting for sale or negotiating for the sale of supplies or war materials to the specified
government departments. They merely provide that, if a retired
officer engages in any of the prescribed activities, he will not be
entitled to receive retired pay for the period involved. (JAG:II:2:
JAC:mks of 5 March 1956) Although a retired officer forfeits his
retired pay only while he is engaged in such a manner, once the
Navy Department determines that he is so occupied, he will be
considered in that status until he proves that he has discontinued
his selling activities.

Navy Judge Advocate General, Reference Guide to Employment Activities of Retired Naval Personnel, September 1957. *Cf.*, however,
38 DECS. COMP. GEN. 470, 473–74 (1959).

68 Stat. 1142 (1954), 5 U.S.C. § 740c (1958)

In 1954 Congress enacted the "Hiss Act" prohibiting retirement
payments to any person convicted of violating various laws. These include 18 U.S.C. §§ 216, 281, 283, 284, and 434. The statute thus re-
inforces the conflict of interest restraints on retired military officers.

1963 LEGISLATION

The definitions appearing in Section 202 of Law 87–849 make no
mention of retired officers. To the extent that they are given special
attention, reference must be made to the individual substantive provisions of the new act.

The most important section of the new act specifically dealing
with retired officers is Section 206. This section exempts retired officers from the restrictions contained in Section 203 (the successor to
Section 281) and Section 205 (the successor to Section 283). The
matter does not stop here, however. Section 2 of Law 87–849 contains the repealer provisions of the new act. Under this section, which
repeals substantially all of the former conflict of interest statutes, it
will be found that Sections 281 and 283 have not been entirely

repealed. In so far as Sections 281 and 283 apply to retired officers of the armed forces, they continue in effect under the new act. This means in substance that the second paragraph of Section 281 and the second paragraph of Section 283, discussed above, remain applicable to retired officers of the uniformed services. The Section 206 exemption of such officers from the force of the new Sections 203 and 205 meshes with the limited repealer contained in section 2 of the new act and leaves retired officers in *status quo ante* under present Sections 281 and 283.

Still open for examination is the question of the applicability of the other substantive provisions of the 1963 legislation to retired officers—that is, Sections 208, 209, and 207.

Section 208 does not raise a practical problem for the retired officer. That section requires government employees to disqualify themselves from acting for the government in matters in which they have a personal economic interest. Retired officers not on active duty are not called upon to act for the government, and it would not appear that any question would arise regarding the applicability of Section 208 to retired officers.

Substantially the same thing is true of Section 209, which forbids government employees from receiving outside compensation for the performance of their governmental official duties. Having no special duties, the retired officer not on active duty will not encounter Section 209.

But Section 207 is awkward. Section 207 imposes restraints upon the activities of former government employees. The basic problem in applying this section to retired officers is that in one sense they are former employees, while in another sense they are considered to continue as officers of the government because they are at all times subject to recall to duty.

The interpretation of Section 207 as applied to retired officers of the armed services can be most easily examined by considering the perhaps atypical case of an Army officer who goes through three different stages in his career. In stage 1 of this assumed case the officer is on active duty; in stage 2 he assumes the status of a retired officer; in stage 3 he resigns from his status as a retired officer and severs all connections with the military.

While in stage 3, the erstwhile officer is clearly a former officer or employee of the United States government, and the provisions of Section 207 are applicable to him as they would be to any former

government officer or employee. While the officer is in stage 1, on
active duty, it is equally clear that Section 207 does not apply to him
because he is not a former officer or employee. The difficult question
arises while he is in stage 2. Did his shift from active status to retired status operate to make him a former employee for purposes of
Section 207?

Two arguments suggest that the officer on retired status is not
subject to Section 207. The first is the literal argument that, being
still an officer of the United States, he is not a former officer of the
United States. The second argument is based on the fact that the
new act maintains in effect the special provisions of Section 281 and
283 applicable to retired officers. Arguably, the specific retention of
these restraints upon the activities of retired officers indicates that
they are not also to be subject to the general post-employment restraints contained in Section 207.

The other side of the argument is apparent. In some respects the
bar imposed by Section 207—particularly under subsection (a) of
that section—is more restrictive than the special rules applicable to
retired officers appended to Sections 281 and 283. Realistically, too,
the active officer who moves to a retired status can for some purposes
be viewed as a former employee regardless of the fact that for other
purposes, such as recall, he remains under certain governmental discipline. It is hard to find any reason why the principle of disqualification contained in Section 207 should not apply in the same way
to the group of personnel known as officers of the armed services as
it does to the broader group of persons known as officers of the
United States government.

Neither Congressional report nor floor discussion casts any light
whatever on the applicability of Section 207 to the uniformed services. There is no way to resolve the legal obscurity on this issue.
The safest answer obviously is for the retired military officer to com-
ply not only with the limitations contained in the second paragraphs
of Sections 281 and 283 but also with the restraints imposed by Section 207—restrictions that are basically sound, sensible, and not un-
duly onerous.

2. Enlisted personnel

As stated earlier, the position of regular enlisted men was uncertain under the pre-1963 conflict of interest statutes. The position of
retired enlisted personnel was even more uncertain. The problem

here, however, was limited in scope. Sections 1914, 434, 99, and 284 would not by the nature of their substantive provisions apply to enlisted personnel on a retired and inactive status. The problem that remained was whether retired enlisted personnel were subject to the special paragraphs that apply to retired officers under Sections 281 and 283. On this point there was at least the directly relevant statement from the House of Representatives Committee on Military Affairs explaining the meaning of the amendment made to Section 281. The statement is quoted in ¶ A.2 of this appendix. It reveals that the House Committee assumed that Section 281 did not apply to enlisted men at all and, in particular, that the 1940 amendment relating to retired officers was not intended to apply to enlisted men. There was no similar statement in the history of the second paragraph of Section 283, the paragraph that in substance matches the second paragraph of Section 281 and deals with retired military officers. It was not likely, however, that any court would hold that Section 281 applied to retired enlisted men while Section 283 did not—or vice versa. On balance, therefore, the stronger indication was that neither of the sections applied to retired enlisted personnel.

Law 87–849, effective January 21, 1963, specifically exempts enlisted men from the substantive provisions of the 1963 conflict of interest legislation. See ¶ A.2 of this appendix.

C. Reservists

The problem of the application of the conflict of interest laws to military reservists is best discussed as a whole.

In *Simmons v. United States*, the court concluded that an attorney who was also a lieutenant colonel in the Reserve Corps of the United States Army, inactive status, was not an officer of the United States under Section 283 and hence could prosecute a claim against the United States in the Court of Claims. The court said:

The act of June 3, 1916, 39 Stat. 189, creates certain reserve corps and defines the status of officers of the Reserve Corps of the Regular Army. It provides, among other things, that a member of that corps "shall not be subject to call for service in time of peace, and whenever called upon for service shall not, without his consent, be so called in a lower grade than that held by him in said Reserve Corps," and the provision fixing an age limit is expressly declared to be inapplicable to appointment or reappointment of officers of the Judge Advocate and some other sections. Unlike an officer on the retired list, an officer of the Reserve Corps has no salary or emolument of office. He is not in time of peace, except perhaps while discharging some duty to which he may have been lawfully called and assigned under the act of June 3, 1916, or other act, amenable to the Army regulations or court martial. He has no defined duties to discharge; his position is more analogous to that of an officer honorably discharged from the service than to that of a retired officer. [55 Ct. Cl. 56, 57 (1920).]

Whether a court would hold this analysis applicable under the other conflict of interest statutes was resolved in 1956 by 70A Stat. 632 (1956), as amended, 72 Stat. 1557 (1958), 5 U.S.C. § 30r(d) (1958).

That section provides that:

> When he is not on active duty, or when he is on active duty for training, a Reserve is not considered to be an officer or employee of the United States or a person holding an office of trust or profit or discharging any official function under, or in connection with, the United States because of his appointment, oath, or status, or any duties or functions performed or pay or allowances received in that capacity.

Thus any reserve officer or enlisted man, whether or not retired, was declared to be beyond the reach of all the conflict of interest statutes when he was not actually on active duty or was on active duty for training only. When the reservist goes on extended active duty for purposes other than training, he ceases to be treated in any special way under the conflict of interest laws and is subject to the same regulations as regular military personnel on active duty.

The 1963 statute, as we have seen, exempts enlisted men from the conflict of interest laws. And it applies to reserve officers on active duty somewhat different categories from those used formerly, utilizing the distinction between regular government employees and Special Employees that appears recurrently throughout the provisions of the 1963 legislation. See the discussion in ¶ 1A–3.2.2b. By force of Section 202, the new statute provides in substance that:

(1) Despite the provisions of 5 U.S.C. § 30r(d) discussed above, a reserve officer or National Guard officer who is not otherwise an

officer or employee of the United States is treated for purposes of
the provisions of Law 87–849 as a Special Employee when on active
duty solely for training;

(2) A reserve officer or National Guard officer involuntarily on
active duty is similarly treated as a Special Employee;

(3) A reserve officer or National Guard officer voluntarily serving a period of extended active duty in excess of 130 days is treated
as an "officer of the United States."

This means that a reserve officer or National Guard officer who is
serving involuntarily or who is on active duty for training only—
regardless of the period of service—is subject to the 1963 act, but
only to the less stringent restraints applied by the act to Special
Employees. The reserve officer or National Guard officer who serves
less than 130 days is also, by force of the general provisions of Section 202 of the new act, a special government employee restricted
only by the more limited restraints applicable to Special Employees.
Only the reserve officer and National Guard officer who serves voluntarily beyond the 130-day limit is viewed as an "officer of the
United States" subject to the full body of restraints imposed by the
1963 legislation upon regular government employees generally. Except as modified with respect to reserve officers and National Guard
officers on active duty solely for training purposes, 5 U.S.C. § 30r(d)
continues in effect so that reserve officers and National Guard officers
who are not on active duty are not for this purpose to be considered
"officers of the United States."

D. NATIONAL GUARDSMEN

Generally speaking, the members of the National Guard units in
the States are not considered federal employees. See, *e.g.*, Storer
Broadcasting Company v. U.S., 251 F.2d 268 (5th Cir.) *cert. denied*,
356 U.S. 951 (1958). Moreover, under present law the National
Guard is a part of the reserve armed forces. 66 Stat. 501 (1952),
10 U.S.C. §§ 3077, 8077 (1958). As such, members of the National
Guard enjoy the special exemption for reserves in general discussed
under ¶ C above. When a National Guard unit is activated, its
officers become subject to the conflict of interest statutes to the
same extent as reserve officers on active duty. See ¶ C above.

A special problem exists with respect to National Guardsmen of
the District of Columbia. The last sentence of Section 281 and the
last sentence of Section 283 provide that those sections "do not

apply to any person because of his membership in the National Guard of the District of Columbia." This provision probably was intended to mean that members of the National Guard of the District of Columbia should be treated in the same way as members of the National Guard in the states; that is to say, the peculiar federal character of the District of Columbia should not result in the imposition of special restrictions on members of the District of Columbia National Guard units. Unfortunately, (1) there are no similar exemptions in the conflict of interest statutes other than Sections 281 and 283 although it is in general true that employees of the District of Columbia are subject to all the conflict of interest statutes; and (2) the exemptive language in Sections 281 and 283 with regard to District of Columbia National Guardsmen does not distinguish between their status before and after activation. Read literally, these exemptive provisions would have the result of leaving District of Columbia National Guard personnel under all the conflict of interest statutes except Sections 281 and 283, but freeing them from the restrictions of Sections 281 and 283 even when they are fully activated and on active duty—though all other National Guard units and reserve units are subject to the restraints of the conflict of interest statutes when on active duty only to the extent discussed in ¶ C. No conceivable justification for such a distinction exists. It may be hoped that a court confronted with the problem would find room for an interpretation that would apply the conflict of interest statutes coequally to National Guard units of the states and National Guard units of the District of Columbia.

APPENDIX C. PARTNERS AND
ASSOCIATES OF FEDERAL EMPLOYEES

None of the conflict of interest statutes requires government employees to drop all their business connections. Federal personnel often maintain not only business investments but active participations in enterprises as partners or corporate managers. If an employee of the United States belongs to such a private business partnership, do the limitations imposed upon him by the conflict of interest laws apply to his partners as well? The question is of vital importance, especially in the case of the intermittent governmental employee who lends an occasional advisory hand to the government but who makes his livelihood in a private business or profession. For example, a lawyer practicing in a partnership would find it difficult to accept an appointment as a government consultant or other intermittent employee if acceptance meant that his partners would be subject to the disabilities of Section 281, for in that case they could not help to represent clients in matters such as taxation and antitrust arising in an executive forum. See *Conflict of Interest and Federal Service,* chapter 7.

Because of the independent and recurrent importance of the problem, this appendix reviews the position of partners and associates of current and former federal employees under Law 87–849, effective January 21, 1963, and the predecessor federal conflict of interest laws. The statutes are considered here in the same sequence as in the main text of the book.

1. Assisting Outsiders in Governmental Dealings

1A. 18 U.S.C. § 281 and Section 203 (1963)

It appears that partners' acts are covered by Section 281.[1] Their acts will, it is said, be "imputed" to the partner in government service and he will be in violation of the section.[2] The language of "imputation" indirectly expresses the conclusion that the policy of the statute would be undercut if a government employee could avoid its restrictions by having his partners do the acts that are forbidden to him.

When a member of a partnership contemplates accepting a government appointment he will want to consider closely whether the partnership is apt to want to assist its clients or customers in their dealings with the executive branch of the government. If so, his safest procedure is either to decline the appointment or resign from the partnership. Another route also appears to be sanctioned. One requisite element in a violation of Section 281 is that the proscribed services be compensated. If the partner entering government service can make sure that he does not receive, directly or indirectly, any of the compensation received by the partnership from its client

---

[1] 4 Ops. Att'y Gen. 47 (1842) (predecessor to 18 U.S.C. §431 (1958)); 38 Ops. Att'y Gen. 213 (1935) (predecessors to 18 U.S.C. §§ 431 and 432 (1958)); 40 Ops. Att'y Gen. 183 (1942) (predecessor to Section 281); 40 Ops. Att'y Gen. 289 (1943) (predecessor to Sections 283 and 281); United States v. Quinn, 111 F. Supp. 870 (E.D.N.Y. 1953), 116 F. Supp. 802 (E.D.N.Y. 1953), 141 F. Supp. 622 (S.D.N.Y. 1956) (Section 281). In the *Quinn* case, a member of Congress whose partners rendered compensated services before the Bureau of Internal Revenue on behalf of certain taxpayers was indicted under Section 281. Defendant's motion for acquittal was granted on the ground that the evidence failed to establish that, in receiving a share of partnership profits, Quinn had received compensation with knowledge that it was for services which as a member of Congress he could not have legally performed under the section. But the court assumes without difficulty that it made no difference that Quinn had not personally participated in rendering the services. The court said: "It is acknowledged that none of the clients have retained him, met him or in general that he had any contact with them. However, this circumstance in and of itself is no bar to a prosecution, providing that the Government establishes prima facie the essential elements of the offense sufficient to send the case to the jury." *Id.* at 624–25.

[2] If it can be shown that the partner was simply acting "for" his associated government employee, no theory of "imputation" is required, for Section 281 specifically covers services performed by the employee "himself or another."

or customer for services which the government employee is forbidden to perform by Section 281, it appears that he will not be held to be in imputed violation of the section as a result of his partners' activities.[3] Adopting this approach, a lawyer entering government service might resign from his partnership, then form another partnership with the same partners, the only difference between the two being that all work relating to the government would, during the time he is in government service, be carried on by the partnership of which he is not a member and from which he receives no compensation.[4]

One recent case further indicates that even where the partner on government duty shared in the compensation from the forbidden activities of his partners, their acts will not be "imputed" to him for purposes of Section 281 if there is no basis for a finding that he received the compensation with knowledge that it was for the services which he could not have legally performed himself. It is doubtless easier for the Attorney General, or the counseling lawyer, acting in advance, to declare the rule of imputation than it is for a judge to send a man to jail after the fact for an imputed crime arising out of acts by his partners that were not illegal as to *them*, and acts that he may not even have known to have occurred.

But may not the partners of the federal employee themselves be indicted under Section 281 for providing compensated services which the employee is forbidden to provide? Probably not, though there is nothing more to go on than the language of the section itself, and the judicial tradition against casual extensions of criminal statutes.[5] Whether in some situations the partners might be indictable as aiders and abettors is another question.

[3] 40 Ops. Att'y Gen. 289 (1943) (Section 283); 4 Ops. Att'y Gen. 47 (1842).

[4] Perhaps it would be dangerous for the government employee's percentage of participation in the new partnership to be greater than it had been in the original partnership.

[5] There is a single phrase in 40 Ops. Att'y Gen. 289 (1943) that may suggest that the partners might be independently covered. The Attorney General said: "To avoid the provisions of . . . [Sections 283 and 281], the purpose and wording of the proviso require that *both the Consultant and his partners* shall refrain from prosecuting any claim against the Government during the period of an appointment. Case v. Helwig, 65 Fed. (2) 186." (Emphasis added.) *Id.* at 293. But opinions are different from indictments, and even the opinion quoted does not make it clear that the criminal penalty falls on the partners rather than (or as well as) the appointee.

A federal employee may have other kinds of business associates than partners. He or his partnership may have employees; or he may be a director, officer, or shareholder in a corporation. So far there is no immediately relevant indication of how far the courts will go in talking "imputation" as among these relationships. The discourse of partnership law lends itself most readily to doctrines of "imputation." But, as a matter of policy, there is no reason why a government employee should be allowed to circumvent conflict of interest restraints by acting through an incorporated enterprise any more than by acting through a partnership.

Section 203 of Law 87–849, the direct successor to Section 281, says nothing about partners, though it contains essentially the same language as Section 281 regarding the receipt of compensation "directly or indirectly." But Section 207 of the new legislation contains in subsection (c) special substantive rules governing the conduct of partners of government employees. Subsection (c) then provides that the provisions of Section 203 shall apply to partners of government employees only to the extent provided in the subsection. By the back door, therefore, the new legislation does provide something about the applicability of Section 203 to the partners of a government employee. The substantive rules prescribed by subsection (c) of Section 207 are discussed at ¶ 5 of this appendix.

Neither Section 203 nor any other section of the new legislation offers further guidance on the applicability of conflict of interest restrictions to associates of a government employee other than partners.

1B. 18 U.S.C. § 283 and Section 205 (1963)

The situation of partnerships under Section 283 may be even more precarious than under Section 281, since the former does not require compensation as an element of the offense. Section 283 is violated if the forbidden services are performed by the partners of the government employee and if a court "imputes" the services to him—even though the employee-partner received none of the compensation paid to the outside partners, and perhaps even though they receive no compensation.

There is very little authority to go on here. The most direct statement on the point comes from the opinion of the Attorney General quoted in note 5. It is true that Section 281 specifically refers to the possibility of services performed by the employee "or another," a phrase that is missing in Section 283. But the same dogmas of partnership doctrine govern both statutes, and no policy reason supports a differentiation in the treatment of partnerships under the two statutes. Altogether, the likelihood is great that the Attorney General would be upheld in his view that Section 283 reaches the employee whose partners perform the services he is forbidden to perform. This conclusion is obviously of most significance to the legal profession, because of its traditional use of the partnership, and because more than any other profession it is engaged in the prosecution of claims.

As in the case of Section 281, it would not appear that the partners of the government employee are themselves subject to indictment under Section 283 if they perform acts forbidden to the employee by the section.

Law 87–849, effective January 21, 1963, treats partners of government employees subject to Section 205 in the same manner that it treats them under Section 203. They are not specifically referred to in these sections, but the general provision in subsection (c) of Section 207 has the effect of applying restraints somewhat like those of Section 203 and Section 205 to partners of government employees in certain situations. See ¶ 5 of this Appendix.

1C. 18 U.S.C. § 216

As an institutional matter, the partnership problem that is so acute under Section 281 is relatively unimportant in the context of Section 216. It is normal practice to pay compensation for the kinds of representational activities that are involved in Section 281, most commonly to law firms; impropriety arises only when a government employee is in some way involved. But it is far from common practice to pay compensation to *anyone* in order to procure a government contract. Section 281 is dangerous in the partnership situation because it can be violated by an innocent transaction in the ordinary course of business. The offense under Section 216, involving direct bribery or at least graft, comes much closer to the common law notion of an act said to be *mala in se*—an act that everybody knows he is not supposed to do.

One can only speculate on the response of a court asked to "impute" a partner's acts to another partner under Section 216. The elements do not quite fit. The offense under the first paragraph of the section declares the receipt by the government employee to be the crime—not the services. Even under Section 281, the receipt of the compensation has not yet been imputed—only the services performed by the partners. Further, there is no language in Section 216 corresponding to the reference to services "by himself or another" appearing in Section 281. And, finally, there is something about the flavor of Section 216 that seems to call for a more personal guilt: the overlap into bribery; the immediate odor of graft; the personal character of the sanction of permanent attaint. There are clearly more obstacles to imputed liability in the case of Section 216 than in the case of the other conflict of interest statutes.

There is no new successor to Section 216, repealed by Law 87–849. See ¶ 1C–5.

2. SELF-DEALING: 18 U.S.C. § 434 AND SECTION 208 (1963)

Section 434 would not appear to have any application to partners and other business associates of the government employee. The proscribed offense under the statute is official action; the employee is required not to take certain official acts if he has certain private interests. His outside private partners cannot violate the statute.[6]

These statements are equally applicable to the successor provision, Section 208.

3. OUTSIDE COMPENSATION: 18 U.S.C. § 1914 AND SECTION 209 (1963)

The problem of the government employee's partner is not serious under Section 1914. Under this section, the illegal act is the payment and receipt of salary by a government employee in connection with or for his government services. No one other than the employee himself could perform the acts necessary to the offense. While the employee could arrange to have the money paid to one of his partners, this stratagem does not raise a serious point of construction of the statute; if the employee is the ultimate beneficiary of the payment, the device of indirect receipt of the payment will not serve to insulate him.

Section 209 of Law 87–849 makes no change in the law in this respect.

---

[6] Perhaps with effort one could conjure up a case of back-scratching where two contracting officers work together, each helping along the company in which the other is interested.

4. POST-EMPLOYMENT RESTRICTIONS

4A. 18 U.S.C. § 284 and subsections (a) and (b) of Section 207 (1963)

If a former government employee is prohibited from certain action by Section 284, are his business partners and associates similarly prohibited from taking the action? Doubtless they are, where the former employee is the active party and merely acts through his partners as dummies. But the harder question is whether his statutory disability is to be "imputed" in any way to others.

As noted earlier, the likelihood is that the restrictions contained in Sections 281 and 283 extend to the partners of a government employee, but the language in those provisions provides more support for such a conclusion than can be found in the language of Section 284.[7] There is also force to the view that it is more necessary to curtail activities of the partners of a government employee while he is actually in office; it is easier for them to trade upon his inside position while he is there than after he has left.[8]

There is no direct authority passing upon the applicability of Section 284 to the partners and associates of former employees. For many persons most interested in an answer, one has been provided from a different source. In the case of lawyers, partners of former government employees will be barred from certain activities by Canon 36 of the American Bar Association's Canons of Professional Ethics, whether or not they are barred by Section 284. That canon reads in part:

A lawyer, having once held public office or having been in the public employ, should not after his retirement accept employ-

[7] Section 281 refers to services rendered by the employee "or another"; Section 283 at least contemplates the presence of partners and associates when it forbids the employee to share the compensation received for the forbidden services where he did not himself render them.

[8] Under a similar statute restricting activities of former employees who had worked for the government in the disposition of surplus properties, the Attorney General concluded that the former employee would not "be prevented from accepting employment as an officer of a corporation which acquires surplus property if he does not participate in the negotiations with his former agency." Unpublished Ops. Att'y Gen., Nov. 13, 1944. Compare, too, the discussion in Appendix B of the position of retired military personnel under the second paragraphs of Sections 281 and 283.

ment in connection with any matter which he has investigated
or passed upon while in such office or employ.

The scope of the restriction contained in the canon is obviously
somewhat different from that contained in Section 284. But the
significant point is for present purposes that it seems to be unchallenged that if the canon bars a lawyer from certain activity, it
also bars his partners and his law firm. In a relatively recent case,
discussed in ¶ 4A–4.1.2, the court arrived at this conclusion almost
by assumption.[9] Lawyers are not the only persons who as a professional matter might be expected to be called upon to provide
services in connection with "claims." But they are the most likely
group to be so involved. For this reason, the courts will probably
not ever be called upon to pass on the applicability of Section 284
to the activities of partners. A change in Canon 36, or a change in
its interpretation, could focus immediate attention upon this aspect
of the interpretation of Section 284.

One can speculate, without much basis in authority, that a court's
decision in this question might depend upon the remedy or recourse
being sought. In a criminal prosecution against a partner, a court
might well conclude that Section 284 did not reach out to cover
him; in a proceeding to disqualify the partner of the former government employee from appearing on behalf of a client who could not
under Section 284 be represented by the former employee, the
court might well conclude that Section 284 demands the disqualification of the partner. The whole question, therefore, of whether
Section 284 covers partners of the former employee may in a sense
be a false question, or at least one that must be broken down into
smaller pieces before it can be considered and weighed.

Neither Section 207 nor any other section of Law 87–849 contains restrictions on the activities of partners of former government
employees.[10] Indeed, the last sentence of subsection (c) of Section
207 explicitly negates any implication that any statutory restrictions
other than those specified in the subsection might apply to partners.
Of course, restrictions arising from other sources, such as the American Bar Association's Canons of Professional Ethics, are not affected
by Law 87–849.

[9] United States v. Standard Oil Co. 136 F. Supp. 345 (S.D.N.Y. 1955).
[10] See S. Rep. No. 2213, 87th Cong., 2d Sess. 13 (1962), referring to
the deletion of a provision on the point contained in the House version of
the bill that ultimately became Pub. L. 87–849.

4B. 5 U.S.C. § 99

The discussion of partners under Section 284 is equally applicable to Section 99 unless conceivably the absence of a criminal penalty under Section 99 makes some difference. A court that would balk at extending the criminal provisions of Section 284 to the partners of a former government employee might nonetheless conclude that the partners should be disqualified from representing a claimant if the former government employee with whom they are associated is so barred. Similarly, a court might be more willing to impose such a disqualification under Section 99, where it can be certain that no criminal sanction would be implied by its decision.

There is no counterpart to Section 99 in Law 87–849.

5. 1963 Restrictions on Partners—Section 207(c) (1963)

Subsection (c) of Section 207 of Law 87–849 is the only provision of the new statute that deals explicitly with the position of partners of government employees. Structurally this subsection is badly placed because it does not deal with the problem of post-employment activities to which the rest of Section 207 is addressed.

Subsection (c) applies to any person who is a partner of an officer or employee (including a Special Employee) of the executive branch of the United States government, of any independent agency of the United States, or of the District of Columbia. This language of coverage conforms to that of subsection (a) of Section 207. See ¶ 4A–3b. For discussion of the statutorily defined term "Special Employee," see ¶ 1A–3.2.2b.

Regrettably, the substantive restrictions imposed upon partners of an employee covered by subsection (c) are rather intricate. Further, they do not match the restrictions imposed by the rest of the new statute on the employee himself.

Subsection (c) forbids the partner to act as agent or attorney for anyone other than the United States in connection with a particular matter or transaction that meets the criteria set out in the subsection. Thus the language in subsection (c) defining the act forbidden to partners of current employees is identical to the language in subsection (a) of Section 207 defining the act forbidden to former employees. The discussion at ¶ 4A–4.2.1 concerning the meaning of "act as agent or attorney" under subsection (a) thus applies with equal force to the partner under subsection (c). As is discussed at

¶ 4A–4.2.1, however, the prohibition in subsection (a) of Section 207 against acting as agent or attorney in connection with a sensitive transaction is a different standard of prohibition from that found either in Section 205 or Section 203 with respect to the current employee or in subsection (b) of Section 207 with respect to the former employee. As a consequence, the act forbidden to the partner of a current employee under subsection (c) of Section 207 is different from that forbidden to the employee himself under either Section 205 or Section 203.

This is not the only source of difficulty in subsection (c) of Section 207, however. What are the matters as to which the employee's partner is forbidden to act as agent or attorney? It will be observed upon close reading that the statutory standards for determining sensitive transactions under subsection (c) are unique to that subsection—they are not the same standards which the employee himself is required to apply in order to determine which transaction he must avoid. Under subsection (c), the partner is prohibited from acting as an agent or attorney in connection with "any judicial or other proceeding, application, request for a ruling or other determination, contract, claim, controversy, charge, accusation, arrest, or other particular matter in which the United States is a party or has a direct and substantial interest *and* in which such officer or employee of the Government or special Government employee participates or has participated personally and substantially as a Government employee through decision, approval, disapproval, recommendation, the rendering of advice, investigation or otherwise, *or* which is the subject of his official responsibility" (emphasis added). Up to the italicized word "and," the recitation of transactions and dealings appearing in subsection (c) of Section 207 is the familiar one appearing in several places in Law 87–849.[11] But the "and" and the language following it are unique, having no parallel in any other section. In a variety of circumstances, therefore, it will be found that the partner can act where the employee could not. In some cases, such a distinction is understandable, and deliberate—the employee being placed under a substantially tighter control than his privately employed partner. In other cases, however, particularly with regard

[11] It appears in substantially this form in Section 203 (but limited to matters in an executive forum), in clause (2) of Section 205 (though the act forbidden is different from that in subsection (c) of Section 207), and in Section 208.

to partners of Special Employees, subsection (c) of Section 207 is not too satisfactory. Under both subsection (c) of Section 203 and the third paragraph of Section 205, for example, the Special Employee is not disqualified unless the transaction involves specific parties. The rule under subsection (c) of Section 207 imposes a harsher standard upon the partner by omitting the requirement that the transaction be one involving specific parties. The significance of the difference is pointed out at ¶ 4A–4.2.2.

Furthermore, the Special Employee is not affected at all by subsection (c) of Section 203 or the third paragraph of Section 205, unless the particular question is one in which he personally and substantially participated as a government employee, or unless it was pending in his own department or agency (if he served more than 60 days out of the preceding year). But the standard for the partner's exclusion is totally different; he is barred from acting as agent or attorney if his partner, the Special Employee, participated in the matter as an employee or if the matter is subject to the official responsibility of the Special Employee.

This kind of hairsplitting hardly seems necessary, and it is hard to predict just how these different standards might work out in practice. If the Special Employee has served more than his 60 days, it is likely that he would be barred from acting in his private capacity on some matters that were pending before his agency while his partner would be able to act on them so long as the matters were not subject to the official responsibility of the Special Employee himself. Conversely, particularly where the Special Employee has not served the 60 days, he would be free to act privately on a matter that was under his official responsibility so long as he did not personally participate in his governmental capacity, while his partner would be barred from acting as agent or attorney in the matter since the matter is subject to the Special Employee's responsibility.

The disparities between the rules applicable to Special Employees and the rules applicable to the partners of Special Employees will probably have only occasional practical impact. Most Special Employees are consultants, and as such have no "official responsibility" as that term is defined in subsection (b) of Section 202. In most cases, too, the most practical advice would be that the partner of a government employee should not become involved in any matter which the employee himself is forbidden to become involved in. But this is not a totally satisfactory answer. Not all Special Em-

ployees are consultants and some of them do have "official responsibility." Moreover, the very existence of subsection (c) of Section
207 demonstrates beyond argument that the statute did not intend
that the partners of government employees should be subject to the
same limitations and prohibitions as the employees themselves. This
comment brings us to the last paragraph of subsection (c) of Section 207.

The final paragraph of subsection (c) of Section 207 makes it
explicit that partners of government employees shall be governed by
subsection (c) and by nothing else in the statute. The paragraph
reads:

> A partner of a present or former officer or employee of the
> executive branch of the United States Government, of any in-
> dependent agency of the United States, or of the District of Co-
> lumbia or of a present or former special Government employee
> shall as such be subject to the provisions of sections 203, 205, and
> 207 of this title only as expressly provided in subsection (c) of this
> section.

This says in so many words that unless the partner's act is prohibited by subsection (c) of Section 207 it is not to be considered to
be forbidden by Section 203, Section 205, or Section 207. The
reference in the quoted paragraph to Section 207 itself is remark-
able; since there is nothing in subsection (c) of Section 207 that
restricts the activities of partners of former government employees,
the result of the quoted paragraph is that partners of former government employees are subject to no statutory restrictions of any kind
by Law 87–849. See ¶ 4A of this appendix.

A final point. ¶ 1B–4.7 discusses a series of special exceptions to
the rules laid down by Section 205. There is no corresponding set of
exceptions for the partners of employees. To give an example, a federal employee may, under the first exception in Section 205, act
as agent or attorney for any person in a disciplinary or loyalty proceeding; but there is no indication under subsection (c) of Section
207 that his partner could undertake the same case. There is probably a good place here for the invocation of *pari materia*.

APPENDIX D. A NOTE ON
SANCTIONS AND ADMINISTRATION

Statutes do not enforce themselves. They call for administration and policing, and they often evoke a supplementary pattern of regulation and administrative sanctions. This is the topic to which this appendix is devoted, divided into three subtopics: criminal sanctions; civil sanctions; regulations and administrative sanctions.

I. CRIMINAL SANCTIONS

A. CRIMINAL SANCTIONS AGAINST THE GOVERNMENT EMPLOYEE

With the exception of 5 U.S.C. § 99, all the general conflict of interest statutes discussed in this book bear criminal penalties. Though there have in fact been very few indictments or convictions under these statutes, the ever-present threat of criminal penalty and conviction hangs over those who are in government service or who are considering entering it and undoubtedly has some effect upon their conduct.

For no reason other than the accidents of history, the criminal penalties under the conflict of interest statutes have varied considerably. Sections 281, 283, 216, and 284 provide for a maximum fine of $10,000. Section 434 provides for a maximum fine of $2,000. Section 1914 sets the maximum fine at $1,000. All six statutes provide for a penalty of imprisonment that may be imposed either in substitution for or in addition to the fine. Sections 281, 434, and 216 set a maximum prison term of two years; Sections 283 and 284 set a maximum of one year; and Section 1914 provides for a maximum prison term of six months. In addition to these penalties, Sections 281 and 216 go to the lengths of providing, in slightly varying language, that any person convicted under these sections shall forever be disqualified from holding any office of honor, profit, or trust under the United States.

The usual difficulties in the interpretation and application of criminal statutes arise under these criminal provisions. What degree and kind of "intent" is required? What kinds of penalties may be imposed cumulatively? These and other such questions are touched upon in the discussion in ¶ 1C–4. For a recent case raising a number of procedural questions under Section 281, see United States v. Johnson, 215 F. Supp. 300 (D.Md. 1963). There is no basis for discussing the administration of criminal sanctions within the narrow category of conflict of interest statutes. The same basic questions run through the whole of the criminal law, and no special flavor or refinement has been given to them in the conflict of interest context.

Under Law 87–849, effective January 21, 1963, the criminal provisions applicable to the conflict of interest statutes are consolidated, though deliberately not made uniform. Under the new act, Sections 203, 205, 207, and 208 impose a maximum fine of $10,000 or two years in prison or both. Section 209 distinguishes as a lesser offense the receipt of compensation from outside sources and provides for a $5,000 penalty or one-year imprisonment or both. The new statute gives no new guidance on matters such as intent and cumulative offenses.

B. Criminal Sanctions Against Third Parties

Section 1914 provides for a criminal penalty to be imposed not only upon the government official who receives a forbidden supplement to his salary but also upon the outside person paying the supplemental compensation. In substance, Section 216 also forbids the payment as well as the receipt of compensation for the procurement of a government contract, and thus provides for a criminal sanction applicable not only to employees of the government but to third persons as well. None of the other older conflict of interest statutes provides for such criminal sanctions. Pursuit of third parties for offenses involving the conflict of interest statutes must in these cases be predicted upon a theory of conspiracy, or upon the general statute on aiding and abetting, reading: "Whoever promotes an offense against the United States, or aids, abets, counsels, commands, induces, or procures its commission, is a principal." 18 U.S.C. § 2(a) (1958). One case has, however, held this approach unavailable as a way to reach a payor of compensation forbidden by Section 281. United States v. Bowles, 183 F. Supp. 237 (D. Me. 1958).

Under the 1963 legislation, three sections specifically apply criminal sanctions to third parties who are not government employees. Subsection (c) of Section 207 imposes a penalty of $5,000 or one year's imprisonment or both upon the government employee's partner who violates the restraints applicable to partners under that subsection. Subsection (b) of Section 203 and the second paragraph of subsection (a) of Section 209 impose a criminal penalty upon the payor of compensation to a government employee that is forbidden by these two sections. To the extent that any outside payment may be involved in a violation of Sections 205, 207, or 208, recourse for a sanction against the third party payor must continue to be made to the general statutes on conspiracy and aiding and abetting, if at all.

II. CIVIL SANCTIONS

In a number of ways, the courts have found themselves called upon to enforce the principles or policies of the conflict of interest statutes by means other than the imposition of criminal sanctions.

Section 216 provides that the President may declare void any contract or agreement entered into in violation of the section. No cases have arisen under this section.

Precisely this principle was invoked by the government, however, in *Mississippi Valley Generating Company v. U.S.*, 364 U.S. 520 (1961), where the government claimed the right to cancel a contract that was tainted by the activities of a government employee violating Section 434. The case is discussed in ¶ 2–4.2a. Though there were other difficult problems in the case, the Supreme Court had no difficulty in concluding that, if the government's case could be proved, it could properly invalidate and rescind the contract on general principles of equity. Thus the specific provision in Section 216 appears not to be necessary; the civil sanction of contract cancelation is available wherever a violation of a conflict of interest statute can be shown.

With relative frequency, court cases have arisen in which the plaintiff is suing for a fee for services and is met with the defense that the services rendered violated the conflict of interest statutes. Apparently, no court has questioned the premise underlying this defense. It seems to be unchallenged that if the services are in violation of the conflict of interest statute, the third party for whom the services were performed may raise the point as a defense and thus receive the services without paying for them. If this were widely understood, it might have some useful preventive effect; but once the services have been performed, it does seem a strange result to permit the third party—often the instigator of the transaction—to be the beneficiary of the government employee's infraction.

In *United States v. Standard Oil Co.*, 136 F. Supp. 345 (S.D.N.Y. 1955), the government claimed that a lawyer who had formerly been a government employee should be disqualified from acting as counsel in the case, and his firm with him. The case is discussed in ¶ 4A–4.1.2. The court's opinion proceeded on an interpretation of the lawyers' Canons of Ethics. Without the canon, however, adequate basis for disqualifying the lawyer would have arisen from the conflict of interest statutes themselves, assuming the facts to be as alleged. Such disqualification thus offers another form of civil sanction to the conflict of interest laws.

Section 218 of Law 87–849, effective January 21, 1963, provides more explicitly than any of the present conflict of interest statutes that the President or, under regulations prescribed by him, the head of any department or agency involved, may declare void and rescind any contract or other government action in relation to which there has been a final conviction for violation of any of the provisions of the act. Section 218 further provides that the United States may recover, in addition to any penalty prescribed, any amount paid out by the government with regard to the contract or things of value transferred, or the reasonable value thereof. After the holding of the Supreme Court in the *Mississippi Valley Generating Co.* case, it cannot be said that Section 218 significantly expands present law, for the Court found substantially this same proposition to inhere in traditional principles of equity jurisprudence. Perhaps more interesting is the fact that Section 218 calls for the President to set forth regulations under which such rescissions can be effected by department and agency heads. In practice, rescission can be a drastic and harsh recourse, hurting or ruining innocent persons who have become economically involved in a large-scale governmental transaction quite unaware that some other person has in the long course of the transaction conducted himself with impropriety.

III. REGULATIONS AND ADMINISTRATIVE SANCTIONS

Chapter 4 of *Conflict of Interest and Federal Service* is devoted to a broad discussion of regulations and administration in the conflict of interest field. As the chapter points out, no central office in the executive branch has responsibility for controlling or coordinating the administration of ethical conduct among government employees. Since the publication of that book, the White House has taken further affirmative action in the area. On February 9, 1962, the President issued a memorandum to all Departments and agencies of the executive branch entitled "Preventing Conflicts of Interest on the part of Advisers and Consultants to the Government." 27 Fed. Reg. 1341 (1962). At the instance of the President, there was distributed to all agencies a lengthy opinion of the Attorney General dated January 31, 1962, providing an interpretation of the conflict of interest statutes. 42 Ops. Att'y Gen. No. 6 (1962). With the enactment of Law 87–849, effective January 21, 1963, the Attorney General distributed another general memorandum on that date regarding the changes in the law made by the 1963 legislation. 28 Fed. Reg. 985 (1963). And on May 2, 1963, the President circulated and published another special memorandum dealing with consultants and advisers. 28 Fed. Reg. 4539 (1963).

It remains true, however, that major responsibility for regulations, and for administrative enforcement of regulations, in the field of conflict of interest is vested in the individual departments and agencies. The Civil Service Commission plays no central role in this regard. The record of the individual departments and agencies continues to be uneven. A few agencies have done little or nothing in the field; a large majority have done something by way of issuing regulations but have been unenergetic in their administration; a small number of agencies have developed more refined and imaginative regulations and have enforced them with some vigor. Among the agencies that have been particularly active in the area are the Housing and Home Finance Agency, the Atomic Energy Commission, the Small Business Administration. See, in particular, the regulations of the Department of Justice, 28 Fed. Reg. 7698 (1963). In a category of its own is the Department of Defense, which has shown an awareness of the special risks inherent in the administration of multi-billion dollar procurement programs. See *Conflict of Interest and Federal Service*, chapter 4.

The only generalization that can be made is that administrative regulations regarding ethical conduct of federal employees are widespread and vary greatly from agency to agency. The administrative sanctions used to enforce these regulations and to regulate the conduct of current employees, former employees, and outside parties dealing with the agencies cover a wide range. The stringency with which these regulations are enforced varies depending on the agency involved. When a problem arises—and, more important, if problems are to be avoided—the employee, former employee, or non-employee dealing with a government agency must familiarize himself with the current regulations and practices of the agency involved.

APPENDIX E. ABSTRACTS OF LEGISLATIVE HISTORY

This appendix contains abstracts of the legislative history of the federal conflict of interest statutes reviewed in this book.

The abstracts are for reference and research. They do not contain a textual analysis or interpretation of the developing stages of the statutes. The general history of the statutes is recounted in the main text. The abstracts are designed for the lawyer or judge faced with a concrete situation that he hopes may be illuminated by historical research. In this situation he is not interested in secondary editorialization, and cannot be content with a check of a few selected sources; he needs the basic raw legal data from which he can draw his own interpretation to meet his particular problem. For his needs, the abstracts, which collect these data in one place for quick access, should prove a useful timesaver.

The historical material concerning each statute is treated separately, except that the material on the new Law 87–849 is treated as a single unit. The material grouped under each statute is listed chronologically.

5 U.S.C. § 99 (1958)

1. Background

The original predecessor of 5 U.S.C. § 99 (1958) was enacted in 1872. For earlier background, see the legislative history of 18 U.S.C. § 283 (1958), this appendix.

2. The 1872 Act

For debate, amendatory proposals, and action on the original act, see: CONG. GLOBE, 42d Cong., 2d Sess. 1584, 1846, 3109–13, 3133 (1872); Act of June 1, 1872, ch. 256, § 5, 17 Stat. 202.

3. The Revised Statutes of 1873

The language of the 1872 act was altered in the technical revision of the United States Statutes in 1873–74. See REV. STAT. § 190 (1873). GOULD & TUCKER, NOTES ON THE REVISED STATUTES OF THE UNITED STATES (1889) does not mention the change or the reasons for it. For the limited authority of the statutory revision committee, see 2 CONG. REC. 129 (1873).

4. Subsequent History

5 U.S.C. § 99 (1958) retains the language of REV. STAT. § 190 (1873) intact. Efforts to amend REV. STAT. § 190 (1873) gave rise to 18 U.S.C. § 284 (1958), for the legislative history of which see this appendix.

18 U.S.C. § 216 (1958)

1. Background

The original predecessor of 18 U.S.C. § 216 (1958) was enacted in 1862. For earlier background, see: H.R. REP No. 2, 37th Cong., 2d Sess., pts. 1 and 2, *passim,* and especially pt. 1, at 1, 40–41, and pt. 2, at 46–48 (1861); S. EXEC. DOC. NO. 17, 37th Cong., 2d Sess. 1 (1862); H.R. MISC. DOCS. NOS. 34 and 44, 37th Cong., 2d Sess. (1862); H.R. EXEC. DOC. NO. 151, 37th Cong., 2d Sess. 2–7 (1862); S. MISC. DOCS. NOS. 12 and 34, 37th Cong., 2d Sess. (1862); CONG. GLOBE, 37th Cong., 2d Sess. 306–08, 2478, 2774, 3403 (1862); ch. 33, § 2, 12 Stat. 412 (1862).

For debate, amendatory proposals, and action on the 1862 act, see: CONG. GLOBE, 37th Cong., 2d Sess. 2957–59, 3129, 3260–61, 3325, 3378 (1862); Act of July 16, 1862, ch. 180, 12 Stat. 577.

2. The 1863 Amendment

For debate and action on the amendment made in 1863, see:

CONG. GLOBE, 37th Cong., 3d Sess. 371, 1018, 1306 (1863); Act of Feb. 25, 1863, ch. 61, 12 Stat. 696.

3. The Revised Statutes of 1873

The language of the 1862 act, as amended in 1863, was altered in the technical revision of the United States Statutes in 1873–74. See REV. STAT. § 1781 (1873); GOULD & TUCKER, NOTES ON THE REVISED STATUTES OF THE UNITED STATES 455–56 (1889). For the limited authority of the statutory revision committee, see 2 CONG. REC. 129 (1873).

4. The Revision of 1909

In the general revision of the criminal laws in 1909, REV. STAT. § 1781 (1873) was amended. For debate, amendatory proposals, and action, see: S. REP. No. 10, 60th Cong., 1st Sess., pt. 1, at 18, and pt. 2, § 114, at 121 (1908); 42 CONG. REC. 755, 757, 804, 986, 1763–64, 2123–25 (1908); 43 CONG. REC. 3219, 3824 (1909); Act of March 4, 1909, ch. 321, § 112, 35 Stat. 1108.

5. Related Legislation in 1926

In 1926 Congress adopted additional criminal provisions respecting the sale of office or influence. It is questionable whether these changes should have been construed to repeal the similar provisions of the 1909 act as the revisers of the 1948 Criminal Code assumed. H.R. REP. No. 304, 80th Cong., 1st Sess. A–19 (1947). In any case, for the history of the 1926 legislation, see: 67 CONG. REC. 6419, 10841, 12612 (1926); H.R. REP. No. 1366, 69th Cong., 1st Sess. 1 (1926); Act of Dec. 11, 1926, ch. 3, 44 Stat. 918.

6. The 1948 Criminal Code

In the substantive revision and consolidation of the Criminal Code adopted as Title 18 in 1948, § 112 of the 1909 act was amended. See: H.R. REP. No. 304, 80th Cong., 1st Sess. A–19 (1947); 93 CONG. REC. 5048–49, 5121 (1947); 94 CONG. REC. 8075, 8721–22, 8864–65, 9367 (1948); 18 U.S.C. § 216 (1948). See generally: HOLTZOFF, PREFACE TO TITLE 18, UNITED STATES CODE ANNOTATED VI (1950); *Hearings on H.R. 5450 Before the House Committee on Revision of the Laws*, 78th Cong., 2d Sess. (1944); H.R. REP. No. 152, 79th Cong., 1st Sess. (1945); H.R. REP. No. 304, 80th Cong., 1st Sess. (1947).

7. Other Related Laws

The history of 18 U.S.C. § 216 (1958) has tended to run concurrently with the development of other criminal sections dealing with bribery and other related offenses. See, in particular, 18 U.S.C. §§ 204, 205, 214, and 215 (1958).

18 U.S.C. § 281 (1958)

1. Background

The original predecessor of 18 U.S.C. § 281 (1958) was enacted in 1864. The 1864 act arose out of the same background and atmosphere as did the predecessors of 18 U.S.C. §§ 216 and 283 (1958), for the legislative history of which see this appendix.

2. The 1864 Act

For debate, amendatory proposals, and action on the original act, see: Cong. Globe, 38th Cong., 1st Sess. 93 (1863); Cong. Globe, 38th Cong., 1st Sess. 460, 555–62, 2778, 2894 (1864); Act of June 11, 1864, ch. 119, 13 Stat. 123.

3. The Revised Statutes of 1873

The 1864 act was amended slightly in the technical revision of the United States Statutes in 1873–74. See: Rev. Stat. § 1782 (1873); Gould & Tucker, Notes on the Revised Statutes of the United States 455–56 (1889).

4. The Revision of 1909

In the general revision of the criminal laws in 1909, Rev. Stat. § 1782 (1873) was amended. See: S. Rep. No. 10, 60th Cong., 1st Sess., pt. 1, at 18, and pt. 2, § 115, at 121 (1908); 42 Cong. Rec. 755–57, 804–05, 986, 1763–65, 1895–99, 1977, 2123–25 (1908); 43 Cong. Rec. 3217–20, 3735–36, 3788–92, 3824 (1909); Act of March 4, 1909, ch. 321, § 113, 35 Stat. 1109.

5. The Amendment of 1940

Following upon the decision of the court in Morgenthau v. Barrett, 108 F.2d 481 (D.C. Cir. 1939), 35 Stat. 1109 (1909) was amended in 1940. See H.R. REP. No. 2330, 76th Cong., 3d Sess. (1940); 86 CONG. REC. 3263, 7071, 8407, 8459, 9555, 12757, 13463 (1940); Act of Oct. 8, 1940, ch. 762, 54 Stat. 1021.

6. The 1948 Criminal Code

In the substantive revision and consolidation of the Criminal Code adopted as Title 18 in 1948, § 113 of the 1909 act, as amended by 54 Stat. 1021 (1940), was further amended. See: H.R. REP. No. 304, 80th Cong., 1st Sess. A–23 (1947); 93 CONG. REC. 5048–49, 5121 (1947); 94 CONG. REC. 8075, 8721–22, 8864–65, 9367 (1948); 18 U.S.C. § 281 (1948). See the general sources cited in paragraph 7 of the legislative history of 18 U.S.C. § 216 (1958), this appendix.

7. The Amendment of 1949

A technical revision act in 1949 amended 18 U.S.C. § 281 (1948). See: H.R. REP. No. 352, 81st Cong., 1st Sess. 1–3 (1949); S. REP. No. 303, 81st Cong., 1st Sess. (1949); 95 CONG. REC. 3072, 3546, 3813, 3837, 5020, 5826–27, 6249, 6283–84, 7255 (1949); Act of May 24, 1949, ch. 139, § 5, 63 Stat. 90.

18 U.S.C. § 283 (1958)

1. Background

The original predecessor of the 18 U.S.C. § 283 (1958) was enacted in 1853. It is thus the oldest of the seven conflict of interest statutes. For earlier background, see CONG. GLOBE, 32d Cong., 1st Sess. 59 (1851); CONG. GLOBE, 32d Cong., 1st Sess. 1128, 1258–59, 1337–40, 2100–01, 2301–05, 2413–14, 2418 (1852).

2. The 1835 Act

For debate, amendatory proposals, and action on the original act, see CONG. GLOBE, 32d Cong., 2d Sess. 242, 289–90, 295–96, 391–92, 805 (1853); CONG. GLOBE, 32d Cong., 2d Sess. 64, 67, 117 (Appendix, 1853); Act of Feb. 26, 1853, ch. 81, § 2, 10 Stat. 170.

3. The Revised Statutes of 1873

The 1853 act was amended in the technical revision of the United States statutes in 1873–74. See REV. STAT. § 5498 (1873); GOULD &

TUCKER, NOTES ON THE REVISED STATUTES OF THE UNITED STATES 1038 (1889). By force of REV. STAT. § 5596 (1873), subsection (8) of the 1853 act was dropped in the revision without comment, though the revision committee's stated authority did not extend to substantive changes. See 2 CONG. REC. 129 (1873).

4. The 1901 Amendment

An exemption was written into Section 5498 in 1901 and reenacted in 1905. See: Act of March 1, 1901, ch. 670, 30 Stat. 844; 33 Stat. 911 (1905).

5. The 1909 Revision

In the 1909 revision of the criminal laws minor changes were made in Section 5498, as amended in 1901, but without debate or comment. See Act of March 4, 1909, ch. 321, § 109, 35 Stat. 1107.

6. The 1948 Criminal Code

In the substantive revision and consolidation of the Criminal Code adopted as Title 18 in 1948, Section 109 of the 1909 act was amended. See: H.R. REP. No. 304, 80th Cong., 1st Sess. A–23–24 (1947); 94 CONG. REC. 8075, 8721–22, 8864–65, 9367 (1948); 18 U.S.C. § 283 (1948). See the general sources cited at paragraph 7 of the legislative history of 18 U.S.C. § 216 (1958), this appendix.

7. The Amendment of 1949

Further amendments were made in 1949 to 18 U.S.C. § 283 (1948). See: H.R. REP. No. 846, 81st Cong., 1st Sess. (1949); Act of June 28, 1949, ch. 268, 63 Stat. 280. The changes were parallel to, but not identical with, the changes made in 1940 and 1949 to the predecessor of 18 U.S.C. § 281 (1958). See paragraphs 5 and 7 of the legislative history of 18 U.S.C. § 281 (1958), this appendix.

18 U.S.C. § 284 (1958)

1. Background

Unlike the other conflict of interest statutes, 18 U.S.C. § 284 (1958) did not assume form until very recently. The main strands in its history are the following:

a. See the legislative history of REV. STAT. § 190 (1875), as amended, 5 U.S.C. § 99 (1958), this appendix.
b. Legislation in 1919 following upon 31 OPS. ATT'Y GEN. 471 (1919). See: 58 CONG. REC. 1735–36 (1919); Act of July 11, 1919, ch. 8, 41 Stat. 131.
c. Attempts in the 1920's to amend REV. STAT. § 190 (1873). See: H.R. REP. No. 455, 67th Cong., 1st Sess. (1921); 65 CONG. REC. 303, 1963, 2801 (1923); 65 CONG. REC. 3139–40, 3150, 6006, 6706, 7332–33, 7429–30 (1924).
d. Section 403(j) of the Renegotiation Act of 1942, ch. 619, 56 Stat. 985 (1942), providing for limited exemption from 5 U.S.C. § 99 (1940). See: War and Navy Departments Memorandum, *Hearings on Section 403 of Public Law 528 Before a Subcommittee of the Senate Committee on Finance*, 77th Cong., 2d Sess. 45 (1942); 88 CONG. REC. 8439–40 (1942); 40 OPS. ATT'Y GEN. 289, 293 (1943).
e. 1944 amendment to Section 403(j) of the Renegotiation Act of 1942, 56 Stat. 985 (1942). See H.R. REP. No. 871, 87th Cong., 1st Sess. 88 (1943); 90 CONG. REC. 88 (1944); Act of Feb. 25, 1944, ch. 63, 58 Stat. 90. 58 Stat. 78 (1944) extended the Renegotiation Act to five additional agencies that were not cabinet departments and were not therefore covered by 5 U.S.C. § 99 (1940) as interpreted by 25 OPS. ATT'Y GEN. 6 (1903).
f. Section 19(e) of the Contract Settlement Act of 1944, 58 Stat. 668. See 90 CONG. REC. 6138, 6517–19. See also, with respect to this provision, the statement of the Comptroller General in *Hearings on H.R. 131 Before the House Committee on Expenditures in the Executive Departments*, 79th Cong., 1st Sess. 14 (1945); H.R. REP. No. 725, 79th Cong., 1st Sess. 4 (1945); S. REP. No. 104, 79th Cong., 1st Sess. 3 (1945).
g. Spot legislation granting limited exemptions from, or extending, post-employment restrictions. See Wheeler, *Restrictions on Activities of Personnel During and After Government Service*, 6 FED. B.J. 333, 337 (1945); Act of Oct. 3, 1944, ch. 479, § 27, 58 Stat. 781.

2. The 1948 Criminal Code

In the substantive revision and consolidation of the Criminal Code adopted as Title 18 in 1948, the revision committee drew upon the sources listed above in paragraph 1, especially Act of July 11, 1919, ch. 8, 41 Stat. 131, and Contract Settlement Act of 1944, 58 Stat. 668, and put together 18 U.S.C. § 284 (1948). See: H.R. REP. No. 304, 80th Cong., 1st Sess. A–24 (1947); 94 CONG. REC. 8075, 8721–22, 8864–65, 9367 (1948); 18 U.S.C. § 284 (1948). See the general sources cited at paragraph 7 of the legislative history of 18 U.S.C. § 216 (1958), this appendix.

18 U.S.C. § 434 (1958)

1. Background

The original predecessor of 18 U.S.C. § 434 (1958) was enacted in 1863. It shared the same Civil War background as the predecessor of 18 U.S.C. § 216 (1958), for the legislative history of which see this appendix.

2. The 1863 Act

There was no direct debate on this section of the broader bill in which it was contained. See CONG. GLOBE, 37th Cong., 2d Sess. 952–58 (1863); CONG. GLOBE, 37th Cong., 3d Sess. (1863); H.R. REPS. Nos. 49 and 64, 37th Cong., 3d Sess. (1863); Act of March 2, 1863, ch. 67, § 8, 12 Stat. 698.

3. The Revised Statutes of 1873

The 1863 act was amended in the technical revision of the United States Statutes in 1873–74. See REV. STAT. § 1783 (1873). No comment on the changes appears.

4. The 1909 Amendment

In the general revision of the criminal laws in 1909, REV. STAT. 1783 (1873) was amended. See: S. REP. No. 10, 60th Cong., 1st Sess. 15 (1908); 42 CONG. REC. 662–63, 777–78 (1908); 43 CONG. REC. 3824 (1909); Act of March 4, 1909, ch. 321, § 41, 35 Stat. 1097.

5. The 1948 Criminal Code

In the substantive revision and consolidation of the Criminal Code adopted as Title 18 in 1948, Section 41 of the 1909 act was amended. See: H.R. REP. No. 304, 80th Cong., 1st Sess. A–32 (1947); 93 CONG. REC. 5048–49 (1947); 94 CONG. REC. 8075, 8721–22, 8864–65, 9367 (1948); 18 U.S.C. § 434 (1948). See the general sources cited at paragraph 7 of the legislative history of 18 U.S.C. § 216 (1958), this appendix.

18 U.S.C. § 1914 (1958)

1. The 1917 Act

The original predecessor of 18 U.S.C. § 1914 (1958) was enacted in 1917. For debate, amendatory proposals, and action, see: 54 CONG. REC. 2039, 2041, 2043, 2045–46, 2515, 2886, 3996, 4011–12, 4017, 4404 (1917); H.R. REP. No. 1540, at 2, No. 1548, at 2, No. 1576, at 3, 64th Cong., 2d Sess. (1917); Act of March 3, 1917, ch. 163, 39 Stat. 1106.

2. The 1948 Criminal Code

In the substantive revision and consolidation of the Criminal Code adopted as Title 18 in 1948, the 1917 act was amended slightly. See: H.R. REP. No. 304, 80th Cong., 1st Sess. A–130–31 (1947); 93 CONG. REC. 5048–49 (1947); 94 CONG. REC. 8075, 8721–22, 8864–65, 9367 (1948). See the general sources cited at paragraph 7 of the legislative history of 18 U.S.C. § 216 (1958), this appendix.

PUBLIC LAW 87–849

1. Background

The President's Special Message of April 27, 1961, and attached draft bill, 107 CONG. REC. 6835 (1961).

2. Hearings on H.R. 8140

Hearings of June 1 and 2, 1961, before the Antitrust Subcommittee (Subcommittee Number 5) of the House Judiciary Committee, 87th Cong., 1st Sess., ser. 3, on Federal Conflict of Interest Laws.

Hearings of June 21, 1962, before the Senate Judiciary Committee, 87th Cong., 2d Sess., on Conflicts of Interest.

3. Reports

H.R. Rep. No. 748, 87th Cong., 1st Sess. (1961). S. Rep. No. 2213, 87th Cong., 2d Sess. (1962).

4. Debate and Action

107 Cong. Rec. 14774 (1961); 108 Cong. Rec. 21269, 21640, 21975, 21992, 22311, 23160, 23264, 23423, 23544 (1962). 76 Stat. 1119 (October 23, 1962), effective January 21, 1963.

INDEX

The material in this book is closely outlined by topic and subtopic in a pattern of numbered paragraphs recurring in each chapter. Paragraph captions in the table of contents will usually lead the reader directly to the discussion of the particular subtopic in which he is interested. Items appearing in the table of contents have not, therefore, been included in this index.

Index 285